The Smaller Bulbs

Brian Mathew

The Smaller Bulbs

B. T. Batsford Ltd · London

ISBN 0 7134 4922 5

Typeset by Keyspools Ltd, Golborne, Lancs.

Printed by
Anchor Brendon Ltd
Tiptree, Essex
for the Publisher
B.T. Batsford Ltd
4 Fitzhardinge Street
London
W1H 0AH

Contents

List of illustrations

List of drawings

Acknowledgements

I hesitate here to mention any individual names at all for two reason; firstly because there are so many kind friends, colleagues and passing acquaintances who have helped me with my interest in bulbs over the years that the list would run into several pages, and secondly because I am concerned about leaving someone out. There are many people to whom I am clearly indebted who would form the core of such a list but there are many, many others who may have given me just one plant or a snippet of information which has helped to put the 'icing on the cake', so to speak. So, I extend my thanks to everyone who has in any way nourished my knowledge of the world of bulbous plants and, in particular, I would like to remember those who are no longer with us but selflessly passed on their knowledge for the future; we must learn a lesson from their example and not take it all with us when we depart from this world.

Having said that I would not mention names I am going to break my own rule, which is one of the perks of being the author! You will see that I have dedicated the book to E.B. Anderson. The reason for this is not only that he was one of the best growers of rare bulbs that I have ever known, and one of the most generous who would always share his latest rarity, but also because he was the person who really guided me into writing. It was he who was asked to write the book on bulbs in the late 1960s which turned into my first book called *Dwarf Bulbs*, because he felt that he could not take it on himself at the time and recommended me to the publishers instead. It is with some pride that I can claim to have known 'EBA' and shared in his extensive knowledge and enthusiasm. It is also fitting that this book, which is intended as a replacement for the long-out-of-print *Dwarf Bulbs*, is published by the same house as approached Bertram Anderson some 20 years ago. My typist Maggie undertook the task of converting my heap of paper into something the publisher could recognize – and corrected my spelling of Latin names, grammar, punctuation, and even unsplit infinitives – whilst also giving encouragement. So, thank you Maggie, I hope this one wasn't too messy! And thanks also to our son Paul for his regular interruptions to come and see the latest trap on his carnivorous plants; it maintains a very necessary sense of proportion, although perhaps retarding the manuscript delivery date!

The photographs are taken by the author, except for 21 *Cooperia drummondii* by T. Walker, 41 *Fritillaria michailovskyi* by H. Esslemont, 50 *Gynandriris sisyrinchium* by Paul Furse, 85 *Sternbergia candida* by T. Baytop, 93 *Tulipa montana* by J.S. Ingham.

Introduction

Although intended as a replacement for *Dwarf Bulbs*, I found that during the preparation of this book it rapidly took on a character of its own and has ended up as a completely new book, much more comprehensive in dealing with the hardy bulbs than its predecessor. In order to make room for the many species which have been added I have deliberately culled those genera which were optimistically included in *Dwarf Bulbs* as being on the border lines of hardiness, such as *Tigridia*, *Hesperantha* and *Ferraria*. These do not survive even the mildest winter in my Surrey garden and only thrive if given a fair amount of heat in the greenhouse, so I felt that it was better to omit these and concentrate on giving fuller details of the hardier popular groups like *Tulipa*, *Corydalis*, *Crocus* and *Fritillaria*. Within such genera I have tried to describe or at least mention as many species as possible so that the enthusiast, confronted by a name in a catalogue, seed list or book can find some information about it, even if it is only briefly compared with another similar species.

In trying to give fairly comprehensive treatment to some genera I have inevitably felt obliged to include some of the taller species for the sake of completeness, and a few home-made rules have been applied. An example is with *Fritillaria*, where there are many dwarf species and the genus is very popular at the present time. It would be very unsatisfactory to pick out those up to, say, 15cm in height and leave out other closely allied ones of 20cm, so I have attempted to include them all. Genera in which nearly all the species are tall and dwarfness is an exception have been left out – *Lilium* is the obvious example; in any case there are many good books on the market devoted entirely to Lilies.

Orchids are not included, although a few are unquestionably hardy and certainly bulbous in the broad sense. However, the vast majority are not outdoor plants in temperate countries, or are non bulbous, so I have left them out on the basis that there are plenty of specialist books available on this popular subject.

Although the arrangement of the book is predominantly alphabetical, it should be borne in mind that I have frequently broken this rule by inserting species which are similar to those above, indented to keep the main sequence alphabetical. It is important, therefore, to use the index and not rely entirely on the sequence in the text to find names.

It will be noticed that I have used the terms spring, summer etc. instead of precise months. This is mainly because the flowering time varies widely from year to year and from garden to garden, even within one small country like England. Bulbs in my own cold garden can be flowering several weeks later than identical ones at Kew only ten miles away. In parts of the country spring comes in February, whereas in Toronto and Edmonton, Canada (where there are many bulb enthusiasts) it may not arrive until April, May or June. In the southern hemisphere, of course, where good bulb growers also abound, the seasons are reversed, so I feel fully justified in using this apparently vague system as it is more accurate in a world-wide context to say, for example, 'early spring' than 'March or April'.

Cultivation notes are usually given in the introduction to each genus or in some cases under the species, where there are differing requirements. Obviously these are generalizations only, for each garden has its own set of conditions and idiosyncracies, and what seems almost impossible to cultivate for one person may be increasing too rapidly for another. By and large I have tried to write about plants which I grow or have tried to grow – yes, I have plenty of failures too – but it would be nonsense to leave out all the species which I have not yet had the opportunity to try out. So, there are a certain number of items which I have observed in other gardens and in some cases, as with very rare subjects, I have resorted to herbarium specimens for further information. I am of course indebted to my 'home from home', the Royal Botanic Gardens, Kew, for the use of the herbarium and for providing the living collections in the gardens where many rare species are skilfully cultivated.

Names of Chinese provinces are given in the current Pinyin form, with the older 'post office' form in brackets, thus: Xinjiang (Sinkiang) province.

I hope you, the reader, will enjoy the following pages and get as much fun out of growing small bulbs as I do. There is no end to the range you can try, for even if you think you have obtained all the species there are countless variations, and then there is hybridization to start on – but please do keep accurate records of who the mother and father are!

The cultivation of bulbs

The following notes are intended as a general guide to cultivation methods for the bulbs described in the book, rather than precise instructions as to how to grow individual species. In fact it is almost impossible to say exactly how a particular plant should be treated, since each garden differs slightly from the next in its microclimate, soil and situation and what may be found ideal in one area will probably not apply in another.

Bulbs in grass

To me this constitutes one of the most natural and attractive ways of cultivating bulbs, since I have seen so many species in the wild growing in just such conditions. Over the years, in a small patch of rough grass, literally only a few metres square, I have experimented in a very unscientific way by planting out a few surplus bulbs left over at repotting time to see which species enjoy this treatment. The results have surprised me for I was expecting most of the smaller ones to be choked by the rather coarse grasses of which the turf consists. The main thing to remember is that the grass cannot be mown early in the year and must be left until the bulbs have seeded and died down naturally, usually not until late May or June at the earliest, and later still if late-flowering subjects such as *Tulipa sprengeri* and *Allium stipitatum* are included. Rather than being annoyed about this I have taken the view that it is an interesting feature and have encouraged various other plants such as the early umbellifer *Anthriscus sylvestris* (Cow Parsley), and the blue Borage *Pentaglottis sempervirens*; these too can be cut down in summer. For the summer months the mowing of the area is taken in with the rest of the lawn, without any ill effects on the bulbs. If autumn-flowering species are planted then a careful watch must be kept from late August onwards for the 'noses' of Colchicums and Crocuses pushing through – and mowing stopped immediately they are spotted.

The planting methods I have adopted are of the simplest and appear to be satisfactory. For single bulbs I merely make a slit with a trowel or spade and push the bulb down it. Larger numbers can be planted in colonies to give a natural effect and in this case I remove a whole strip of turf with a spade, loosen the soil beneath and plant the bulbs in an irregular pattern, replacing the turf and treading it down again. This is carried out in late summer or early autumn when the bulbs are still dormant.

The following have been successful to date: *Anemone blanda*, *A. nemorosa*; *Biarum tenuifolium*; *Colchicum autumnale*, *C. speciosum*; *Crocus* in a wide range of species, spring and autumn-flowering, and the *C. chrysanthus* cultivars; *Cyclamen hederifolium* (where the grass is sparse under shrubs); *Iris histrioides*, *I. reticulata*; *Narcissus asturiensis*, *N. cyclamineus* and cultivars, *N. poeticus*; *Fritillaria meleagris* vars; *Galanthus* species and vars: *Romulea ramiflora*; *Ornithogalum* species; *Muscari neglectum*; *Leucojum aestivum*, *L. vernum*; *Corydalis solida* vars; *Tulip sprengeri, T. greigii* vars; *Scilla siberica, S. greilhuberi.*

Besides planting bulbs, surplus seeds can be scattered – but it will be several years before any results can be detected.

Bulbs in borders

Bulbs are really only successful in areas which are not cultivated frequently, such as in shrub borders or at the front of borders containing hardy perennials like Hellebores. However, they can also be used for short-term bedding displays; the Hyacinths and Tulips are of course the prime example here. In general, bulbs planted in beds which have to be dug over from time to time are a nuisance and rarely thrive. Shrub borders on the other hand are ideal, since these are planted and left undisturbed for many years. Few bulbs will thrive in deep shade right underneath the shrubs but in the dappled-shady areas beneath deciduous shrubs certain bulbs such as *Scilla, Chionodoxa, Eranthis* and *Galanthus* thrive, and may well increase to form drifts. In the more open areas *Crocus, Iris, Narcissus* and *Tulipa* can be planted in groups to great effect.

In open sunny borders the summer-flowering bulbs can be bedded out in groups and lifted again for the winter. On the whole, however, these tender, taller, subjects have not been included in this book.

Borders against sunny walls

Beds which are backed by a wall facing the sun are one of the most treasured sites in a garden and, since they are warm and sheltered, they extend the range of bulbs which can be grown successfully. It is well worth retaining such sites for really special plants which will not thrive elsewhere in the garden. A mixture of bulbs with other plants should be used, so that there is an interest throughout the year, and many of the slightly tender grey and silver leaved plants are ideal since they act as a foil for the bulbs. The bulbs which benefit most from being planted in such a site are those which are dormant in summer, during which time their bulbs need to be warm and dryish in order to form flower buds for the coming season.

Among the bulbs which will appreciate this kind of treatment are: *Sternbergia lutea, S. clusiana; Fritillaria imperialis, F. persica; Zephyranthes candida; Iris magnifica, I. bucharica; Hermodactylus tuberosus; Nerine bowdenii; Leucojum autumnale; Galanthus reginae-olgae; Muscari muscarimi; Tigridia pavonia; Pancratium illyricum.*

Raised beds

These can be made into an attractive garden feature, fitting into an overall design, or they can be purely functional and tucked away out of sight and regarded purely as a practical means for growing a collection of bulbs. Whichever view is taken the principle is the same; to provide an area in an open sunny position which is raised above the existing ground level, filled with a soil mixture which is free-draining so that it dries out somewhat in summer when the bulbs are at rest. A good range of small bulbs can be grown in such conditions which would otherwise not thrive in the open border, usually because they are shaded by other coarse summer-growing plants and do not receive the warmth they require. A raised bed need not be dull in summer when the bulbs are dormant, for it is an ideal place for growing small rock plants, or alpines as they are loosely called. Careful planting will mean that these do not cover and shade the bulbs.

The soil mix for a raised bed should be 'open' and free-draining and, although it is not essential to be precise, something near to the following proportions will be satisfactory: 3 parts (by volume) sieved loam, 1 part coarse gritty sand, 1 part sieved moss peat; if some fine gravel is obtainable, 1 part of this is also valuable, and this can be used for a topping as well. The overall height of the bed above ground level is not critical, but something between 30 and 60cm (1–2ft) will be fine. Anything much higher than this will dry out too much and anything much lower is scarcely worth doing. The surround can be built of a variety of materials, depending upon the availability, cost, and the effect required. One of the most attractive ways is to use natural walling stone and build dry walls, leaving crevices for rock plants to trail down. The outline can be regular or informal in shape, depending upon the site and the overall design of the garden; gracefully curved beds can be a most attractive feature in their own right. The many brands of reconstructed stone walling blocks are very useful and here again, holes can be left for planting, even if the blocks are cemented together. If the structure is to be made rather rigid, by cementing, then concrete footings will be necessary but these do not have to be very deep, even for a wall 60cm in height. Ordinary bricks can be used, but take advice from the local supplier or builder as to which ones to use, since some types will shatter during frosty weather; concrete blocks are also suitable.

Whichever method is used, the beds are filled in the same way. First a layer of drainage consisting of broken crocks, clinker, brick rubble or similar material is placed on the bottom; this layer should not be less than 8cm deep. Over this place a layer of coarse fibrous peat, or turf turned upside down, to prevent the compost washing down into the drainage material. Finally, fill up to the top of the wall surround with compost mixed up in the proportions given above. Some settling is inevitable, but the bed can easily be topped up again at a later date.

The choice of plants for such a bed is not limited to bulbs, but anything else which is planted must be fairly compact, so that it will not shade the bulbs too much, and it must enjoy sun and dryish conditions in summer since you will not want to water the bed frequently whilst the bulbs are dormant. It is best to plant these in autumn so that they are fairly deep-rooted by the time the first summer comes round. Trailing plants can be chosen for the crevices and edges of the bed – to fall down over the walls and break up the outline.

For the more functional 'botanical collection' type of bed I find it preferable to plant the bulbs in straight lines, alternating the various bulbs so that they can be separated more easily when digging up again at a later date. For example, *Crocus* corms look quite different from *Fritillaria* bulbs, so would make good contrasting companions. A plan of the bed can also be made as a safeguard against loss of labels; I find that cats are the greatest nuisance, for the newly made bed in particular is an ideal scratching ground and labels easily become scattered. A layer of fine mesh wire netting, buried just beneath the soil surface but above the bulbs, is a reasonable deterrent against digging animals.

An ideal method of planting is to grow the bulbs in the smallish basket-type pots which are sometimes available; these are pot-shaped but made of a plastic mesh similar to the larger ones sold as water-lily baskets or 'Clematis pots'. These can be buried completely in the soil and the label can be tied on to the mesh securely, there is no root restriction as in ordinary pots and when it is time to re-make the bed it is the simplest matter to lift all the pots, complete with their contents of bulbs. The main problem is finding a source of supply.

Bulbs in rock gardens

Rock gardens are in effect a series of raised beds or pockets, filled with a well-drained soil mixture, and arranged in an informal way so that there are many different aspects and situations in which to plant a range of subjects with differing requirements. Much the same comments apply here as were made for the raised beds described above but the scope for planting is much wider and any bulbs which are planted must be able to tolerate the same conditions as the rock plants around them. The choice of planting positions can range from open sunny spots with sharp drainage to semi-shaded damper corners, and from well-protected beds at the foot of sunny rocks to cooler spots on the shady side of rocks. If a stream is incorporated this extends the possibilities even further to give damp positions for the few moisture-loving bulbs.

The actual construction of the rock garden is a subject too large to deal with here and, rather than treating it superficially, I refer the reader to one of the many specialist books available.

Bulb frames

Although not the most attractive of garden features, the covered bulb frame represents an excellent method of growing those species occurring in areas which have a hot dry summer during their dormant period. In most of the cooler temperate countries the summers are just not warm enough or dry enough to encourage good results out in the open garden, but with slight protection from the elements a whole range of delightful bulbs can be grown – including such fascinating treasures as the Juno and Oncocyclus Irises, tuberous Anemones, Tulip species and dwarf Fritillarias.

In effect, a bulb frame is just a raised bed with provision for frame lights to be fitted when necessary. The construction is exactly the same as for raised beds but the measurements are dictated by the type of frame light used, which can range from sheets of corrugated plastic to more expensive glass Dutch Lights or metal-framed ones such as the 'Pluie' and 'Access' types. These last types are advantageous in being easy to ventilate and they have extra height to allow taller bulbs to develop properly. The frame itself can be made in a variety of materials from railway sleepers, which are very frost-proof, to brick, breeze-block, concrete or stone – and the choice is almost a matter of personal preference.

Since bulb frames are usually of practical rather than ornamental value it is wise to plant in rows and keep a plan for reference, and prevent things from seeding into each other, or chaos soon results. The 'perforated pots' mentioned above under raised beds are an excellent way of growing them, or slates and tiles on edge can be used to keep the various species separate from each other.

With most Mediterranean, Middle Eastern and North American bulbs the annual sequence of treatment consists of keeping the lights on through the summer months, in order to keep the dormant bulbs warm and relatively dry, then removing them in autumn and giving several good waterings to encourage root action. The lights are replaced and no further watering is necessary (unless there is exceptionally warm sunny weather in late autumn) until early spring. In late winter and early spring the lights can be removed completely or opened (if of the type with ventilation) whenever the temperature is above freezing. Water should be provided frequently to prevent drying out throughout the spring during the growing and flowering period. As soon as the foliage begins to die back and the seeds have been gathered the lights are put on again for the whole of the summer. The bulbs may be left undisturbed for three or four years before replanting, but an annual feed of bone meal in autumn is beneficial during the interim years. Replanting, carried out in summer or early autumn, can be a laborious process but it can be great fun seeing what has survived, what has increased, and the depth to which bulbs have pulled themselves down.

Bulbs in pots under glass

The great appeal of growing bulbs in pots is that they are easily kept separate from each other so that they can be given individual treatment, and they can be moved for closer inspection, for photographing or for showing. However, it is not always the best way to grow certain species and there is a lot of work involved in maintaining a collection in good condition.

The pots may be clay or plastic. I would recommend plunging both types up to the rim in sand, gravel or similar material to protect the bulbs from frost and, in the case of clay, also from excessive drying out. The compost must be free draining, so I add to any proprietary compost, be it a loam-based one like John Innes or a peat-based one, coarse gritty sand in the proportions of 2/3 compost to 1/3 sand (by volume). Broken crocks are placed in the bottom over the drainage hole. The bulbs are planted or repotted in late summer or early autumn and should be placed well down in the compost, about 2/3 of the way down the pot, for very few thrive if planted near the surface. A final topping of chippings gives an attractive appearance and stops the soil getting washed about and compacted during watering. The pots are then plunged in a cold frame or greenhouse bed, but if placed on the bench are best given at least a layer of sand or grit on which to stand since this will retain a little moisture around the base of the pot where the roots are. Hardy species are perfectly happy in a cold frame or alpine house with no heat at all, providing they are plunged in sand, but any slightly tender species must be kept frost-free or nearly so. Small electric fan heaters are very good since they keep the air moving and can be set to cut in just above freezing point. Paraffin and gas heaters generate a certain amount of moisture, which is not good for difficult bulbs like the Juno Irises which rot off at the very slightest sign of moisture on the leaves.

Species which are grown entirely for display in the alpine house, such as the *Iris reticulata* and *Crocus chrysanthus* cultivars, are best obtained fresh each year from the nurseryman since they are fairly cheap; the old bulbs can be planted out in the garden after flowering.

Propagation by seed

Tremendous fun can be had by propagating your collection of bulbs, thus having spares to pass on and exchange for others. Initially the aim should be to raise a good batch of each item, especially the rarer ones, so that there are several bulbs of each to experiment with in different planting positions. Once the species is well established some crossing can be tried, which can result in some interesting variations, but please do keep accurate records of the parents and, if the hybrid is something really good, give a note to one of the societies' journals or bulletins so that the information is not lost.

Growing from seed has some very important points in its favour, although it can be a very long process. The first point is that you get a lot of bulbs from one capsule of seeds – but more important is that the resulting plants will almost certainly vary slightly from each other, perhaps not in appearance but in some miniscule or hidden way. During the course of growing the young bulbs on to flowering size some will probably do well, others not so well and some will die; this is selection in progress and the survivors are those most suited to your particular garden and cultivation method.

If time permitted I would sow seeds as soon as I collected them from the capsules since this is what happens in nature. However, with majority of hardy autumn, winter and spring flowering bulbs nothing much is to be lost by delaying sowing until the following autumn (for summer-flowering bulbs such as *Tigridia* sow in spring). They will then be watered along with the parent bulbs in autumn, receive a cold period in winter and (hopefully!) germinate; some will appear in autumn, others in spring.

My method of sowing is the same for all bulbs, into pots filled with a free-draining mixture such as described above under 'Bulbs in pots under glass'. The seeds are sown thinly since the young bulbs may have to stay there for a season or two, and then covered with a thin layer of grit which gives an ideal surface for the young shoots to push through. With this covering the soil surface is protected from heavy rain which may compact it and wash out the seeds; it also discourages mosses and liverworts from growing. With all hardy species I place the pots out in the open to receive frost and rain through the winter, at least until germination is seen to be taking place; when this happens they are moved into a cold frame or the greenhouse for protection and are fed several times with very weak liquid tomato fertilizer for the rest of their growing season. In summer they are allowed to dry out a little in a frame but are not sunbaked since the tiny bulbs can shrivel away to nothing.

The seedlings are left for one to three years in the same pots giving liquid feeds every two or three weeks during the growing season. After this they are large enough to handle and can be potted on as for mature bulbs in the autumn, or can be planted out in the garden. Sometimes instead of leaving them in pots, I plant out the whole pot full of seedlings into a bulb frame soon after germination to grow on undisturbed, and this method seems to be quite satisfactory.

The time taken to reach flowering size varies widely between the various types and the growing conditions. Three to five years is an average but some will flower in two years while others may take seven.

Natural bulb increase

That well worn phrase 'by division of established clumps' is marvellous if you are in the happy position of having grown your bulbs so well that they are forming patches of their own accord!

The advantage of natural bulb increase is that all the offspring will be identical with the parent so that named clones can be perpetuated, whereas from seed there may be variation and names cannot be applied to individual forms so accurately. Young bulbs (corms etc.) may be formed when a parent bulb splits up, or they may be produced as 'offsets' around the base of the parent, or in the leaf axils (e.g. Lilies) or sometimes in the inflorescence. These bulbs can be removed at repotting time and grown on in exactly the same way as the mature bulbs; with hardy species the clumps can be divided and planted back into the same site.

Artificial inducement of young bulbs

Bulbs which do not increase naturally may be encouraged to do so by damaging the parent in some way, new bulblets forming on the damaged surfaces. On a small scale,

Fritillaria bulbs can be broken into two and repotted, each of the two scales then forming a young bulb in the next growing season. Commercially, *F. imperialis* bulbs are cut into many pieces, giving rise to a lot of youngsters – but I would not recommend this unless you have plenty of bulbs to experiment with! Many of the true bulbs which consist of scales may be increased by making cross cuts into the basal plate, or even slicing the bulb lengthways into several pieces, each with a piece of the solid basal plate. New bulblets form along the cut surfaces and can be removed and potted up at the end of the growing season.

As with natural bulb increase, these methods are useful if a particular form is selected and requires cloning.

Pests and diseases

Fortunately for the dwarf bulb enthusiast there are very few pests and diseases which cause any serious damage, and usually if the plants are being cultivated well there is not likely to be much trouble. Plants in poor health become subject to attacks by various diseases and may then require treatment, but in the first instance, if a plant looks poorly, the method of cultivation should be questioned. Obviously some troubles are unavoidable, such as attacks by aphids and slugs, but in general the cause is easily recognized and a visit to the nearest garden centre or shop is the best way to find out which insecticide or fungicide to use. It is always best to attempt a cure first without the use of chemicals, turning to these only as a last resort. A small attack of aphids can usually be kept under control by simply squashing them. Botrytis often appears as a result of damp still air in a greenhouse or frame, so avoiding these conditions is advisable to prevent the trouble appearing. With virus diseases there is no cure, and the only course is to destroy the plants before they spread to the rest of the stock, but it is as well to remember that many viruses are spread by aphids and if they are kept under control the incidence of virus attack is less likely.

Rather than attempting to describe all the pests and diseases which can attack dwarf bulbs, and recommend treatments which may well be out of date in a couple of years, I would rather refer the reader to other publications which deal with the subject in more accurate detail. The Ministry of Agriculture bulletin *Diseases of Bulbs* is very useful, published by H.M.S.O., and Collins' *Guide to the Pests, Diseases and Disorders of Garden Plants* by Buczacki and Harris is a good all-round work. The R.H.S. Dictionary also gives quite a lot of information.

The Bulbs

Albuca

On the whole this rather interesting group of African bulbs are too tender to be cultivated in cool temperate regions, even in an alpine house. They have racemes of flowers which are distinctive in appearance, with the inner three segments held together around the style and stamens, almost forming a tube, while the outer three spread out. They are mostly fairly tall with yellow, greenish or white flowers, often with a darker green or brownish stripe on the segments. One dwarf species is worth growing in the protection of an alpine house.

A. humilis from Lesotho has small white bulbs producing one or two narrow cylindrical basal leaves and a flower stem up to 10cm tall, carrying only one to three flowers. These are white with a green stripe on the outer segments and yellow tips to the inner ones. It is a native of the Lesotho Drakensberg Mountains, and was introduced by Mrs Milford, probably in the 1930s.

Allium

The onions are an enormous group of bulbs, probably bordering on one thousand species, and containing some very useful members such as the onion, leek and garlic, some very ornamental, a great many of no particular value at all and some which can be bad weeds in the garden. All have one feature in common and that is the umbel of flowers, where the flowers all arise at the same point at the top of a stem – a feature it shares with various other genera such as *Brodiaea*, *Triteleia* and *Dichelostemma*, which are dealt with in this book. Nearly all the *Allium* species have the characteristic onion smell when leaves or bulbs are crushed, which most of the other genera do not have.

This is obviously not the place to describe in detail a vast number of species, many of which would be of no aesthetic value, however interesting botanically. I have therefore picked out just a few of the 'better' ones which are fairly small in size, and known to be reasonably hardy; this does not mean that I scorn the superb taller ones such as *A. giganteum*, *A. rosenbachianum*, *A. christophii* (*A. albopilosum*) and *A. regelii*, for these are excellent garden plants.

All those mentioned are reasonably easy to grow in a sunny situation, but where there are specific needs I have made extra comments. These bulbous species mostly occur in dryish stony places in the wild but the Himalayan ones are often plants of alpine pastures.

A. acuminatum is usually 15–25cm in height with 1cm wide deep pink or lilac-pink flowers produced in spring in an umbel about 4–6cm in diameter; the segments are pointed, the outer three recurving somewhat. Widespread in the Pacific North West of North America.

A. *crispum* is not unlike A. *acuminatum* but has very undulate or crisped segments, bright purple-pink in the form sent to me by Wayne Roderick, California.

A. *murrayanum* is an excellent garden plant, having large flowers with broad segments in bright pink. It is of unrecorded origin but seems to be a variant of A. *acuminatum*.

A. akaka   A very striking dwarf species, rather like a small version of the frequently cultivated A. *karataviense*. It has one or two broad grey-green basal leaves lying on the ground, on which sit a large umbel 3–10cm in diameter, consisting of many whitish to pinkish starry flowers, each about 1cm in diameter. Originates from E. Turkey, Iraq and Iran in scree conditions. It requires a hot sunny well-drained position and flowers in spring.

A. *mirum* is similar in its habit and leaves but the spherical umbel, about 5–8cm in diameter, consists of many papery-looking flowers with broader segments than those of A. *akaka*. The colour is white to purplish, with a darker vein on each segment. Afghanistan.

A. amabile   This has a rootstock consisting of small rhizomes, forming dense clumps with tufts of grassy leaves. The flower stems are 10–15cm in height and carry two to six reddish-pink flowers, each about 0.5–1.0cm in diameter; they are often funnel-shaped with slightly recurving tips. It is a native of Yunnan Province, China. It flowers in late summer and is easily cultivated in sun or semi-shade.

A. *mairei* and A. *yunnanense* are names met with in cultivation; they are given as synonyms in the *Flora of the People's Republic of China*, but W.T. Stearn in the *European Garden Flora*, vol. 1 maintains A. *mairei*; this has paler rose coloured flowers which are all held in an erect position.

A. beesianum   This is one of the most attractive of the smaller Alliums, suitable for a rock garden and flowering in late summer. It makes clumps of slender bulbs with linear leaves and stiff 15–25cm stems carrying drooping umbels of up to ten bright blue flowers, which are bell-shaped and 1–1.5cm in length. W. China.

A. *sikkimense* (A. *kansuense*, A. *tibeticum*) is similar but smaller, with flowers usually less than 1cm long. E. Himalaya and China.

A. callimischon   An interesting little plant, not showy but flowering in autumn. From its rounded bulbs it produces thread-like leaves and wiry stems carrying few-flowered umbels of small papery white or pale pink flowers. In subsp. *haemostictum* from Crete they are red-spotted inside and the plant is about 5–15cm in height. Subsp. *callimischon* is from the Greek mainland and is taller with unspotted flowers. Both do well in a sunny well-drained position.

A. cernuum   A clump-forming species with narrow elongated bulbs and tufts of narrowly linear leaves. The nearly white to deep pink or purplish-red flowers are carried in summer on 15–30cm stems in a pendulous umbel about 3–5cm in diameter and are almost globular in shape, about 5mm long with the stamens protuding. Easy in the open border. N. America, widespread.

A. cyaneum (A. purdomii)   An attractive little plant forming clumps, with thread-like leaves and 10–15cm stems bearing few-flowered umbels. The small flowers, under 1cm in diameter, are deep cobalt blue with conspicuous stamens, produced in late summer. W. China. It is suitable for the rock garden or sink garden and not at all difficult.

A. cyathophorum Probably not yet in cultivation but a variety of it, var. *farreri*, is frequently seen and is easily grown in the border or rock garden. I find that it seeds too freely and the flowers are best removed as they fade to prevent seeding. It is clump-forming, with narrowly linear leaves and stems 15–25cm in height. The umbels bear up to thirty wine-red coloured flowers in summer about 0.5–1cm long. W. China.

A. falcifolium A dwarf species with a round bulb producing one or two narrow, sickle-shaped grey-green leaves. It is usually less than 10cm in height with a fairly dense umbel, 4–5cm in diameter, of bell-shaped rose-pink to purple-pink flowers about 1.0–1.5cm long. It needs a well drained sunny place, or a bulb frame. W. United States.

A. flavum A very variable species, forming small clumps of bulbs. It may be dwarf, at about 5cm, in height, or up to 30cm with few to many flowers in the umbel. These are pale to deep yellow, bell-shaped and about 5mm long, carried on long pedicels with the outer ones pendulous and the inner more or less erect. The short forms are good for a sunny rock garden and may be found under the names 'Nanum', 'Pumilum' or 'Minus'; some forms are nicely fragrant. Europe, W. Asia.

A. karataviense A very ornamental species for sunny places in borders, where it can be very striking as a foliage plant alone. Although of large size it is fairly dwarf, with stems 10–20cm in height with the two or three broad (up to 15cm wide) elliptic blue-grey leaves almost resting on the ground. The umbel is usually about 10–15cm in diameter, carrying many starry pale purplish-pink flowers about 1.0–1.5cm in diameter. Soviet Central Asia.

A. moly There are not many yellow-flowered Alliums which are good garden plants, but this is excellent and useful for naturalizing in sun or semi-shade beneath deciduous shrubs. It has rounded bulbs which produce offsets freely. The leaves, one or two per bulb, are grey-green, lanceolate and up to 3cm wide. It has 15–25cm stems bearing umbels 5–7cm across of large bright yellow flowers each about 1.0–1.5cm in diameter. S.W. France, E. Spain, in light woodland.

  A. scorzonerifolium is very similar, but with narrower leaves not more than 7mm wide. Spain, Portugal.

A. narcissiflorum (A. pedemontanum) This is usually confused with the similar *A. insubricum* in gardens and the latter is more frequently cultivated. *A. narcissiflorum* has a clump-forming habit, with elongated slender bulbs on a rhizome and narrowly linear leaves about 5mm or less wide. The flowering stems reach usually 15–25cm and carry a pendent umbel of five to eight large bell-shaped pinkish-purple flowers about 1.0–1.5cm long. It is a native of the south-west European Alps of N. Italy and S. France in rocky places.

  A. insubricum differs in having only three to five flowers in the umbel, and they are larger at about 1.8cm long. There is also a difference in the bulb tunics, fibrous in *A. narcissiflorum*, papery in *A. insubricum*. N. Italy, between Lakes Como and Garda.

  Both of these are among the most attractive of all Alliums and are not difficult to cultivate in a well drained sunny rock-garden position.

A. oreophilum (A. ostrowskianum) One of the best of the dwarf species, with a rounded bulb, narrow linear leaves at ground level and 5–15cm stems carrying 4–6cm wide umbels of large purple-pink flowers, each about 1cm in diameter. The cultivar 'Zwanenberg' is a deep carmine-red. It is a native of Central Asia and is very hardy, requiring only a sunny well-drained position.

A. paradoxum   In a good form this is a most attractive species but it is more usual to see ones which have mostly green bulbils instead of flowers. It is 10–25cm in height with one basal leaf and a small umbel of pendent wide bell-shaped white flowers, over 1cm long. The best forms I have seen come from the Elburz Mountains in N. Iran, but it also grows in the Caucasus. It is very easy in the open garden.

A. pulchellum   The form found in gardens this is actually *A. carinatum* subsp. *pulchellum*. *A. crinatum* subsp. *carinatum* should be avoided since the umbel has many bulbils and it can become a weed. Subsp. *pulchellum* is a graceful plant usually about 20–40cm in height, rather slender with very narrow leaves and loose umbels of many purple-pink flowers on long down-curving pedicels; there is also a white form. It is a useful mid-to-late summer-flowering bulb, very easily cultivated in the open border. S. Europe.

A. senescens   A clump-forming species with slender bulbs grouped on short rhizomes. There are several narrowly linear leaves per bulb, so the impression is of a very leafy plant, especially when a clump has formed. The flower stems usually overtop the leaves, very variable in height from 5–30cm, carrying tight many-flowered 2–5cm wide umbels of pale to deep pink flowers in summer. There are many forms of this and some pleasing mountain forms have grey-green twisted leaves almost prostrate on the ground. Several subspecies have been described and the most frequently seen European variant is subsp. *montanum* (*A. montanum*). It is a widespread species in Europe and Asia and a very good tough plant for the rock garden or border.

A. triquetrum   An attractive species but it should be kept for naturalizing beneath shrubs, since it can increase very rapidly. It has rounded bulbs with channelled basal leaves and three-angled stems 10–20cm in height, bearing few-flowered umbels of drooping tubular bell-shaped flowers 1–2cm long. They are white with green stripes. W. Mediterranean region.

A. unifolium   This has small bulbs each producing only one falcate leaf overtopped by 15–30cm stems which carry umbels 5–6cm in diameter, of sizeable widely bell-shaped pink flowers about 1.5–2.0 across, in late spring. It is worth growing on the rock garden in a sunny position. California and Oregon.

A. virgunculae   An excellent little species, uncommon in cultivation but not difficult to grow in a well drained sunny place, and excellent for the alpine house since it flowers in the autumn. It is 5–15cm in height with thread-like leaves and 2–3cm wide umbels each carrying up to twelve starry flowers. The best form I have seen is a dwarf one with white flowers, but it may also be pink. Japan.

Alrawia

A genus of two species related to *Bellevalia*, not very showy but could be described as being enthusiasts' plants! They are from regions with hot dry summers and thus in cooler climates require bulb frame or alpine house cultivation, with the bulbs dried out during their dormant period. Although easy to cultivate they do not increase very readily.

A. bellii (Scilla leucophylla, Bellevalia dichroa) Medium-sized bulbs produce several strap-shaped basal leaves, almost flat on the ground, hairy on the margins. The stems are 10–25cm in height with short racemes of pendent bell-shaped flowers, violet and with whitish tips to the lobes. They are 1cm or less long with a very short tube only one quarter the length of the whole flower. Occurs only in W. Iran on open hills and fields.

A. nutans Rather like *A. bellii*, but has slightly longer tubular flowers 1.0–1.3cm long, and the tube is about half the length of the whole flower. The leaves are not hairy on the margins. N.E. Iraq.

Amana

The few species forming this small eastern Asiatic genus are usually included with *Tulipa* and this approach is probably correct, although there is no difficulty in recognizing them and they are geographically distinct. They have small Tulip-like bulbs and in flower are also just like miniature Tulips, except for the linear bracts just below the inflorescence and the fact that there is a distinct style between the ovary and stigma; in *Tulipa* the stigma is sessile, sitting immediately on the ovary. They are very easy to cultivate and increase quite rapidly vegetatively. The small flowers require a good sunny day to encourage them to open fully. The Tulips do not extend farther east than the western Himalaya, whereas Amana is not found west of E. China.

A. edulis (A. graminifolia) This flowers in early spring, with stems 5–10cm in height carrying several white, yellow-eyed flowers about 1.5–3.0cm long, which open out flat to a starry shape; the exterior is strongly veined reddish-brown. There are two narrow (4–7mm wide) leaves per bulb, grey-green with a pair of (rarely three) linear bracts, just below the flowers. The bulb, like some Tulips, has its tunics densely lined with hairs. It is a native of Japan, Korea and E. China on open hillsides.

    A. latifolia is very similar in flower but has shorter, broader (6–11mm wide) leaves with a pale silvery or whitish stripe along the centre, and three or four bracts in a whorl below the flower. It is a native of Japan. It is easy to cultivate but does not increase especially quickly.

    A. erythronioides from China also has broader leaves and three or four bracts; the two leaves are unequal in width, the narrowest 1.0–1.5cm and the broadest 1.5–2.2cm, so it does look a little different from the other two species in which the leaves are nearly equal in size. Probably not in cultivation.

Androcymbium

A small, horticulturally fairly uninteresting genus related to *Colchicum* and *Merendera*. Some of the African species are more showy but are not hardy, whereas the Mediterranean ones are hardier but insignificant. They differ from both the above

genera in having a whorl of wide bract-like leaves surrounding the flowers, forming a
sort of involucre which is sometimes whitish with darker veining. The funnel-shaped
flowers have no proper tube, the segments being free from each other, as in *Merendera*.
They are little known in cultivation and are best if given alpine house or bulb frame
treatment, with a long hot dry period in the summer.

A. europaeum   The small Colchicum-like corms with tough blackish tunics produce a
rosette of leaves almost flat on the ground, the lower part of each leaf widened to about
1cm to form the involucre and the upper part tapered to a long point. There are several
widely funnel-shaped white or pink flowers 2.0–2.5cm in diameter resting in the centre of
the leaves, usually produced in winter or very early spring. They have long-pointed
segments. Spain, in rocky or sandy places.

   A. gramineum (*A. punctatum*) from North Africa is very similar, as is *A. palaestinum* from
the E. Mediterranean. They have larger capsules, over 1cm long.

   A. rechingeri, known only from W. Crete and the adjacent islet of Elaphonisi, is like
A. europaeum, but has shortly pointed perianth segments and the capsule does not split
open to release the seeds; instead it slowly rots and breaks up.

Anemone

Although the majority of the Anemones are non-bulbous, and do not fall within the
scope of this book, there are a considerable number which have swollen storage organs
and are offered by bulb nurseries. Most are spring-flowering with delightfully simple
flowers, providing some of the most attractive early spring plants. The well-known
species such as *A. blanda* and *A. apennina* are ideal for the rock garden or for naturalizing
beneath shrubs but the tuberous species from the Middle East are usually best treated as
bulb frame or alpine house plants where they can be dried off in summer.

   Anemones are propagated by division of clumps, in cases where increase takes place
naturally in this way, or by seed which should be sown when fresh.

A. apennina   An excellent species for growing in semi-shade under shrubs in humus-
rich soil, or in grass. It grows up to 15cm in height with dissected stem leaves overtopped
by the 3.0–3.5cm diameter flowers which have ten to twenty narrow petals. Blue is the
usual colour but white and pinkish forms are also known. The rootstock is a rather
elongated rhizome, unlike the rounded or knobbly tuber of *A. blanda*. Wild in Southern
Europe in semi-shady places, flowering in early to mid spring.

A. biflora   This is one of the gems of the genus but is not an easy plant to cultivate since
it comes from rocky hillsides in Iran, where its tubers become dry and sunbaked in
summer. Mis-shapen tubers produce stems 5–10cm in height, carrying very dissected
leaves and cup-shaped flowers 3–5cm in diameter. The most common colour is red, in
various shades, but yellow and coppery forms are also occasionally seen in the wild. It
inhabits mountain regions at altitudes up to 3000m in stony soils.

   A. biflora is very rarely seen but, thanks to the skill of Mrs Molly Dawson, I know that
the species is still in cultivation. Those which she grows are derived from an introduction
which I and my colleagues made on the Bowles Scholarship expedition to Iran in 1963.
The tubers are cultivated in pots in an alpine house and dried out in summer;
propagation is by seed.

   A. biflora is part of a confusing complex of 'species' from the Middle East and Central

Asia, some of which have been introduced into cultivation in recent years. They are mainly distinguished by the characters of their basal leaves and whorl of stem leaves and a summary of the supposed differences is as follows:

(a) Leaflets of stem leaves narrowed to a flattened or winged stalk; basal leaves with three distinctly stalked leaflets – *A. biflora*, *A. petiolulosa*, A. bucharica and *A. baissunensis*.

    A. petiolulosa from C. Asia has yellow flowers backed with red, about 2.5–4.5cm in diameter; the three leaflets of the basal leaves have very long stalks, all 3 stalks roughly equal in length, whereas in *A. biflora* they are shorter and unequal.

    A. bucharica also from C. Asia has red flowers and purple anthers, sometimes very large, 3.5–6.0cm in diameter. The three leaflets are very dissected, more so than in *A. biflora*, looking very carrot-like; the central one is on a longer stalk than the two lateral ones, as in *A. biflora*.

    A. baissunensis is a yellow version of *A. bucharica*.

(b) Leaflets of stem leaves as in the above group; basal leaves with three more or less unstalked leaflets – *A. gortschakowii*, *A. almaatensis*, *A. oligotoma*.

    A. gortschakowii from C. Asia (Tien Shan Mountains) has smallish yellow flowers about 1.5–2.0cm in diameter; the middle leaflet of the basal leaves has about 9–13 teeth.

    A. almaatensis, also from Tien Shan, is similar but has the leaflets more dissected, with up to 17 teeth.

    A. oligotoma from the Pamir-Alai range has leaflets less divided than in *A. gortschakowii* with only 5–9 teeth. I have not seen this plant and rely on descriptions only.

(c) Leaflets of stem leaves and the three leaflets of the basal leaves not at all stalked – *A. tschernjaewii*, *A. eranthioides*, *A. seravschanica*.

    A. tschernjaewii from the Pamir-Alai has white or pale pink flowers 2.5–4.0cm in diameter, with a darker stain in the centre, and dark purple stamens (see also p. 9).

    A. eranthioides also from Pamir-Alai has yellow flowers backed greenish or reddish with yellow anthers.

    A. seravschanica has small yellow flowers only 1.0–1.5cm in diameter, and glabrous, whereas the others have the tepals hairy on the outside.

All of these species require bulb frame or alpine house cultivation so that their tubers can be warm and partially dry in summer.

A. blanda Perhaps the best-known of the spring anemones, a highly desirable species for growing in half-shade or in grass. The knobbly tuberous rootstock produces dissected leaves and large flat flowers 3.5–4.5cm in diameter, which have ten to twenty petals. The fruiting heads bend over whereas in the otherwise similar *A. apennina* they remain erect. The flowers vary enormously in colour from pale blue to deep blue, various shades of pink, and white. Several of the variants have been given names: 'Atrocaerulea' (deep blue), 'Charmer' (deep pink), 'Ingramii' (deep blue), 'Pink Star' (bright pink), 'Radar' (magenta), 'Scythinica' (white, blue outside), 'Violet Star' (amethyst), 'White Splendour' (white, pinkish outside).

    A. blanda is native to the Balkans and Turkey in scrub, rocks or grassy places; it flowers in early to mid spring.

A. caucasica This is like a miniscule *A. blanda*, with flowers only 1.5–2.0cm in diameter; a real enthusiast's plant! It grows wild in the Caucasus and the Talysh

Mountains of N.W. Iran, where I have seen it in oak scrub with *Paeonia wittmanniana* and Snowdrops.

A. coronaria   A showy Mediterranean species from which the St Brigid, De Caen and other strains have been developed, particularly for the cut flower industry. The knobbly tubers produce finely cut, almost carrot-like leaves and red, blue or white flowers, 3.5–6.5cm in diameter, with 5–8 petals in the wild forms, on 10–20cm stems. The stem leaves are also much-divided, unlike those of *A. hortensis* and *A. pavonia*, its closest relatives. *A. coronaria* normally flowers in spring or early summer, but in cultivation the tubers produce finely cut, almost carrot-like leaves and red, blue or white flowers, market. Many colour forms, single and double, have been selected.

   A. coronaria is a warmth-loving species and needs to be planted in a sheltered sunny position if it is to thrive.

A. fulgens   This is considered to be a hybrid between *A. pavonina* and *A. hortensis*. Like them it has knobbly tubers and foliage which is less divided than in the related *A. coronaria*. The flowers are brilliant red and 4–5cm in diameter with rather narrow petals. The selection 'Multipetala' has many more petals; 'Annulata Grandiflora' has red flowers with a yellowish centre. Like its relatives it requires a warm sunny position.

A. hortensis   This relative of *A. coronaria* is similar but can be distinguished by having twelve to twenty narrow petals and stem leaves which are undivided or have only a few coarse lobes. The 3–4cm diameter flowers occur in mauve and pinkish shades. It occurs in S. France to the Balkans, flowering in spring. Like its relative it requires a warm sunny situation.

A. nemorosa   Although the rootstock of the Wood Anemone is a long thin rhizome and should not be dried out, this species is nevertheless usually offered by the bulb nurserymen. These stick-like rhizomes are best planted in early spring before growth commences, or in autumn when dormant; being a woodland species it does well in semi-shaded humus-rich soil. It is a common late spring-flowering European and British plant, having three deeply lobed leaflets and, in its common wild form, has snowy white flowers on 10–15cm stems, 2.5–4.0cm in diameter with five to eight petals. Several varieties have been selected and named: 'Alboplena' (double white), 'Atrocaerulea' (deep purplish-blue), 'Allenii' (lavender blue), 'Bowles Purple' (purple), 'Hilda' (semi-double white), 'Leeds Variety' (large white), 'Robinsoniana' (pale blue), 'Rosea' (white, fading pink), 'Royal Blue' (violet).

   All of these are suitable for cool positions under shrubs or in the large rock garden, but they can form extensive patches.

A. pavonina   A relative of *A. coronaria*, but differs in having the stem leaves undivided or only slightly lobed; from *A. hortensis* it differs in the flowers, having ten or less broader petals. Like *A. coronaria* the wild forms have been developed and many large-flowered strains selected, notably the 'St Bavo' strain. The wild forms, which occur in open stony places in the Mediterranean region from France to Turkey, have flowers in early spring, 4–5cm in diameter in red, pink or purple shades, often with a yellowish or white eye.

   Like its relatives *A. pavonina* requires a warm sunny situation if it is to thrive.

A. ranunculoides   In general growth habit and appearance, this spring-flowering species resembles *A. nemorosa*, but has bright yellow flowers 1.5–2.0cm in diameter, with five or six petals. It occurs in European woodlands and is thus best grown in semi-shade in humus-rich soil. 'Flore Plena' has double flowers.

A. × seemannii A hybrid between *A. nemorosa* and *A. ranunculoides*. It is similar in overall appearance to these but has flowers of a delightful soft creamy-sulphur shade.

A. trifolia This is a close relative of *A. nemorosa* and resembles it in flower and in the rhizomatous rootstock, but the leaves consist of three undivided leaflets, not lobed as in the Wood Anemone. It occurs in woodlands in south-east Europe and is known only in its normal white-flowered form; it is easily cultivated in semi-shade.

A. tschernjaewii The first time this charming species came to my notice was when Paul Furse introduced tubers from Afghanistan in the 1960s. Since then further introductions have been made from Kashmir, under the erroneous name of *A. biflora*, and I have seen it on open sunny hillsides in central Asia, in Uzbekistan, so it is a widespread species in the wild. The leaves are dark green with few divisions, overtopped by 5–10cm stems bearing cup shaped flowers 2.5–4.0cm in diameter in white or pale pink with a darker reddish stain in the centre and the anthers are also a dark purple. It flowers in spring and requires alpine house or bulb frame cultivation where the tubers can be dried out in summer.

Anoiganthus

This is now included in the genus *Cyrtanthus* and can be found on p. 65.

Anomatheca

Only one species of this small South African genus of the Iridaceae is cultivated to any extent, and is hardy in most areas where the ground does not freeze more than a few inches deep. The genus is related to *Lapeirousia*, a much larger more widespread group in Africa, none of which is however at all hardy.

A. laxa (Lapeirousia cruenta) This grows between 15 and 30cm in height, with a fan of flat leaves clustered at the base of the stem. The stem is simple or with a few short branches and bears flattish flowers about 2cm in diameter with a long slender tube; the usual colour is red with darker markings on the lower segments, but there is also a pure white form, and a pale blue form with purple blotches in the throat. The relatively large seeds are bright red.

A. *laxa* is a native of the eastern parts of southern Africa in dampish places and is winter-dormant, commencing to grow in late spring, and flowering in mid to late summer. It does best in a light soil in an open sunny border, where it can be left permanently, although in cold districts it is best to lift the corms for the winter. Propagation is simply by division of clumps which build up fairly quickly, or by seed – which will give flowering corms in one or two years.

Arisaema

An interesting and large group of summer-flowering Aroids, they are widely distributed in the world and have a considerable number of species which are hardy enough to be grown without protection in cool temperate climates. Most of these hardy species originate in the Himalaya, China, Japan and North America. Arisaemas produce large flattish tubers, which lie dormant in winter and begin to grow in spring or early summer, producing an aerial 'stem' of sheathing leaf stalks crowned by attractively lobed, sometimes mottled leaves. The flowers are of typical Aroid make-up with a large hooded spathe, usually greenish or purplish, enclosing the pencil-like spadix which bears the minute flowers at its lower end, hidden down inside the tube. The upper end is elongated into an 'appendix', which may be anything from club-like at its apex to long-tapering and whip-like. In late summer the fruiting heads can be attractive, large dense heads of orange or red berries.

Most Arisaemas come from summer rainfall areas in partial shade and seem to be best in cool growing conditions. I find that a peat garden in semi-shade is ideal, or a humus-rich border with Hellebores. Their tubers need to be planted deeply, at about 15–25cm, in soil which is fairly open with plenty of leafmould – a little sand should be placed around them at planting time.

Unfortunately not many of the species are in general cultivation, but a few are becoming more widely known among enthusiasts.

A. candidissimum   This is by far the best species for gardens, showing up well with its large white spathes, and is very hardy, increasing by offset tubers to form clumps. It is about 30cm in height when in leaf, but the inflorescences are shorter and are produced before the large three-lobed leaves expand. The spathes are about 8–10cm long on a 15cm stem and are tubular, with an expanded hood over the apex which has a shortly pointed 'tail'. They are predominantly white with a pinkish suffusion and striping, sometimes with greenish suffusion, and the pencil-like spadix is white or yellowish-green. It is a native of W. China.

I have had this growing well in a variety of situations, sun or shade, damp or dry but find that it does best in a sunny position in soil which is rich and well supplied with humus. The tubers do not come into growth until early summer.

A. consanguineum   A very robust species which may produce a stout, attractively spotted stem up to a metre in height, crowned by an umbrella-like leaf which consists of many narrow radiating long-pointed leaflets. Just beneath the leaf the spathe is produced, deep green with a slightly brownish tinge, about 15–20cm in length with a long-tapering point at the apex. The green spadix is almost hidden in the tube. An extra bonus is the large cluster of red berries which should be gathered for propagation purposes, since offset tubers are not produced freely. China, Taiwan, E. Himalaya. This does well in the semi-shaded peat garden with the tuber planted deeply.

A. costatum   A little-known species in cultivation, but not difficult to grow and forming clumps by offsets when doing well in humus-rich, semi-shaded conditions. It is about 25–35cm in height, with a very conspicuously veined leaf consisting of three leaflets which often have reddish margins. The spathe, carried below the leaf, is a deep purple-brown with white stripes, hooded over at the apex and drawn out into a long point. A curious feature of the spadix is that it is extremely long and tapering into a whip-like appendix, which twists and coils, dangling down to touch the ground. Nepal, Himalaya.

A. propinquum is a little like this in its three-lobed leaves and spathe colouring, but is altogether smaller and the spathe ends rather abruptly in a short point; the slender appendix dangles out of the mouth of the hooded spathe, but is not as long – not reaching the ground. E. Himalaya, and a very common plant in Sikkim, where I had the fun of seeing it in 1983 on the Alpine Garden Society's expedition.

A. flavum   Not a showy plant, but very distinctive with its small yellow spathes. It will reach 30cm in height when growing well, but is usually less. It has one or two leaves per tuber, each consisting of about five to ten leaflets. The small, 3–4cm long spathes are yellow or greenish-yellow, with the sharply-pointed apex turned over abruptly at right angles so that it lies horizontally, completely hiding the tiny spadix inside. It is widespread from the Arabian Peninsula eastwards through the Himalaya to China.

I find it very hardy, easily grown in the sun or partial shade and producing seeds freely.

A. griffithii   A very dramatic plant but not very hardy, certainly in my cold garden, best grown with protection or lifted for the winter. It has large three-lobed leaves overtopping the short-stemmed spathes, which are tubular in the lower part but widen out in the upper portion into elephant-ear like flaps; the colour is greenish or purplish, with a strong netted pattern of paler veins. It is made even more curious by the tail-like appendix dangling down to the ground. E. Himalaya, but keeping to the forest at lower altitudes.

A. utile is very similar but has slightly smaller spathes with less widely developed 'ears'.

A. jaquemontii   A fairly mediocre garden plant, but easy enough to grow and fun for those who like green-flowered plants. It is a slender species to about 30cm in height, with leaves consisting of three to nine narrow leaflets, usually over-topped by the green spathes which have a hooded, long-pointed apex. The spadix protrudes slightly from the mouth of the spathe but does not have a greatly elongated appendix. Himalaya.

A. kiusianum   An interesting species, often quite dwarf in cultivation and proving to be reasonably hardy to date. It has one leaf with up to 13 leaflets which are pointed at the apex. The spathe is dark purple, hooded over at the apex and abruptly narrowed to a point; the spadix protrudes considerably and is elongated into a slender appendix. It is a native of Japan.

A. ringens   An early-flowering species which must be grown with some protection in frosty areas since it emerges in early spring. It has large leaves with three broad leaflets, which taper to long points. The spathes are shorter than the leaves, greenish or purplish with paler stripes, the upper part curved over into a dome-like shape and usually coloured a much darker purple-black; the whitish or cream spadix is hidden within the spathe.

Simon Mayo, the Aroid specialist at Kew, has likened the curious domed part of the spathes to the helmet of a nineteenth-century cavalryman!

A. serratum (A. japonicum)   A very variable species which at times has been divided up by botanists into many separate species. The leaf stalks, forming a stem, are usually attractively mottled and lined pale and dark green and carry up to twenty leaflets in a pedate arrangement. The spathes may be green to purple, sometimes striped or spotted, hooded over at the apex and drawn out into a point, hiding the club-shaped spadix inside. It is a native of China, Korea and Japan and is a fairly hardy plant, but in districts where the ground freezes to a great depth it is best lifted for the winter or grown in the protection of a frame or greenhouse.

A. sikokianum   An exciting species, proving to be hardier than I expected but not unfortunately producing offsets or seeds very freely. It is about 25–35cm in height with two leaves per tuber, consisting of three to five leaflets, usually overtopped by the spathe which is dark brownish- or blackish-purple, suffused green inside. It is hooded over at the apex and long-pointed, but has a wide open mouth, displaying the large white spadix which has its apex much-expanded like the clapper of a bell. It is a native of Japan. Tubers planted out in a semi-shaded border have now survived two winters with temperatures down to $-12°C$.

A. speciosum   An attractive species but rather tender, even in my Surrey garden. It has large leaves with three red-margined leaflets, the two lateral ones lopsided and different in shape from the centre one, which is regularly shaped. The spathe is hidden beneath the leaves and is purple with pale stripes, hooded over at the apex and drawn out into a long tip, but this is much exceeded by the spadix which has a long trailing dark purple tail-like appendix hanging from the mouth down to the ground. It occurs widely in the eastern Himalaya and W. China.

Var. *mirabile* differs only in having a very much thickened base to the appendix and is rough on the surface at this point.

A. tortuosum (A. helleborifolium)   A stout species with a well-developed, often green-spotted stem bearing two or three pedate leaves with up to seventeen leaflets. The spathe is usually a rather pale green overlaid with a greyish 'bloom' and the pointed apex is either hooded over or stands erect. The name is derived from the green or purplish spadix appendix which is S-shaped, protruding from the spathe with its tip held upright. It is a widespread plant in the Himalayan region, India and W. China.

A. triphyllum   Jack-in-the-Pulpit. This produces one or two leaves on a spotted stem, each with three leaflets, equalling or overtopping the hooded green spathe which may be suffused with purple, or striped lengthways with white or green. The spadix is visible inside the 'cowl' of the spathe and is upright, pencil-like or slightly club-shaped, and green or purplish. It is a native of eastern North America and is very hardy, suitable for a peat garden or semi-shaded border.

Arisarum

A small group of Arums which are known for their curiosity value, rather than beauty, since their spathes are small and of subdued colours.

A. proboscideum   This produces in spring a mat of dark green arrow-shaped leaves less than 10cm in height, amid which are carried strange 2–3cm long blackish-purple spathes which have a tapered whip-like apex up to 15cm in length. It is sometimes called the Mouse Plant since, to some, they look like small black mice diving for cover among the leaves! It needs a humus-rich soil in semi-shade. Italy and Spain, in semi-shaded places.

A. vulgare   A common Mediterranean species with plain green, silvery-zoned or mottled, arrow-shaped leaves and greenish to brown striped spathes up to 6cm long on stems 15–20cm high. It flowers in winter or early spring and requires a sheltered sunny position where it will dry out in summer.

Arum

A very interesting group of hardy tuberous plants, but many of them have little ornamental value and they are not cultivated to any extent except by specialists. Their leaves, which may be plain, spotted or marble-patterned are of characteristic shape, like broad arrowheads with two basal lobes; these appear in autumn or spring followed in spring by the sail-like spathes. One species produces spathes in autumn. The common British native *A. maculatum* is a typical member of the group and on the whole is best avoided in gardens since it can become quite a pest; in the wild garden it can be worthwhile however, first for its fresh young leaves in late winter, then for the dense spikes of bright red berries which last into the early autumn.

The flowers of the Arums are carried at the base of the pencil-like spadix which protrudes from the spathe, and are in two whorls like collars around the spadix, the lower ones female and the upper male ones bearing the pollen.

The following species are among the more striking and are easy to cultivate in sunny situations.

A. creticum   This is to me the best of them all. It has plain green leaves over-topped in spring by deep yellow or white, rather narrow, pointed spathes, 8–15cm long – the blade of which is often twisted and recurved, leaving the similarly coloured spadix protruding. They are often fragrant. The yellow and white variants should possibly be regarded as different species but this is a group in need of specialist study before decisions can be made. It is a native of Crete in rocky places. Although its leaves appear in autumn and winter I have never known them to be damaged by frost.

A. dioscoridis   This is a very variable plant in its spathe colour, with some very striking variants. The background colour is often pale green overlaid with deep purple blotches, this form being called var. *smithii*. I have also seen forms in Turkey with large velvety-purple spathes, blotched darker, which are probably referable to var. *spectabile*. They unfortunately have a disgusting smell. The leaves are unmarked green. E. Mediterranean, often in rocky scrub.

A. italicum   This is frequently cultivated in its variety *pictum* (*marmoratum*) for its beautifully creamy-veined arrow-shaped leaves which appear in autumn and remain in a decorative state through the hardest winter weather until the spring or summer. It is very hardy and will grow in a wide range of situations, but the pale green spathes seem to be produced only if it is in a warm sheltered place. It is a widespread plant of woods and hedges in Europe, N. Africa and Asia Minor, but wild forms are sometimes not marked so attractively on the leaves.

A. petteri (A. nigrum)   Not a very showy plant, since the spathes are usually almost hidden by the plain green foliage. They are short-stemmed, about 15–20cm long, and are deep purplish-maroon or blackish-purple with a very thick dark purple spadix. It is very easy to cultivate in a sunny situation. Yugoslavia, especially in the coastal mountains in stony scrubland.

A. pictum   A very interesting species but unfortunately the leaves, which appear in autumn, are very easily damaged by frost. It is unusual in producing blackish-purple spathes in autumn, 15–25cm long, with a deep purple spadix. The leaves are most attractive, thick and leathery shiny green with creamy veins, and it is worth growing in a deep pot in the protection of an alpine house for its foliage alone. The name should not be confused with *A. italicum* var. *pictum*. It is a native of the Balearic Islands, Corsica, Sardinia and Italy in rocky places.

Begonia

Most Begonias are of course not at all hardy and are grown as pot plants or for summer bedding. One species, *B. grandis*, is reliably hardy in milder districts and will tolerate a considerable amount of frost if its dormant tubers are not too wet. It needs a sheltered position in sun or partial shade and as a precaution against loss some loose peat or bracken should be placed over the dormant tubers in winter. Propagation is by bulbils which are produced in the leaf axils.

B. grandis (B. evansiana)   The tuberous stock produces fleshy stems to 20–35cm in height, bearing cordate leaves about 15cm long which are tinged pink beneath. The loosely branched inflorescence carries four-petalled pinkish flowers (white in the cultivar 'Alba') in late summer. It is a native of China.

Bellevalia

A group of *Muscari*-like bulbs from Europe and the Middle East, which on the whole have little value as garden plants, interesting as they are. Mostly they have racemes of dull, brownish, dirty white or dingy purple tubular flowers, with six small perianth lobes. The leaves are all basal and strap-like or linear. Unlike *Muscari*, the flowers are not constricted at the mouth and the anthers are held just within the entrance to the tube, whereas in the related *Hyacinthus* they are carried well down inside the tube.

Of the considerable number of species, the following, with brighter colours, are attractive and on the whole easy to cultivate; they all flower in mid spring after the first flush of early bulbs is over.

B. atroviolacea   This has a 15–20cm flower stem with a dense raceme of tubular deep indigo blue flowers, each about 8mm long with short spreading lobes. It is a native of Northern Afghanistan and the adjacent parts of Soviet Central Asia.

B. turkestanica, also from C. Asia, is very similar but has lighter blue shorter flowers.

B. forniculata   An exciting species, 15–30cm in height, bearing a loose elongated raceme of intense mid-blue flowers, one of the most startling blues in a bulbous plant that I know. The individual flowers are shortly tubular, almost bell-shaped. It grows in waterlogged meadows in clay in E. Turkey, but does not seem to demand particularly wet conditions in cultivation in order to flourish.

B. hyacinthoides (Strangweia spicata)   Rather different from the rest in having short (5–10cm) dense spikes of blue flowers, which have only a short tube, about a third to half as long as the spreading lobes, thus giving a more open flower, and the stamens have their filaments toothed at the base. The leaves are linear, about 5mm wide and ciliate at the edges, usually flat on the ground. It is a native of Greece, in rocky places. This is an attractive little plant, very suitable for an alpine house or bulb frame.

B. kurdistanica   I am growing under this name an attractive species introduced by Oleg Polunin, either from Iraq or Lebanon. It has many-flowered racemes of white flowers in mid spring, 20–30cm in height; it is perfectly happy in an open sunny situation and increases well. Peter Boyce has recently introduced the true species from Syria and it is clear that the two are different, the former thus requiring further study.

B. paradoxa   In *Dwarf Bulbs* I confused this species with *B. forniculata*. *B. paradoxa* has stems 15–25 cm tall, carrying short dense racemes of flowers of a deep, dull, almost navy shade of blue; in fact they are so short as to be more or less globose. It also occurs in N.E. Turkey in damp alpine pastures and in the adjacent parts of Caucasia. It is like a compact version of the more common *B. pycnantha*, and possibly should be regarded as such.

B. pycnantha   This is the best-known of the blue-flowered species, since it is readily available from nurseries. It is robust, with dense elongated conical racemes on stems up to 30cm; like *B. paradoxa* the flowers are a dark navy blue and they have a yellowish rim to the six lobes. It is a more widespread species than the others, in E. Turkey, W. Iran, N. Iraq and the southern Caucasus, growing in wet meadows. I also have a white form collected for me by John Ingham in Iran. In cultivation *B. pycnantha* can be grown in the open border or rock garden.

B. rixii   An interesting little species named after Martyn Rix, who collected it on one of his many expeditions in the Middle East. It is a dwarf plant, only 5–10cm high, with the short grey-green leaves lying on the ground and somewhat twisted. There are few flowers in a short dense raceme and these are bright blue at first, changing to a dark blue and then brownish as they age. It grows in rocky places in the mountains of S.E. Turkey and, although hardy, requires a position where its bulbs can dry off and become warm in summer – so a bulb frame or raised bed cultivation suits it best.

B. tabriziana   An attractive little species which has been known as a *Hyacinthus* and *Hyacinthella*, at one time quite well-known in cultivation but now rather rare. It is 5–10cm in height, with three or four narrow linear leaves and short dense racemes of small bell-shaped flowers 6–7mm long, half the length being a tube. The form which was in cultivation had blue flowers but it varies, according to Per Wendelbo, from white to lilac or blue. It is a native of N.W. Iran – in the region of Tabriz in dry stony places – and in cultivation is best grown in a bulb frame or alpine house.

Biarum

A small fascinating genus of the Araceae from the Mediterranean and Middle East. Unlike most Aroids they are autumn-flowering, the frequently blackish evil-smelling spathes appearing before the leaves which emerge in late autumn and remain green until the following spring. The leaves are entire, without the arrow-like lobes at the base which Arums have. The spathes are almost stemless and rest directly on the ground with the blade upright or sometimes folded back and pressed to the soil, leaving the pencil-like spadix standing erect. The arrangement of flowers at the base of the spadix is important in distinguishing between the species. There are two 'collars' of flowers around the spadix, the lowest being female, the upper male (pollen-bearing); these two groups are separated by a gap which usually has hair-like sterile flowers on it, and there may also be sterile ones above the collar of male flowers. The fruits do not appear until spring and are like a cluster of small white eggs at ground level.

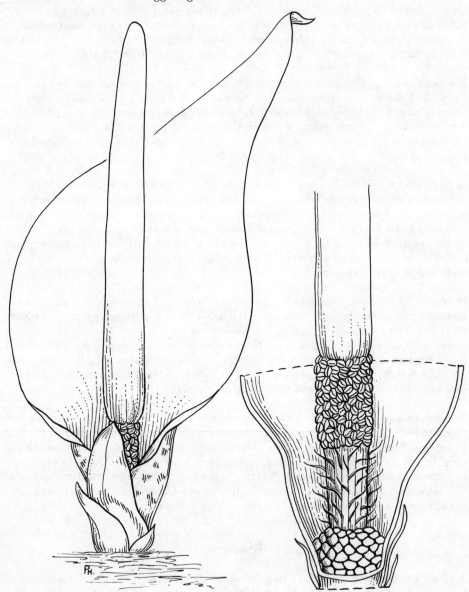

BIARUM

A Biarum *inflorescence showing (left) the spathe and spadix and (right) cutaway to show the female flowers at base, sterile hair-like flowers in the centre and the male (pollen-bearing) flowers at the top*

Biarums are usually plants of rather sunbaked places and the majority of them are best treated as bulb frame or alpine house plants where, in the confined space, the impact of the smell can be experienced to the full! *B. tenuifolium*, however, is easy to grow in any sunny situation and is very hardy.

B. carduchorum This has deep blackish purple lanceolate spathes, 10–20cm long, the margins of which are folded in and fused at the base into a cylindrical tube about 5cm long. The leaves usually appear at the end of flowering time and are roughly elliptical, about 7–15cm long with a long petiole. S. and E. Turkey.

B. davisii A small species, unusual in being fragrant and in having creamy or yellowish spathes spotted with pink inside; they are bottle-shaped at the base with a hooded apex and the slender spadix is reddish, only slightly protruding from the mouth of the spathe. The small leaves follow later in autumn and are only 2.5–7.0cm long. Crete and S. Turkey. I find that the Turkish form is much easier to grow and flower than the Cretan, and it is larger.

B. eximium A lovely species, if that adjective can be considered suitable for this genus! It has deep purple spathes 8–10cm long which become recurved, leaving the blackish spadix protruding. The base of the spathe is folded into a bottle-shaped tube but the margins are only actually joined together right at the very base. The leaves which follow have a blade up to 20cm long. S. Turkey.

B. bovei is similar but has a more slender spadix not more than 3mm thick; in *B. eximium* it is at least 5mm thick. S. Turkey, Lebanon, Israel.

B. pyrami, also from S. Turkey, is like *B. eximium* in having a stout spadix and bottle-like base to the spathe, but differs in the arrangement of the sterile whisker-like flowers on the spadix; in *B. eximium* they are scattered evenly while in *B. pyrami* they are in a cluster just above the female (bottom) flowers only. The spathe of *B. pyrami* is usually about 18–20cm long and may be purple or greenish flecked and suffused with purple.

B. carratracense should be mentioned here also; it has deep reddish-purple spathes and a purple spadix. The tube of the spathe is more cylindrical than bottle-shaped and the lamina rather narrow in proportion to its length. Some people regard it as related to or a variant of *B. bovei*. S. Spain.

B. spruneri I find that this is the earliest-flowering species, usually in mid to late summer. It has a rather short deep purple spathe, 10–15cm at most, and it stays almost erect with the erect blackish spadix about the same length. The leaves follow much later in autumn, long after the spathe has disappeared. S. Greece.

B. tenuifolium This is the most commonly cultivated species, very easy to grow and increasing rapidly by small offset tubers. It does well in open sunny positions and has even taken to growing in a patch of rough grass in my garden. The spathes, which are produced in late summer or autumn are rather long and narrow, often twisted lengthways and usually about 10–20cm long, greenish or purplish with a cylindrical whitish tube at the base. Unlike all the other species mentioned there are hair-like sterile flowers both above and below the cluster of male (upper) flowers. The leaves follow much later and are very variable, usually linear and often undulate at the margins, but some forms in S. Greece have short oblong leaves and ones I have seen in Crete have very narrow ones with attractively crisped margins. It is widespread in the Mediterranean region.

Var. *abbreviatum* has short greenish spathes which are strongly hooded at the apex.

Bloomeria

A genus of few species from North America, related to *Brodiaea* and *Triteleia*. It is rarely seen in gardens, although an attractive summer-flowering bulb. The main feature distinguishing it from other genera is that each of the six stamens has a small cup at the base of its filament. Although hardy, the bulbs require a warm sunny situation to ripen them during their dormant period in late summer.

B. crocea   This has one long linear basal leaf, which dies away by flowering time, and wiry stems 25–45cm in height carrying a many-flowered umbel 5–15cm in diameter. Each flower is about 1.5cm in diameter, flattish and starry, yellow-orange with a purple or greenish line on each segment; there is no perianth tube. It is mainly Californian but reaches northern Mexico in Baja California.

Var. *crocea* has the filament cup double-notched at the apex; in var. *aurea* the cup has two acute teeth: var. *montana* is an extreme where the two teeth are extended into long points.

Bongardia

A member of the Berberis family, unusual in having a tuber and dying down in summer. It is related to *Leontice* and *Gymnospermium*, which are also dealt with in this book, but differs noticeably in its leaves – which are pinnate in shape. It is easily cultivated in an alpine house, bulb frame or open sunny place where it will be hot and dry during its dormant period; it flowers in spring to early summer.

B. chrysogonum   The corky rounded tuber produces several basal leaves which are pinnate, bearing opposite grey-green leaflets, each of which has a brown-red zone near its base; it is thus quite a handsome foliage plant. Several yellow flowers are carried in a leafless, loosely-branched inflorescence, 20–50cm in height. These are flattish and about 1.5cm in diameter, followed by inflated bladder-like fruits. It is a native of Turkey, stretching eastwards to Soviet Central Asia and Pakistan, growing in fields and open sunny hillsides.

Brimeura

A small genus of bulbous plants containing only two species formerly regarded as Hyacinths but clearly not very similar to *H. orientalis*. Both species are worth growing, especially *B. amethystina*, which will do well on a rock garden or in semi-shade. *B. fastigiata* is small and less showy and is better grown in the alpine house, where it can be seen more closely.

B. amethystina (Hyacinthus amethystinus)   This is 10–20cm in height, with several narrowly linear green basal leaves and a loose one-sided raceme of narrow horizontal or drooping bell-shaped flowers, about 1cm long with six short lobes; it thus looks rather like a miniature Bluebell. The colour varies from pale to deep blue, some forms being a very bright vibrant blue, and there is also a white form 'Alba'. It flowers in mid to late spring. Pyrenees, in grassy places.

B. fastigiata (Hyacinthus fastigiatus, H. pouzolzii)   A dwarf plant only 5cm or so in height, with narrowly linear basal leaves and short dense racemes, of up to ten flowers which face upwards. The lower pedicels are slightly longer than the upper giving the inflorescence a wide appearance. The flowers are about 7mm long with the tube and lobes about equal in length and they vary from white to pale lilac-blue or even pinkish. It is a native of Corsica, Sardinia and Menorca.

Brodiaea

One of a group of closely related genera from North America which have their flowers carried in umbels on leafless stems, looking rather like Alliums. Their rootstock consists of a corm covered with fibrous tunics and their leaves are mostly rather long and linear – only one or two per corm in many cases. The other genera are *Triteleia*, *Dichelostemma*, *Bloomeria* and *Muilla* which will be found here in their appropriate alphabetical position. The differences between these are not altogether obvious at first, so the following key may be useful in identification.

Key to Brodiaea relatives

A   Fertile stamens (i.e. carrying pollen) 3, plus 3 flattish staminodes
      without any anthers (in 1 *Brodiaea* species no staminodes; in 2
      Dichelostemma species 6 stamens but the stigma is 3-lobed). Flower
      colour blue, violet, purple, pink or red .... B
      Fertile stamens 6, all with pollen-bearing anthers, stigma not lobed;
      flower colour white, yellow, purple, blue........................... C
B   Flowers in loose umbels with rather stiff pedicels; bracts subtending
      umbel colourless; leaves with no angular keel beneath .... *Brodiaea*
      Flowers in tight umbels with flexible pedicels, bracts coloured;
      leaves with a keel beneath... *Dichelostemma*
C   Leaves rounded with no keel beneath; flowers whitish or yellowish... *Muilla*
      Leaves with an angular keel .... D
D   Stamens with their filaments cup-like at the very base; flowers
      yellow .... *Bloomeria*
      Stamens with flattened or thread-like filaments, no cup at base;
      flowers white, yellow, purple or blue................................ *Triteleia*

Brodiaeas are mostly early-summer flowering and, although not very showy plants, are of interest in a warm sunny border, flowering when most other bulbs are ending their display. The umbels of some of the larger-flowered species can be useful when dried for winter decorations. Several of the better known 'Brodiaeas' such as *B. laxa* and *B.* × *tubergenii* will be found under their correct names in *Triteleia* but in literature and nursery lists they may well still be found under *Brodiaea*.

B. californica   A handsome large-flowered species up to 50cm in height, sometimes only 20cm, with umbels 5–20cm across carrying funnel-shaped flowers 3.0–4.5cm long with the segments about three times the length of the tube. The three linear staminodes are flat and whitish or pale lilac. It is variable in colour, usually some shade of lavender or purple, but sometimes pinkish, with a darker mid-vein on the segments. N. California.
   B. leptandra, also with large flowers 2.5–4.0cm long, is not as far as I know in

cultivation; it has narrow perianth segments, 4–7mm wide (up to 10mm in *B. californica*) and the flowers are described as being rosy-violet to pink. N. California.

B. appendiculata is also unknown to me in cultivation. The stamens have filaments which are furnished with two thread-like appendages at the apex; these are lacking in the above two species. The purplish flowers are large, 2.5–4.0cm long. California.

B. coronaria (B. grandiflora)   This is a fairly stocky species, useful for a sunny rock garden. It is 5–25cm in height, with rather few flowers in the umbels. The flowers are 2.5–4.0cm long with a narrow bell-shaped tube which has a slight constriction part of the way up. The perianth segments are slightly more than twice the length of the tube and variable in colour from pale to deep purple or pinkish; the three wide creamy-coloured conspicuous staminodes have their margins rolled inwards. British Columbia and south to California.

Subsp. *rosea* (*Brodiaea rosea*) has pale to deep pink flowers. California.

B. elegans   Another attractive species 10–50cm in height with umbels up to 20cm in diameter and funnel-shaped deep purple flowers 3–5cm long. The segments are slightly more than twice the length of the tube. Unlike *B. coronaria* the staminodes are flat, not with inrolled margins. California and Oregon.

Susp. *hooveri* is a variant from W. Oregon which has the tips of the staminodes curved outwards.

B. kinkiensis and two other species *B. filifolia* and *B. orcuttii* belong to a different section from all the others mentioned. They have smallish flowers which have the staminodes sharply pointed at the apex (blunt or notched in other species) or lacking altogether. *B. kinkiensis* is 20–30cm tall with only one basal leaf. The umbel is up to 15cm in diameter, carrying 2–3cm long starry violet flowers on pedicels 3–8cm long; the segments are slightly longer than the tube. It occurs only on San Clemente Island off the Californian coast.

B. filifolia generally has shorter pedicels 1–4cm long and smaller purplish flowers 1.3–2.0cm long. It is a rare species in California.

B. orcuttii, also Californian, is 8–25cm in height with pedicels 1–5cm long. The flowers are pinkish violet, 1.5–2.5cm long. It differs from the two above species (and from all others) in having no staminodes, just three fertile stamens. I have not grown this or *B. filifolia*.

B. minor (B. nana)   A good species for the bulb frame, dwarf and slender, only 2–10cm in height. The umbel is 2–6cm in diameter, with two to twelve flowers, 1.5–2.5cm long, with the segments slightly more than twice the length of the tube, widely spreading to give a flower diameter of about 1.5cm. The colour is pinkish, lilac-blue or purplish. A distinct feature is that the tube is markedly constricted at the throat. California.

B. purdyi is one I have not grown. It is related to *B. minor* and the flowers also have a constricted throat but it is generally taller, 10–25cm, with narrow perianth segments, the inner ones being only 4–5mm wide (up to 7mm wide in *B. minor*). California.

B. pallida also has flowers with a constricted perianth tube. It is known from only one locality in Tuolumne County, California and differs from *B. minor* mainly in the shape of the anthers.

B. stellaris   A short species with stems 2–6cm tall, carrying umbels to 10cm in diameter of small violet flowers with widely spreading segments, to give a starry appearance; in other small-flowered species such as *B. terrestris* they are more bell-shaped. The tube and segments are about equal in length, giving a total flower size of 1.5–2.5cm long. N. California on rocky hillsides.

B. insignis, also Californian, is related, but differs from *B. stellaris* in having pinkish-purple starry flowers with the segments longer than the tube, and also in various details of the stamens. California.

B. terrestris (B. coronaria var. macropoda) A very dwarf species, one of the best for bulb frame cultivation or for the alpine house. It is less than 10cm in height, the umbels often carried directly on the ground with no obvious stem. There are often rather few flowers on longish pedicels, so the umbels appear very loose. The flowers are lilac or violet coloured, about 1.5–2.5cm long, with the segments slightly more than twice the length of the tube. California and Oregon.

Susp. *kernensis* is a slightly taller variant.

B. jolonensis is taller than *B. terrestris*, with stems up to 15cm, and is distinguished from it in having a purplish ovary (green in *B. terrestris*). California, mainly coastal region.

Bulbocodium

A relative of *Colchicum* and differing mainly in not having three separate styles – instead having one, which divides into three right at the tip.

B. vernum This has small elongate corms producing 3–4cm wide bright pinkish-purple funnel-shaped flowers in spring, resting almost on the ground and accompanied by two or three short lanceolate leaves which elongate later. It is widespread in European mountains from the Pyrenees and Alps to Austria in open alpine meadows.

It is an attractive hardy little plant for cultivation in a sunny raised bed or bulb frame.

B. versicolor (B. ruthenicum) This is like a smaller version of *B. vernum*; the perianth segments each have a pair of appendages at the base. It has a more easterly occurrence, from Italy to the southern USSR.

Calochortus

A sizeable genus of gorgeous plants from North America and Mexico, all of which are worth growing but are not easy. They mostly require a warm, dryish rest period in summer and will not thrive in countries with cooler moister climates. The greatest success I have achieved with them is in the bulb frame or cold house, although in the latter they do become rather tall and lanky and often require support. They are late spring or early summer flowering in the case of most of the species from the W. United States, and these are kept warm and dryish in summer through until about October. The Mexican species however, which are sometimes referred to as *Cyclobothra*, behave in the reverse manner since they come from summer rainfall regions. They are dry and dormant in winter and should be watered in spring for flowering in late summer. *C. barbatus* is the only member of this latter group which is likely to be encountered, although there are several others around in specialist collections.

Their beauty is indicated by some of the vernacular names such as Mariposa Tulip,

Cats Ears, Fairy Lantern and Globe Lily and they are, to me, some of the most exciting and beautiful plants in the whole Lily family.

The study of Calochortus by M. Ownbey in *Annals of the Missouri Botanical Garden* vol. 27 (1940) has not been superseded, although a few extra species have been discovered since then. Unfortunately, of the roughly sixty species described, very few are known in cultivation and are not obtainable from nurseries, but it is possible to get seeds now and again, particularly from the seed lists of the various rock garden societies around the world; they take four or five years to flower but this method probably results in a stronger bulb, more suited to local conditions. Some species, notably the Mexican ones, produce bulblets in the axils of the leaves, and these soon grow into flowering sized bulbs.

The Calochortus flower is, in all its forms, rather distinctive in that the three outer perianth segments are usually narrower than the inner and rather sepal-like. The inner three have a nectar gland at the base, which is often a distinctive shape and is surrounded by brightly coloured zones and tufts of hairs. Some species have large upright flowers while others are smaller, almost globose and pendent; in certain groups the hairs on the segments almost fill the flower, hence the name 'Cats Ears'.

Since they are so different in their treatment I have separated out the species into two major groups, the summer rainfall Mexican species and the North American winter rainfall ones. Within the latter group there are also obvious divisions and, botanically speaking, two Sections are recognized: Mariposa, mainly for the large erect-flowered species which have long narrow seed capsules, and Section Calochortus, for the generally smaller flowered species with rounded or oblong capsules. For the purposes of this book, which is intended primarily for keen gardeners, I think it best to avoid these divisions, which are in some species not very obvious. Instead, I have grouped the North American ones into those with pendent, usually globose flowers and those with upright saucer or cup-shaped flowers, giving three groups in all – including the Mexican summer growers.

The following is only a small proportion of the sixty species, representing those which I have grown or tried to grow, or would have liked the opportunity to try. It is intended as an appetite whetter rather than a definitive account!

All species have narrow linear stem and/or basal leaves and I have therefore not mentioned these in each case.

A   Summer-growing species, dormant in winter; bulbs with netted tunic

C. barbatus (C. flavus, Cyclobothra lutea)   The most well-known of the Mexican species, very easily cultivated and surviving outdoors through the worst winters we have had in Surrey, with winter temperatures down to $-17°C$. It is usually 15–30cm in height with loosely branching stems carrying pendent bell-shaped flowers about 2–3cm in diameter, lined on the inside, and fringed, with long hairs, produced in late summer. The colour form most frequently seen is mustard yellow, but it is a variable species and I have another form with purple flowers tipped golden yellow – not unlike *Fritillaria reuteri*. I grow it in a sunny bed in a sandy soil. Mexico in grass and scrub.

C. pringlei   I am not sure if this is the correct name for the plant which I grow, for the Mexican Calochortus are obviously in need of further study. This is a small species, 15–20cm, with semi-erect flattish flowers in dark reddish-brown, only about 1.0–1.5cm in diameter, the segments covered with similar coloured hairs. I keep this in a frame or cold house in winter whilst dormant. It originally came from Sally Walker, who found it in Mexico.

B   Winter–Spring growing species, pendent flowers

These are dormant from mid summer to late autumn.

C. albus   A beautiful species, usually about 15–20cm high, with several pendent globe-like white or pinkish flowers 2–3cm long; the pointed outer segments are much smaller than the rounded inner ones which are fringed and lined with hairs and have a yellow gland near the base. Var. *rubellus* refers to lovely reddish-pink forms. It is one of the easier species which I have successfully grown outside among heathers. California in rocky scrub and woods.

C. amabilis   This is similar in overall habit and appearance to *C. albus* but the globular flowers are deep yellow, about 1.5–2.0cm long. The inner segments are only fringed with hairs. California.
   C. pulchellus, also Californian, is a lovely plant, similar to *C. amabilis* with its yellow flowers, but they are larger, even more globe-like, about 2.5–3.0cm long, with hairs lining the inner segments as well as fringing them.

C. amoenus   One of my favourites in the genus, with pendent globes of deep rose to purplish-pink; the gland at the base of the inner segments is wide, almost reaching the edges, whereas in *C. albus* it is confined to a smaller area in the middle. California, on scrubby hillsides.

C   Winter–Spring growing species, erect flowers

These are dormant from mid summer to late autumn.

C. caeruleus (C. maweanus)   One of the most charming species, often only 5–10cm in height, with a few flattish flowers more or less in an umbel. They are about 2–3cm across, bluish to nearly white and densely lined with long hairs. Not difficult to grow in a bulb frame. California in open stony soil beneath pines.
   C. elegans, from Idaho, Washington and Oregon, is generally similar but has the inner segments less conspicuously hairy and less fringed.
   C. tolmiei is similar in its flowers to both the above species but has branched flower stems whereas they have stems which are unbranched up to the umbel of flowers. It is widespread, from Washington south to California.

C. clavatus   One of the gorgeous large-flowered species 25–30cm tall with huge erect yellow flowers, about 6–9cm in diameter. The inner segments have a band of hairs on the lower half of the inner surface and brownish markings near the base, where there is a sunken rounded gland. California.

C. gunnisonii   Usually around 20–30cm in height with erect white or soft lilac flowers about 5.0–6.5cm across, deeply bowl-shaped, opening out flattish in the latter stages. The lower part of each inner segment has a beard of long hairs above a sunken oblong gland, and there is often a purple band and blotch across the width. South Dakota south to Arizona and New Mexico, not in the Pacific West States.

C. kennedyi   I include this more out of envy than anything else, for it does seem to be nearly impossible to grow! It has erect 4–6cm diameter bright vermilion-red flowers, sometimes on stems only 10cm in height; there are also orange and yellow forms. On the inner segments there is often a mahogany to nearly black spot and a depressed circular gland surrounded by hairs. Var. *munzii* is the yellow variant. S. Arizona, Nevada and S.E. California in very hot rocky or sandy soil. It obviously requires a sunbaked bulb frame treatment to stand any chance of success in cool climates.

C. luteus   One of the easiest of the large Mariposa Calochortus, thriving in a bulb frame or the alpine house. It is about 15–30cm, with lovely deep yellow erect flowers 4–6cm in diameter, sometimes with a chocolate brown spot and finer dots and lines near the base of each of the inner segments. The gland is not sunken as in *C. clavatus* and it is rather crescent-shaped. California in open grassy places or light woodland.

C. macrocarpus   A gorgeous Mariposa which, thanks to Roy Davidson of Seattle, I have had the pleasure of seeing in the wild, flowering in large numbers in some burnt-off sagebrush country. It is 20–50cm in height, with enormous erect bowl shaped flowers opening out flattish, 6–9cm in diameter in a satin-like lavender with a striking purple band, just above the sunken triangular gland, although this mark may be lacking in some forms; the outer segments are about equal in the length to the inner, or longer than them. It is widespread in the drier parts of western North America, from British Columbia south to California.

   C. nuttallii is perhaps somewhat similar but the flowers are not so large; usually white, sometimes flushed with lavender, and the centre is yellow with a purple or brownish spot near the sunken round nectary. The outer segments tend to be shorter than the large inner ones. It may be only 10–15cm in height but is usually taller. Widespread from North Dakota south to New Mexico in open grassy places. It does not seem to be a difficult species to grow in a bulb frame.

C. monophyllus   A charming, easily cultivated small-flowered species, sometimes less than 10cm tall but variable up to 15cm. It has erect flowers about 2.5–3.0cm across, deep yellow, usually with a brown blotch near the base of each of the inner segments, which are covered with hairs. The sunken gland is a curved band, stretching across the width of the segment. California.

C. nudus   A small slender species 5–15cm tall with upright bowl-shaped white or pale lavender flowers about 2.0–2.5cm in diameter which are nearly glabrous except for a few hairs around the crescent-shaped gland, which is not sunken. California.

   C. minimus is rather similar but is even smaller, with flowers about 1.5cm across which have the inner segments acute (rounded in *C. nudus*) and the capsules are nodding (erect in *C. nudus*). California.

C. splendens   As its name suggests, an impressive Mariposa type, 20–60cm tall with large (5–6cm diameter) erect flowers in pale lavender purple, often with a dark purple blotch on the lower part of the segments which are sparsely covered in the lower half with long hairs just above the small (not sunken) rounded glandular area. California.

C. superbus   A very variable Mariposa, 20–60cm in height, with large showy erect bowl-shaped flowers which may be white, yellow or lavender lined purple with a bright yellow centre and often a brownish or purple spot towards the base of the segments. They are 5–8cm in diameter. The hairy gland is not sunken and is shaped like an inverted 'V'. . California.

   C. vestae is similar in overall appearance but usually larger and has a crescent-shaped gland. California.

C. venustus may also be mentioned here since it is of a similar appearance, but the outline of the gland is a four-sided figure. It is extremely variable and in some forms is among the most spectacular of the Mariposas. The colour ranges from white through yellow, orange, pink, lavender and rose to dark, almost mahogany red. There is often a darker blotch of red-brown above the gland and the 'eye' of the flower is sometimes darker. It is not a difficult species to grow in a bulb frame. California in sandy soils in light woodland or grassy places.

C. uniflorus   An easy species, increasing freely. It is often only 10–15cm high, with several upright medium sized flowers on long pedicels. They are about 3.5–4.5cm in diameter, soft lilac with a darker blotch in the centre of each of the inner segments, which are sparsely hairy. California and Oregon.

C. weedii   One of the Cyclobothra group and therefore having netted-fibrous bulb tunics, but similar to the Mariposas in that the flowers are large and erect. They are 4–5cm in diameter with dense, long hairs on the inner segments – which are deep yellow and often speckled and streaked brown. The gland is rounded and slightly sunken. S. California.

Caloscordum

An Allium relative which is not unattractive for a sunny sheltered position or alpine house, flowering in late summer. Propagation is by seed.

C. neriniflorum   Rounded white bulbs give rise to slender linear leaves, which remain through spring and summer until the loose umbels of small starry bright rose pink flowers are produced. At flowering time the plant is about 20cm in height. An Asiatic species from W. China and the adjacent Pamir mountains.

Chionodoxa

These small Scilla-like bulbs are known as Glory of the Snow because of their mountain-top habitats; consequently they are very hardy and valuable early spring flowering plants, suitable for the rock garden or for naturalizing beneath shrubs. They are best with cool growing conditions where the soil does not become too sunbaked in summer, so it is well to incorporate some humus in the soil before planting.

Unfortunately there has been much confusion over the application of names in *Chionodoxa* and, as my friend and colleague Desmond Meikle has shown, there has to be a complete reversal of usage of some of the names if the original meaning is to be followed.

The genus is distinguished from *Scilla* by having the perianth segments joined into a tube and by the stamens having broad flattened filaments. The Austrian botanist Dr F. Speta considers these features to be insufficient and includes *Chionodoxa* in *Scilla*.

Chionodoxas all flower in late winter or early spring and have two narrow basal leaves, becoming wider towards the apex.

C. albescens   This is one of the two species from Crete. It has one to three small pale lavender flowers with a large white centre, in my experience not opening out widely but remaining shuttlecock-shaped. To make a show, a patch of bulbs is required but it does increase well so this is possible.

C. gigantea   This is a synonym of *C. luciliae*, the true plant of Boissier, not 'C. luciliae of gardens'.

C. lochiae   Named by Desmond Meikle after Lady Loch who collected it in Cyprus where it is an endemic of the Troodos Mountains. It has one to four flowers in a raceme, bright blue without a central white eye like most other species, although the filaments are white; they are about 2.5cm in diameter.

C. luciliae (C. gigantea)   The original *C. luciliae*, as described by Boissier, is a fine plant with usually only one or two large upright flowers about 3–4cm in diameter, in a soft lavender-blue with a small white centre. It is a native of W. Turkey. There is a white form in cultivation.

'C. luciliae of gardens' or 'Maw's Chionodoxa', because George Maw of Crocus fame introduced some bulbs from Turkey during the last century, has for many years been offered in catalogues and cultivated as *C. luciliae* and has become the commonest species in cultivation. It will have to take the name *C. siehei* or *C. forbesii* (see below).

C. nana (C. cretica)   A small Cretan species, rather variable. The one or two pale blue to whitish flowers are only 1.0–1.5cm in diameter, opening out flattish unlike the other small Cretan species *C. albescens*, which remains rather funnel-shaped.

C. sardensis   This is the richest blue Chionodoxa, named after the ancient Sardis in W. Turkey. It has between four and twelve slightly pendent flowers, each about 2.0–2.5cm in diameter in a deep clear blue with almost no white eye in the centre, apart from the filaments.

C. siehei (C. tmolusii)   This appears to be a vigorous version of the plant which has been wrongly grown in nurseries and gardens as 'C. luciliae' for many years and, since the latter cannot take the name *C. luciliae*, it must therefore be referred to as *C. siehei*. Desmond Meikle is of the opinion that both of these are the same as *C. forbesii* (see above), in which case this would be the correct name since it is older than *C. siehei*. However, I am not convinced that *C. forbesii* is the same, having recently received collected material, and will be comparing all these Chionodoxas carefully during the next few seasons.

The original collection of *C. siehei*, cultivated as Glasnevin, is said to have come from Ala Dağ in central Turkey, but this is almost certainly a mistake. Plants exactly like it were collected by John and Susan Allison in W. Turkey and it is now clear that *C. siehei* and 'C. luciliae of gardens' are slight variations of one species. The clone grown in gardens as *C. siehei* is a very vigorous showy plant when doing well, but a patch in my garden which has been left without attention has become less robust and is now indistinguishable from the adjacent collection of the Allisons, and both resemble 'C. luciliae of gardens'.

C. siehei is the best Chionodoxa for gardens, seeding freely and making a fine early spring show. It has up to 12 flowers in a markedly one-sided raceme, each about 2.0–2.5cm in diameter in a strong blue with a large white eye; the colour is definitely on the purplish side of blue when compared with the more intense blue of *C. sardensis*. It is a native of several western Turkish mountains, in alpine habitats near the snowline.

There are several garden forms including 'Naburn Blue', a soft blue, and 'Pink Giant', pink with a white central zone.

C. forbesii is somewhat of a mystery, never introduced to cultivation and not rediscovered in the wild until Vic Horton and Ole Sønderhousen independently collected some bulbs a few years ago and kindly passed some to me. To date they have not given of their best and I have not been able to confirm whether the species is identical with *C. siehei*. So far it appears to be rather fewer-flowered, and the individual flowers smaller and bluer than those of *C. siehei*. It is a native of S.W. Turkey.

× **Chionoscilla**

A variable group of bigeneric hybrids between *Scilla bifolia* and *Chionodoxa siehei* ('C. luciliae of gardens') which have been named × *Chionoscilla allenii*, after James Allen of Shepton Mallet who noted their occurrence in his garden in the late nineteenth century. Some of the variants have been given cultivar names such as 'Fra Angelica'. Like the two parents they are good free-flowering early spring bulbs, with flowers resembling those of *S. bifolia* but slightly larger, at about 2.5cm diameter. The colours range from lilac to a rich violet-blue.

Colchicum

A large genus known mainly for the autumn-flowering species which are often erroneously called Autumn Crocus; they are in fact more related to the Lilies than Crocus. The spring-flowering ones are on the whole much smaller plants and much less easy to grow, although some are attractive subjects for the alpine house. Most of the autumn ones flower before their leaves appear and, although the flowers may be quite small, qualifying easily for inclusion in a rock garden, the foliage can be enormous when fully developed, so care must be taken in their placing in the garden. On the whole the autumnal ones are easily cultivated, requiring sun and good drainage to thrive – although some are equally good when planted in grass; this has the advantage lending support to the leafless flowers during blustery weather. There are two genera related to *Colchicum* which must be mentioned, although they are also dealt with in the appropriate alphabetical place in this book. *Colchicum* has flowers in which the six perianth segments are joined into a long tube giving a goblet-shaped or funnel-shaped flower; there are three separate styles and six stamens (*Crocus* has only three stamens, thus there is no need for any confusion). *Bulbocodium* is a very small genus in which the styles are joined together into one as far as the apex where it becomes three-lobed; it also has the perianth segments free from each other, not forming a proper tube. *Merendera*, like *Bulbocodium*, has the segments separated from each other with no tube but its three styles are like *Colchicum* and separate. There is a good case for 'lumping' all these together into one genus since the other differences are very slight. Work is being carried out on this at present, especially genetical studies, and since this is not yet complete I feel inclined to leave the species where most people will find them in other literature and catalogues, in the three separate genera. The name *Synsiphon* may be encountered in specialist literature, but can be ignored for it is a synonym of *Colchicum* and was a name used for the small spring-flowering Central Asiatic *C. kesselringii*.

I have described the species below in two groups, the autumn ones which mostly are leafless at flowering time and the mainly smaller spring ones in which the leaves appear before or with the flowers; there is a little overlap but this is mentioned where it does occur.

To identify Colchicums it is necessary to note details of flower colour, mainly whether or not there is a tessellated pattern, the colour of the stamena (anthers) and the shape of the tip of the styles and the position of the stigma (× 10 lens probably required); some species have the tips curled over like a shepherd's crook, some have straight styles, and the stigma may be like a dot right at the apex or it may be elongated down the tip of the style for a short distance (up to 3mm). It is also important to note leaf characters and in the autumn-flowering ones this may mean waiting until spring, so the details of the flowers may have to be written down and identification made when the foliage is produced several months later.

It is not an easy genus in which to identify species and I am grateful to Chris Brickell and Karin Persson for the work they have done on Colchicums in recent years, and to Turhan Baytop for the many interesting herbarium specimens he has collected in Turkey.

The distribution of *Colchicum* is almost the same as that of *Crocus*, from Portugal and N. Africa eastwards through Europe and Western Asia to Soviet Central Asia and Afghanistan.

Autumn-flowering (leaves absent in most species)

C. alpinum A diminutive alpine species which is scarcely cultivated and appears to be rather difficult to please. There are one or two small untessellated pale pinkish purple flowers with perianth segments only 1.5–3.0cm long; the anthers are yellow and the style straight, with a dot-like apical stigma. The two or three narrow strap-like leaves are less than 1.5cm wide. It is mainly distributed in mountain meadows in the Alps of France and Switzerland but is also in Italy, Corsica and Sardinia.

C. corsicum is also rather small-flowered but has the stigma slightly elongated down the style, not dot-like, and has three or four leaves. Corsica.

C. pieperanum from Albania has larger flowers and the stigma is elongated along the style for about 1mm.

C. arenarium from Czechoslovakia, Hungary and Yugoslavia has up to five longer leaves. The flowers have generally wider segments 2.5–4.0cm long.

C. macedonicum is rather like *C. alpinum* but appears to have wider leaves, which tend to become widest towards the apex. S. Yugoslavia.

C. autumnale The common Meadow Saffron, often called Autumn Crocus, is not a Crocus and is nothing to do with true Saffron. It is a vigorous early autumnal free-flowering species with large leaves developing later to 15–35cm long, 2–5cm wide. It produces several flowers per corm, pale pinkish-purple, not tessellated, with perianth segments about 4–6cm long; the anthers are yellow and the three styles are curved into a crook at the apex. It is a widespread meadow plant in Europe.

There are several garden selections of *C. autumnale*, including the white 'Album', double white 'Alboplenum' and double pinkish-lilac 'Pleniflorum'. The hybrid 'Waterlily' with large double lilac-pink flowers is said to be a hybrid between 'Alboplenum' and *C. speciosum* 'Album'.

C. neapolitanum from the central Mediterranean region of Europe has perianth segments 3.0–4.5cm long and usually narrower linear-lanceolate leaves 15–25cm long and 1–3cm wide. *C. longifolium* is very similar to *C. neapolitanum*. France, Spain, N. Africa. *C. kochii* is probably a synonym.

C. haynaldii from Romania (Banat) is also clearly related to *C. autumnale*.

C. tenorii may belong here or possibly with *C. lusitanum* (p 29, below); it has purplish curved tips to the styles and the flowers are faintly tessellated. Italy.

C. balansae (C. candidum)   A little-known species in cultivation. It produces several flowers per corm, rosy pink or white with segments 4–7cm long, not tessellated, with yellow anthers and stigmas which are elongated down the style. The four or five leaves which follow are shiny green, up to 30cm long and 7cm wide. A peculiarity of this species is that the corms grow at an extraordinary depth, up to half a metre, with a long neck reaching to the surface. S. Turkey in rocky places.

C. baytopiorum   Named after Professors Turhan and Asuman Baytop, who have discovered many interesting bulbous species in Turkey. It has sizeable clear bright purplish-pink non-tessellated flowers with stamens which have yellow anthers and swollen yellow bases to the filaments; the segments are about 2.5–3.5cm long. The three leaves appear almost at the same time as the flowers and are bright glossy green, about 20–30 cm long and 2.5–4.5 cm wide. S. Turkey in rocky scrubland, Not very hardy.

C. bivonae (C. bowlesianum, C. latifolium, C. sibthorpii, C. visianii)   This is one of the species with markedly tessellated flowers, purplish pink with dark and light squares. The flowers can be quite large, with segments ranging from 5.5–7.0cm long and up to 2cm wide, giving sturdy flowers of good substance; they have pinkish, purplish or brownish anthers. The large erect leaves follow much later, reaching 20–30cm long and 2–4cm wide. It is a widespread and variable plant in meadows and scrubland from Italy eastwards to Turkey and is in all its forms a lovely garden plant. It has been hybridized with other species such as *C. speciosum* and *C. autumnale* to produce some fine cultivars such as 'The Giant', 'Violet Queen' and 'Disraeli'.

C. lusitanum also has tessellated flowers but only slightly so, and the perianth segments are mostly rather shorter, 4–6cm long. It occurs in Spain and Portugal, possibly reaching Italy.

C. boissieri (C. procurrens)   Unusual in having slender corms which travel horizontally rather than remaining erect in one place. It has slender flowers, with segments usually 2.5–3.5 (rarely up to 5) cm long, untessellated, pinkish-lilac with yellow anthers. The two or three leaves are only about 10–20cm long and under 1cm wide. I find it a very easy species to grow in a sunny position in sandy soil, but its corms wander about over the years and it is difficult to find when dormant. S. Greece, W. and S. Turkey in stony places, sometimes beneath pines.

C. sieheanum from the Taurus Mountains in S. Turkey is not unlike this and its corms have a tendency to behave in the same way.

C. psaridis has similar but smaller horizontal corms, almost stolon like. The two leaves are partly developed at flowering time but may reach 5–15cm long, and 0.5–1.5cm wide later on. It is much smaller-flowered than *C. boissieri* with narrow segments 1.0–2.5cm long in non-tessellated pinkish-purple and is more like *C. cupanii* and its relatives in many ways, although these have conventional upright corms. S. Greece, Peloponnese often in olive groves. It requires bulb-frame or alpine-house cultivation.

C. pinatziorum from Euboea in Greece is similar to *C. boissieri*.

C. callicymbium   This is unknown in the wild although it is thought to have originated in Bulgaria. It is leafless at flowering time with the purplish flowers non-tessellated and having segments 2.5–3.5cm long, with blackish anthers. The leaves come later and are 25–40cm long and up to 5cm wide.

C. cilicicum   This is a floriferous, easily cultivated plant, very satisfactory in open sunny borders. Its flowers, which may number up to 15 or more per corm, are lilac-pink to deep pinkish-purple, usually untessellated, with segments 5.0–7.5cm long. The anthers are yellow and the very long styles white with a deep purple tip, not strongly curved at the apex as in some species. It has very large leaves developing soon after flowering, 30–40cm long, 5–10cm wide. S. Turkey, especially Cilicia in stony woodland. A darker rosy-purplish form is in gardens as 'Purpureum'.

C. byzantinum is a similar plant well-known in cultivation for over 400 years, which may be a form or hybrid of C. cilicicum. It has wider leaves with strong veins, looking almost pleated, and they do not develop until the spring.

C. cupanii   This is one of the small-flowered autumnal species with the leaves visible at flowering time. It has two (or rarely three) leaves which are short at flowering time but may reach 10–15cm long and 0.5–1.5cm wide later on. The flowers are pale to deep purple-pink, untessellated, with segments 1.0–2.5cm long and only 3–5mm wide and have purplish-black anthers before they split to reveal yellow pollen. It is widespread from S.E. France to Italy, Greece and Crete in open stony places.

C. cousturieri, from small islands off Crete, differs in having flowers with purple stripes.

C. glossophyllum is a very robust version with wide glossy green leaves.

C. pusillum is similar in its flowers to C. cupanii (although they are often paler to almost white) but differs greatly in its leaves, which may number from three to six and are usually only 1–3mm wide. The flowers tend to have narrower segments about 2mm wide. It varies a lot in the amount of leaf visible at flowering time, the higher altitude forms tending to have no leaves showing, although they appear shortly after the flowers. Chris Brickell and myself have studied many populations in Crete and could find no hard and fast rule about this. It is a native of Crete and possibly S. Greece, growing on open hillsides.

C. cretense is very similar and is the name given to a Cretan high altitude variant with no leaves showing at flowering time.

C. peloponnesianum from S. Greece is similar to C. pusillum, but has yellow anthers and larger flowers with segments up to 3cm long and about 1cm wide.

C. andrium from the Greek island of Andros looks very similar to C. pusillum.

C. stevenii is similar in overall appearance to C. pusillum, with several narrow leaves per corm and pale to deep purplish-pink flowers. They have yellow anthers and are rather larger with segments usually 2–3cm long, but only about 5mm wide. It is apparently a widespread plant from W. and S. Turkey to Cyprus and Syria in rocky places.

C. tunicatum is said to resemble this in its flowers but the leaves do not appear until a few weeks after flowering and they are wider than those of C. stevenii. Israel. I have not seen it.

C. hierosolymitanum   An unusual species in that it has a large number of long narrow leaves per corm produced in a rosette. Prof. Feinbrun notes six to nine but I have counted as many as 20 in S. Turkey; they are 15–20cm long but usually only 0.5–1.5cm wide at maturity in my experience. The sizeable flowers precede the leaves and are pale to deep pinkish-purple, sometimes slightly tessellated, and have yellow anthers; the segments are about 3–4cm long. It occurs in S. Turkey south to Lebanon and Israel in rather hot dry country and is not very hardy. It is possible that I have 'lumped' two species together here – the more northern, Turkish, specimens may belong to C. polyphyllum – but further studies are required.

C. persicum (C. haussknechtii) is rather similar in its flowers but has fewer broader leaves, usually three to five per corm. E. Turkey, W. Iran.

C. kotschyi (C. imperatoris-frederici) A Middle-Eastern species, which seems to be easily cultivated, although not a spectacular plant. It has smallish flowers preceding the leaves, white or pinkish-lilac with segments about 3–5cm long and only 0.5–1.0cm wide, giving a starry flower when it opens in the sun; they are usually not tessellated but I have seen individuals in Turkey with faint chequering. The anthers are yellow. The leaves are not too overpowering, about 10–15cm long and 3–5cm wide. C. and E. Turkey, Iraq, Iran in bushy places on hillsides.

C. lingulatum This is rather distinct when in leaf for they are strap-shaped and flattened on the ground, often rather wavy at the margins, only about 8–12cm long and 1.5–3.0cm wide with a round or blunt apex. They come later, after the flowers which are usually untessellated and some shade of pinkish-purple, with yellow anthers and segments about 3–4cm long. The corm tunics are very tough and blackish and in these, and the leaves, the species resembles *C. variegatum* but there is little similarity between the flowers. W. Turkey, S. Greece in open stony places, sometimes in sparse grassland.

C. parnassicum should also be mentioned here since it has similar flowers to *C. lingulatum*; the stigmas are elongated along the tips of the styles which indicates a probable relationship. The leaves however are not flattened on the ground and the corm tunics are more papery. C. Greece.

C. micranthum A horticulturally rather uninteresting plant with smallish pale pinkish or white flowers, with narrow segments about 2–3cm long and less than 1cm wide; the anthers are yellow. The narrow linear leaves follow later and there are usually two per corm, about 10–20cm long and up to 1cm wide. It occurs in Turkey in the Istanbul area in open stony places. Unlike the small-flowered, few-leaved *C. alpinum* and its allies, the stigma is not dot-like but extended for a short way along the style.

C. borisii from S. Bulgaria appears to be rather similar but has slightly longer flowers and greyish-green leaves.

C. rhodopaeum is a little-known species from S. Bulgaria, which may belong here – but I have seen no specimens.

C. parlatoris A very distinctive little species when in leaf because it has about five to ten narrow linear leaves only 1–4mm wide radiating out at ground level. The flowers precede them and are pale pinkish-purple, non-tessellated with segments about 1.0–2.5cm long, rarely a little more, and under 1cm wide; the anthers are yellow. S. Greece, Peloponnesse, in clearings in scrub.

C. speciosum This is probably the finest garden plant among all the Colchicum species, with well formed sturdy large flowers, and it is very easily cultivated, increasing well into large clumps. The flowers appear long before the leaves and are often as much as 20cm in height with broad segments 6–8cm long, giving a substantial goblet-shaped flower. The colour is untessellated and variable from pale pinkish purple to deep purple, sometimes with a large white zone in the throat, and the superb pure white albino 'Album' is one of the best autumn bulbs there is for the garden. The anthers are yellow in all the forms. The leaves are bright glossy green and by the late spring can be 20–25cm long and 5–10cm wide. It is a native of N.E. Turkey and the Caucasus in meadows and light woodland.

C. giganteum (C. illyricum superbum) is of garden origin and obviously very closely related but said to differ in having funnel-shaped flowers.

C. bornmuelleri is similar but has narrower leaves, less than 5cm wide, and purplish anthers. N. and N.W. Turkey.

C. troodii (C. decaisnei)   A white or pale pinkish lilac flowered species with narrow perianth segments about 2.5–4.0cm long and only 0.5–1.0cm wide giving a somewhat starry flower when it is open; the anthers are yellow. The strap-shaped leaves follow after the flowers have finished and are three to six in number, about 10–20cm long and usually 2–4cm wide. It is common in Cyprus but is also in Syria and S. Turkey. I find it rather tender, liable to be killed off even in a bulb frame in severe winters.

C. turcicum   A rather strikingly coloured species, non-tessellated (or only faintly) deep reddish-purple, flowering before the leaves appear. There are up to eight flowers with segments 3–5cm long and up to 1cm wide, often rather funnel-shaped. The leaves, five to nine in number, are erect and twisted lengthways and rather small, being about 10–15cm long and 1.5–2.5cm wide and greyish green with a ciliate margin. It has yellow anthers. N.W. Turkey, in the Istanbul region, Bulgaria and N. Greece in rocky places.

   C. chalcedonicum, also from N.W. Turkey, usually has only one or two deep rosy purple flowers which are tessellated. The five to nine leaves are grey-green, strap-shaped and about 1cm wide, often lying on the soil surface and undulate.

   The garden plant known as C. atropurpureum is not unlike C. turcicum.

C. umbrosum   A smallish species of no great horticultural value. The flowers precede the leaves and are white or pale purplish-pink with yellow anthers; the segments are 1.5–2.5cm long and 0.5cm or less wide so they appear starry when open. The plants I have seen in Turkey give the impression of having rounded segments which are slightly hooded inwards at the apex and they are not all equal, giving an irregular flower. The leaves are not large, usually strap-like and about 10–15cm long, and 1.0–2.5cm wide. A plant of woods and bushy places in N. Turkey, Crimea, Romania.

   C. fominii is said to have slightly larger flowers and differently shaped corms; not very convincingly different. Romania and adjacent USSR.

   C. laetum is also said to have larger flowers than C. umbrosum with segments 3–5cm long in which case it approaches C. autumnale in size. The stigma however is elongated along the style for a very short distance in both these species (less than 1mm) whereas in C. autumnale and its relatives it stretches along the style apex for over 1mm. S.E. USSR.

C. variegatum (C. parkinsonii)   An unusual species with flowers which open out flattish rather than goblet-shaped and are strongly tessellated purplish-red with purple anthers; the segments are broad at the base and often strongly tapered to the apex, about 4–6cm long and 1–2cm wide. The leaves are carried almost in a rosette, flattish on the ground and are 10–15cm long and 1–2cm wide, often undulate at the margins and slightly greyish- or bluish-green. It is not difficult to grow in a bulb frame but is not vigorous in the open garden, requiring a good hot summer to ripen the corms. Rocky places in the Aegean Islands and S.W. Turkey.

   C. agrippinum is an old garden plant of unknown origin which is similar to C. variegatum in its smallish tessellated flowers but they are more funnel-shaped and paler and the leaves are erect and not so undulate. It is possibly a hybrid between C. autumnale and C. variegatum.

   C. macrophyllum has widely funnel-shaped, tessellated flowers but they are generally paler than those of C. variegatum, with a white throat. The segments are 4.5–7.0cm long and 1.5–3.0cm wide. In leaf it is completely different, for the three or four leaves are 30–40cm long and up to 16cm wide and strongly pleated lengthways. S.W. Turkey, Aegean Islands, Crete in rocky places. Although a striking plant it is a little tender and requires a sheltered spot with plenty of room for its enormous foliage to develop.

Winter–Spring species flowering with the leaves

C. falcifolium   The oldest name for a complex of species which obviously are in need of further study in the wild. It is a small-flowered plant with white to pinkish-lilac segments about 1.5–2.5cm long and less than 0.5cm wide, usually rather pointed at the apex; the anthers are blackish or dark brown before the yellow pollen appears. There are three to five narrow channelled leaves, often coiled on the soil surface, usually less than 5mm wide and varying from glabrous to densely silvery-hairy. E. Turkey, Iran and Syria on open stony hillsides.

Other species which apparently belong to this group include *C. crocifolium, C. fasciculare, C. serpentinum, C. varians, C. tauri, C. hirsutum* and *C. deserti-syriaci*.

C. tuviae from Israel sounds rather similar but I have not seen this.

C. hungaricum   A small, most attractive plant which is one of the best of the spring species. It has two, rarely three, lanceolate, pointed leaves which are short at flowering time but elongate later to 10–20cm long and 1–2cm wide. The flowers are white or pinkish-lilac with blackish anthers (but yellow pollen) and have segments about 1.5–3.0cm long and under 1cm wide. W. Yugoslavia, Albania, Hungary in stony places.

C. doerfleri is like a silvery-hairy leaved version, often with darker purplish flowers and is I find much more vigorous in cultivation. Yugoslavia, Macedonia, south into N. Greece.

C. kesselringii (C. crociflorum, C. regelii)   An exciting little species from Central Asia with the small white flowers, often purple-striped or suffused on the exterior; the narrow segments are about 1.5–2.5cm long and the anthers are yellow. There are up to four leaves, very short at flowering time but even when fully developed not more than 10cm long and 1cm wide. It is from Soviet Central Asia and adjacent Afghanistan growing on mountain slopes. On account of its small size it is best in a bulb frame or alpine house.

C. luteum   This is not difficult to recognize since it is the only yellow-flowered Colchicum! It is fairly small with the leaves short at flowering time but developing considerably afterwards to reach 15–20cm in length and 1.0–1.5cm wide. The flowers are brilliant yellow with segments usually 2–3cm long; in some forms I have seen in Uzbekistan the tube was stained bronze. It occurs in Soviet Central Asia south-east into Kashmir and the Western Himalaya, flowering near the snowline. It is not difficult to grow in a bulb frame or alpine house.

C. ritchii   A mid-winter flowering species which I barely know; it is probably too tender even for a frame or alpine house. It has three or four leaves 1–3cm wide and pale pink to white flowers with brownish-purple or yellow anthers. It inhabits desert sands of Israel, Egypt and Libya, and some of the specimens collected by Mrs Sheila Collenette in Saudi Arabia look very like this species.

C. guessfeldtianum is similar but has narrower hairy leaves 0.5–1.0cm wide. Egypt.

C. schimperi, although it is said to flower in autumn, looks very much the same as *C. ritchii*. Egypt, Israel, Arabia.

C. szovitsii   Another complex like *C. falcifolium*, embracing, according to Chris Brickell, *C. bifolium, C. hydrophilum, C. armenum, C. nivale* and *C. acutifolium*. It has usually two, rarely three leaves, rather short but extending after flowering to 10–20cm long and 2.0–3.5cm wide and one to several small goblet-shaped flowers in purplish-pink, sometimes white with segments 2.0–3.5cm long and 0.5–1.0cm wide; the anthers are purplish-black, chocolate brown or greenish-black with yellow pollen. It is a very widespread plant in the Caucasus, E. Turkey and Iran, where I have seen it in sheets in wet mountain meadows near the snowline. It is a good bulb-frame or alpine-house plant.

C. brachyphyllum (*C. libanoticum*) is like an extremely vigorous version with very broad leaves up to 3cm wide and many flowers produced all together in a bunch. Young specimens are very similar to *C. szovitsii*. Syria to Lebanon.

C. diampolis from Bulgaria has yellow anthers, as does *C. davidovii* (also Bulgarian) which is distinguished from *C. diampolis* by having thin papery corm tunics (tough blackish ones in *C. diampolis*).

C. triphyllum   (C. bulbocodioides,   C. biebersteinii,   C. catacuzenium, C. ancyrense)   As its name suggests, this usually has three leaves per corm, short at flowering time but reaching 10–15cm long and up to 1cm wide later on. The flowers are white or purplish-pink, goblet-shaped like those of *C. szovitsii* and have segments 1.5–2.5cm long and 0.5–1.0cm wide; the anthers are blackish, dark green or purple with yellow pollen. It is a more westerly-occurring species, in W. and S. Turkey westwards through the Mediterranean region to N.W. Africa and Spain, growing in open places and in scrub.

C. burtii is very similar in appearance but its corm tunics are blackish and leathery, ribbed lengthways whereas those of *C. triphyllum* are very thinly papery and brown. It has very narrow erect leaves and normally white or very pale lilac-pink flowers with blackish anthers (before they burst). W. Turkey in open stony soils. It is named after Mr B.L. Burtt who studies, among many other things, *Colchicum* and *Crocus*.

Commelina

A large and fascinating group of plants in the family Commelinaceae, to which the well known *Tradescantia* belongs. Although mostly tropical and non-bulbous, and therefore not qualifying for entry here, there is one Mexican species which has tuberous roots and is fairly hardy.

C. dianthifolia   The cluster of tuberous roots lie dormant in winter, then in late spring send up 10–15cm leafy stems; the leaves are narrowly lanceolate. The flowers are produced in succession over a period of weeks from within boat-shaped bracts and are brilliant blue, with the two upper petals round and larger than the rest, giving the characteristic flower shape of *Commelina* – which has been likened to Mickey Mouse! Each flower only lasts a few hours. It is a native of Mexico, at altitudes of up to 2500m.

C. dianthifolia grows and flowers well in a sunny, well drained border and seeds itself around; it does not however become a problem and any excess plants are easily weeded out.

Conanthera

A small genus from South America, related to *Tecophilaea* and having Crocus-like corms with netted tunics; both species in cultivation are dormant in summer, start to grow in winter, and flower in late spring – so they require alpine-house protection and will not

CONANTHERA CAMPANULATA

tolerate their corms being frozen, so the pots must be plunged in sand. The individual flowers are attractive but are produced on rather lanky stems. They are not difficult to grow and produce seeds freely.

C. bifolia   This produces one or two long narrow basal leaves through winter and spring, dying away by flowering time. The slender flower stems reach 10–30cm and are loosely branched, carrying numerous flowers in long succession so there are a few out at a time; these are blue and about 1.5cm in diameter, pendent and Cyclamen-like with sharply reflexed perianth segments which leave the cone of yellow anthers protruding. It is a native of Chile, growing on rocky hillsides at below 500m.

C. campanulata   Very similar in habit and size, but the flowers are different in being campanulate, with the segments joined into a tube and not reflexed. The colour is deep purple in the form I have, but it varies in the wild from white to greyish-blue to purple, often with dark blotches inside. It also occurs in Chile.

C. parvula is probably only a dwarf, few-flowered form of C. campanulata.

Cooperia

An American genus of Amaryllidaceae, often now included with *Zephyranthes*, since it differs from the latter only in having long-tubed flowers held in an erect position. They are, like *Zephyranthes*, rather tender and require alpine house cultivation with protection from hard frosts.

C. pedunculata   This has a Daffodil-like bulb, producing linear leaves and 10–15cm stems carrying erect solitary white fragrant flowers which are usually flushed pink or purple; they have a slender perianth tube 4–5cm long and the six segments spread out almost flat to give a diameter of about 4cm when fully open. It flowers in mid to late summer and is a native of Texas and Mexico.

C. drummondii is similar but the perianth tube may reach 10cm in length.

Corydalis

Although these are not monocotyledons (in fact they are related to the Poppies or sometimes placed in a separate family Fumariaceae) they usually fall within the scope of interest of bulb enthusiasts and certainly find their way into bulb catalogues. There are many species throughout the northern hemisphere, but only a small proportion of these are tuberous – the rest being annual or fibrous-rooted perennials – and it is these tuberous ones which interest us here. In the last decade or so they have found a great following among alpine gardeners and many species have now been introduced and are being propagated.

The flower of Corydalis consists of four petals, the upper and lower being larger, thus giving a two-lipped appearance to the flower. The upper one has a spur of varying length and shape, depending upon the species, while the lower one is slightly pouch-shaped with an expanded lip, which provides a landing strip for pollinating insects. The two inner petals are small, cupped, and joined at their apex to form a protective shield around the stamens and style; these two are often darker than the rest of the flower, giving a dark eye. The leaves are often grey-green and are compound, consisting of three leaflets in the simplest form, but these are usually subdivided to a varying degree and may be finely dissected; they can be a most attractive feature in themselves.

Cultivation varies considerably, some being easy plants for outdoor cultivation, others requiring a dry summer rest period and therefore needing bulb frame or alpine house cultivation. Propagation is by seed, or in some cases such as *C. solida* and its relatives, by dividing the clumps of tubers which build up by themselves; in a few species, multiple crowns are formed on the tubers so that they can be cut up and divided in this way, one crown per portion.

All the tuberous species mentioned below flower in early to mid spring. They are all small plants, 15cm or less in height, with short racemes of flowers, so these details will not be given in each case. The important features to observe in their identification are (1) whether there is a large scale or not on the stem at or just below ground level; this can be checked by scraping away soil for only a centimetre or two (2) whether the leaves are alternate on the stem or whether they arise at the same point, i.e. are opposite or whorled, (3) the shape of the bracts subtending each flower, in particular whether they are entire (no divisions) or dissected (teeth-like divisions). For brevity and clarity I have noted initially in each species description these details, for example, 'scale absent, leaves opposite, bracts entire'. The flower length given is from the tip of the petals to the tip of the spur.

C. afghanica Scale absent, leaves opposite, bracts entire. An exciting species from Afghanistan which has excellent grey-green foliage pinnately divided and sometimes each leaflet itself pinnately lobed; the margins of the leaflets are margined red when it is grown in strong light. The few white or very pale pink flowers are 3.5–4.0cm long, the spur slender and curved. This is a native of N. Afghanistan in rocky places; it requires bulb frame or alpine house cultivation.

C. aitchisonii Scale absent, leaves opposite, bracts entire. A lovely species with very grey leaves with rather few oval leaflets on long stalks; the few flowers are bright yellow, often changing to orange as they mature, very large, 3.5–5.5cm long, including the long slender spur which is curved at its tip. It needs a dry dormant period, so requires bulb frame or alpine-house cultivation. Propagate by seed. Afghanistan and adjacent USSR, in rocky places.

C. sewerzowii from N.E. Iran, Afghanistan and adjacent USSR and *C. nevskii* from the Pamir-Alai differ only slightly from this in the degree of division of their leaves. In *C. sewerzowii* they are the most divided, being biternate; that is, the three primary divisions of the leaf are again divided into three; in *C. aitchisonii* there are three leaflets only, but the central larger one has three lobes; *C. nevskii* has the least divided leaves with three undivided leaflets. In my experience there is some considerable degree of variation in leaf division in Corydalis and I rather doubt the validity of these distinctions. If these characters are applied, then the lovely plant I saw growing near Ferghana would have to answer to *C. nevskii*, while the introductions of Paul Furse from Afghanistan would, with their more divided leaves, be *C. aitchisonii*.

C. firouzii is also yellow flowered and related to these. It has smaller flowers, at about 3cm long. The leaves are usually biternate more like those of *C. sewerzowii*. It is found in N. Iran on limestone ledges at over 2000m; it grows well in a bulb frame.

C. × allenii Scale present, leaves alternate, bracts (at least the lower) divided. This is an attractive garden plant, apparently easy to grow under glass or in the open garden. It has slightly greyish dissected leaves and yellowish flowers flushed with purple on the lip,

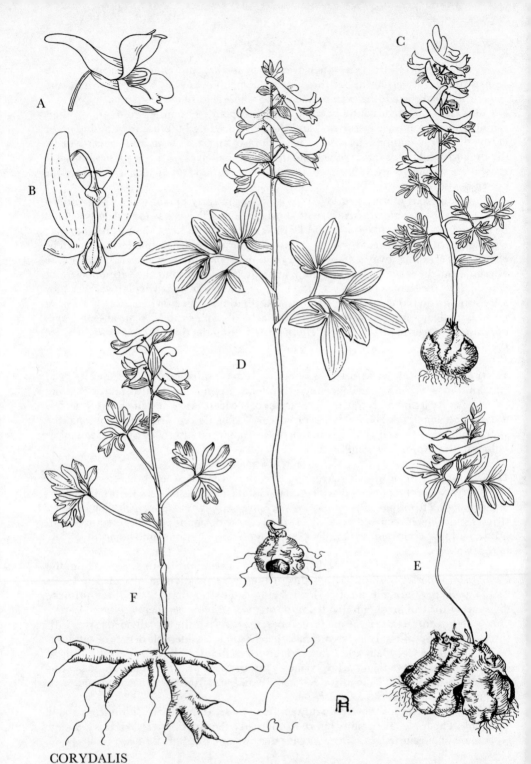

CORYDALIS

(A) *A typical* Corydalis *flower with its two-lipped flower and one spur* (B) *The related* Dicentra *has flowers with two spurs* (C) Corydalis solida *group with a scale-like leaf above the bulb on the stem, and alternate stem leaves; note the toothed bracts adjacent to the flowers* (D) Corydalis bulbosa *group has no scale on the stem; the tuber is hollow beneath* (E) Corydalis rutifolia *belongs to a large group having large corky tubers and opposite leaves; the bracts are usually un-toothed* (F) Corydalis alpestris *has finger-like tubers and several scales on the stem* about 2cm long. It has been suggested that it is a hybrid of *C. bracteata*, presumably with a purplish-flowered species. Garden origin.

C. ambigua Scale present, leaves alternate, bracts entire. This is one of the most exciting tuberous Corydalis in its good forms since it can rival *C. cashmeriana* in blueness of flower, but at the same time has simple cultivation requirements and is easier to grow in drier climates. The leaves are bright green, usually biternate with obovate blunt or rounded lobes, overtopped by the racemes which may have up to 15 flowers held in a slightly drooping position. These are about 2–3cm long with a blunt spur and are variable in colour from violet and lavender to bright blue and rarely white; the best blue colours first came into cultivation as var. *yunnanensis* and var. *jezoensis* (*C. jezoensis*), but these names have no significance and must be regarded as synonyms of *C. ambigua*.

It is a native of Japan, Sakhalin, the Kurile Islands, Kamchatka and N.E. China and is a plant of light woodland or open stony places. In cultivation it requires cool growing conditions and is excellent on the peat garden, although it also makes a fine alpine house plant.

C. lineariloba is very closely related to this but has very narrow linear leaf segments; it has been treated by some botanists as a form of *C. ambigua*.

Some variants of *C. ambigua* have been described, for example var. *rotundiloba* with broad rounded leaf lobes, var. *fumariifolia* (*C. fumariifolia*) with the leaflets more dissected, var. *papillosa* with minutely pubescent stems, var. *glabra*, completely hairless.

C. remota is very similar to *C. ambigua* and appears to have much the same range of variation; the main difference is that the bracts are toothed. It is also eastern Asiatic.

C. repens should also be mentioned since it resembles *C. ambigua* and is from E. Asia. It has entire bracts like *C. ambigua* but the smaller flowers are in the white to pinkish colour range; the leaves have broad rounded lobes.

C. bracteata Scale present, leaves alternate, bracts dissected. To me, this is one of the loveliest of all the tuberous species. It is very like the slightly better known *C. caucasica* in having a rather expanded lip to the lower petal, thus giving a more substantial flower than in *C. solida* to which it is related. The colour, however, differs completely from both and is a delightful shade of soft yellow; the flowers are about 2.0–2.5cm long. *C. bracteata* behaves rather differently from *C. solida* in cultivation; it is very hardy and comes up much later but in mild winters tries to flower as it breaks the surface. The best way, if in a pot, is to grow it in as cool a position as possible until some good spring weather arrives and then bring it into a warmer spot for the stems to elongate; like *C. caucasica* it can be grown on a peat bed or cool part of the rock garden. The tubers divide naturally, or it can be increased by seed. Siberia.

C. bulbosa (C. cava) Scale absent, leaves alternate, bracts entire. A commonly cultivated species and the most easily obtained from nurseries. It is easy to grow in a semi-shaded position in humus-rich soil and will seed itself freely. The tuber becomes large and corky and may be successfully broken up into separate pieces if each has a growing point. The leaves are biternate, not particularly greyish although they are pale green. These are overtopped by dense racemes with ten to twenty flowers, each about 2–3cm long, usually in a dull purplish colour but I have seen pure whites among the coloured ones in wild populations. There is also an albino form in cultivation which has dark purplish bracts and stems which make an interesting contrast with the white flowers. It is a widespread species in Europe, usually in light woodland.

C. bulbosa subsp. *marschalliana* (*C. marschalliana*) is a variant which has cream or pale yellow flowers. I have grown this for many years from a plant I collected in S. Yugoslavia and find it a much more attractive plant than the usual purplish forms. It is native to the Balkans, Crimea, Caucasus and N.W. Iran.

C. bulbosa subsp. *blanda* is a Balkan variant with slightly different details of the leaflets; the central leaflets are on long stalks whereas in subsp. *bulbosa* they are wedge-shaped at the base, but not stalked; it has purplish flowers like subsp. *bulbosa*.

C. buschii   Two scale leaves present, leaves alternate, bracts toothed. This is a rather interesting species, sent to me by Janis Ruksans from Latvia, although it is native in the Far East. It has curious stolon-like tubers with swellings at their tips and is capable of forming patches. The three or four stem leaves are much-dissected with many rather pointed leaflets and are overtopped by dense racemes of pinkish-purple flowers 2.0–2.5cm long. Eastern Asiatic USSR and China, in light woodland.

C. cashmeriana   Scale absent, leaves basal or sometimes also with one on the stem, bracts divided. This is one of the most delightful species, scarely 'bulbous', but with thick fleshy carrot-like roots; there is a slight hint of a bulb with a few tiny loose white scales but such a rootstock cannot be dried out like a conventional bulb. The leaves are green and ternately divided with the leaflets deeply dissected, overtopped in late spring or early summer by dense umbel-like inflorescences (condensed racemes) of four to six brilliant blue flowers, varying in size but about 2cm long; a well-flowered plant can be covered completely, a stunning sight. In the wild the species apparently varies in the colour to a poorer blue with a touch of magenta, but the form in cultivation is of a superb clear blue. It is a Himalayan species from Kashmir eastwards to Nepal, growing in rocky places at very high altitudes and flowering during the monsoon season. It thus requires semi-shade and cool growing conditions on a peat garden or if in a pot, in a cool part of a frame or alpine house. It fares much better in cooler moister climates than in my own relatively dry part of S. England.

C. cashmeriana subsp. *brevicornu* has a shorter spur 4–7mm long (11–13mm in subsp. *cashmeriana*) and comes from the eastern Himalaya in Sikkim and Bhutan.

C. ecristata is a closely related, also bright blue, species which I had the pleasure of seeing on the AGS expedition to Sikkim. It has only two to four flowers in each raceme and these are about 1.5–2.0cm long with a spur 5–10mm long which is strongly curved at its tip (only slightly so, or straight, in *C. cashmeriana*). The lower lip of the flowers is very broad and nearly orbicular and forms a prominent feature. Its variety *longicalcarata* has a spur about 1.0–1.5cm long. Both occur in Sikkim and Bhutan on rocky hillsides and are very rare in cultivation.

C. trifoliata is worthy of a mention here, although I doubt if it is in cultivation. This also has blue flowers but is quite different in appearance because the leaves are divided into three leaflets which are themselves undivided; the bracts also are entire. It is a native of the eastern Himalaya and W. China.

C. polygalina is, I think, the blue-flowered plant I saw in Sikkim in 1983, which has a cluster of elongated tuber-like roots and slender stems bearing a leaf with very narrow linear leaflets. As far as I know this did not get established in cultivation from the material collected on the expedition.

C. juncea. Although not blue-flowered this seems to be related in some way to this group and I would not like to omit it from the book, having seen and enjoyed so much of it in Sikkim. It has a rootstock with bunches of swollen roots like small brown radishes, producing slender stems with racemes of many golden-yellow flowers; the plant is almost leafless at flowering time. Unfortunately it seems rather difficult to grow and I have not succeeded, although others in cooler climates may have done so.

C. caucasica Scale present, leaves alternate, bracts entire. One of the best introductions of recent years. I first had this from Eliot Hodgkin who probably obtained it from the USSR in the 1960s. It is like the common *C. solida* in overall appearance and size but the undissected bracts distinguish it; the main feature however is the expanded lip to the lower petal, giving the flower a more substantial appearance. The flowers are about 2–3cm long with a nearly straight spur and are purplish, or white in var. *albiflora*. The pure white form is by far the best variant, easily cultivated in a peat bed or rock garden, increasing slowly by natural tuber division or by seed, which breeds true. The purple forms are dingy by comparison. Caucasus, in light woods.

C. chionophila Scale absent, leaves opposite, bracts entire. A very rare species in cultivation and slow to propagate by seed; it requires alpine house or bulb frame cultivation. The grey-green leaves are not very divided, sometimes with only three elliptic leaflets but usually more. The racemes are few-flowered with the 2.0–2.5cm long flowers coloured white with purple tips to the petals. It is a native of stony places in N.E. Iran and adjacent USSR, in the Kopet Dağ.

C. conorhiza Several scale leaves present, leaves alternate, bracts entire. This is rather different from the majority of the species mentioned here in that the tubers are vertically elongated and forked into two or three 'fingers', and the stem has several scales on the underground portion. The smallish leaves are ternate, sometimes twice-ternate with many narrowly oblong or oblanceolate lobes; these are overtopped by the racemes which carry three to eight rich reddish-purple or crimson flowers, each about 1.5–2.0cm long with a fat, curved, spur. It occurs in scree conditions in the Caucasus and N.E. Turkey at fairly high altitudes and is not an easy plant to cultivate; it seems to require cool growing conditions without a hot dry period in summer, for the tubers cannot tolerate being dried.

C. alpestris (*C. nivalis*) is related and similar to this in its tuber features. The main difference is that the fewer flowers are bright blue and produced in a short dense raceme. Caucasus and N.E. Turkey in screes at high altitudes, eastwards to the Himalaya.

C. pseudoalpestris, from central Asiatic USSR, is scarcely distinguishable; it has the upper leaf just below the flowers, whereas in *C. alpestris* there is a length of bare stem between the upper leaf and lowest flowers.

C. emanueli from the Caucasus has a similar type of tuber and is apparently very closely related to *C. alpestris*, being blue-flowered but the flowers are larger, at about 2.0–2.5cm long; they are said to have the perfume of jasmin and are held in a vertical position.

C. arctica from E. Siberia and arctic USSR is unknown to me; it is said to resemble *C. emanueli* in having vertical blue flowers. It certainly should be hardy! E. Hulten in *Flora of Alaska* treats this as a synonym of *C. pauciflora* (below).

C. pauciflora clearly also belongs with this group. It is, like *C. emanueli*, a dwarf plant with blue (sometimes violet) flowers; these are held horizontally and are about 2cm long. Hulten, however, says that in Alaska *C. pauciflora* has vertical or horizontal flowers. It is a native of the USSR in the arctic and Siberia, east to Kamchatka and into Alaska and British Columbia. Var. *albiflora* has white flowers.

C. pallidiflora has the same tuber and overall appearance of *C. emanueli* but has sulphur yellow flowers 2–3cm long; it is a native of the Caucasus and is regarded by some botanists as a colour form of *C. emanueli*.

The Corydalis of this group, Section Dactylotuber, seem to be particularly tricky to grow and probably require a cold climate to do well.

C. darwasica Scale absent, leaves opposite, bracts entire. An exciting species when seen in its native screes, but to date it has appeared rather loose and unattractive in cultivation, presumably requiring high light intensity and cool growing conditions to keep it compact. The very grey leaves are biternate with pointed leaflets and the flowers are about 2cm long, white or very pale pink with a dark spot at the apex of the inner petals. It is a native of Central Asia in the Tien Shan and Pamir-Alai ranges, and is also recorded in N. Afghanistan.

C. decumbens   Scale absent, leaves alternate on stem and basal, bracts entire. A rather delicate little Corydalis, not very showy but increasing well by means of small rounded tubers to form patches. It has much-dissected basal leaves on long stalks and two much reduced stem leaves; the raceme is rather loose with a few pinkish to purplish flowers 1.5–2.0cm long. Japan in light woods. The white form, f. *albescens*, might be a better garden plant, but I have not seen it.

C. diphylla   Scale absent, leaves opposite, bracts entire. A fairly well known species, usually obtainable from specialist nurseries, and easily cultivated in a frame or alpine house. It is a graceful slender plant. The blue-green much-dissected foliage has narrow leaflets, often rather pointed. The loose racemes carry pinkish flowers with dark purple lips to the petals, about 2.0–2.5cm long. It occurs farther east than most of the related species, in the N.W. Himalaya, especially Chitral and Kashmir.

C. glaucescens (C. kolpakowskiana)   Scale present, leaves alternate, bracts entire. This is rather rare in cultivation but presumably will not be too difficult to grow and propagate since it belongs to the same group as *C. solida*. The leaves are more or less pinnate with the leaflets deeply divided, overtopped by loose, few-flowered racemes which have pointed bracts. The flowers are purple or pinkish, about 2.0–2.5cm long, with a straight or slightly curved spur. It is a native of Soviet Central Asia, in the Tien Shan and Pamir-Alai ranges.

C. griffithii   Scale absent, leaves opposite, bracts entire. This is not a species I am familiar with and as far as I know it is not yet in cultivation. The leaves are divided into three leaflets, each of which is subdivided into several smaller lobes, but the terminal lobe is always much larger and rounded. The flowers are about 1.5–2.0cm long, pink or nearly white with darker tips to the petals, and have a rather short fat spur; it appears that the lips of the upper and lower petals are widely expanded thus giving a flower of some substance, almost like that of a Dactylorhiza orchid when viewed from head-on. Subsp. *salangensis* has leaves in which the terminal lobe is narrower, not markedly different from the rest.

   C. griffithii is a native of E. Afghanistan and adjacent Pakistan in rocky places.

C. hyrcana   Scale absent, leaves opposite, bracts entire. This is a poorly-known species, seldom collected and not in cultivation to my knowledge. It has biternate green leaves with obovate lobes and loose racemes of five to eight flowers which are 2.5–3.0cm long, pink with darker tips to the petals and a paler upward-curving spur. It appears to be related to *C. verticillaris* and *C. rutifolia*. *C. hyrcana* is a native of N. and W. Iran.

C. integra   Scale present, leaves alternate, bracts entire. This has the general appearance of the commonly cultivated *C. solida*, but the entire bracts distinguish it from the latter. It has biternate leaves with obovate, rounded lobes and racemes of up to twenty flowers. These are 1.5–2.5cm long with a curved spur, pale purple or pinkish with darker tips to the inner petals. It is a native of the eastern Aegean Islands, Turkey and N. Iraq.

C. intermedia (C. fabacea) Scale present, leaves alternate, bracts entire. This is rather like the commonly cultivated *C. solida* in overall appearance but all the bracts are entire, not at all toothed or lobed. It has biternate leaves and short dense racemes of only two to eight small purplish flowers, each about 1.0–1.5cm long; white forms are known. It is a native of north and central Europe, east to Russia in partially shaded places.

C. ledebouriana (C. cabulica) Scale absent, leaves opposite, bracts entire. Perhaps one of the least attractive of the Central Asiatic species, except when seen in its native habitats. It is easy enough to cultivate in a bulb frame or alpine house but often becomes rather 'leggy'; it presumably requires cool conditions and high light intensity to keep it compact, as does the related *C. popovii*. The leaves are grey-green, varying from ternate (three leaflets) to bi- or even tri-ternate, with elliptic or nearly round leaflets. The loose racemes are often rather long with up to ten flowers which are on very short pedicels, about 2–3cm in length, with a rather fat spur which is frequently slightly inflated at its tip and often curved up to the vertical. The colour is pinkish-purple on the lips of the petals, the spur much paler. It grows wild in Soviet Central Asia where it is quite common, and in adjacent N. Afghanistan and Pakistan on rocky hillsides.

    C. cyrtocentra from the W. Himalaya (Chitral) is probably the same but the flowers can be up to 3.5 cm long and an almost U-shaped with the spur in a vertical position.

C. macrocentra Scale absent, leaves opposite, bracts dissected. A very attractive species, rather rare in cultivation and suitable only for a bulb frame or alpine house. The tuber becomes large and corky with several growing points and, as shown by Tony Hall of Kew, can be divided with care; the cut surfaces must be treated with fungicide and allowed to dry before replanting. It has beautiful much-divided blue-grey foliage and contrasting yellow flowers 3–4cm long, only one to three per raceme; the lips of the petals often become orange with age. The divided bracts make this distinct from related species such as *C. aitchisonii*. It is a native of Soviet Central Asia and adjacent N. Afghanistan on rocky hillsides.

C. nudicaulis Scale absent, leaves alternate, bracts entire. A species I do not know in the living state, and it is probably not in cultivation. The leaves have three leaflets which are each divided into several narrowly elliptic, subacute lobes. The many pale purple flowers are carried in loose racemes, each about 1.5–2.0cm long. It is a native of Soviet Central Asia, in the Pamir-Alai range.

C. persica Scale absent, leaves opposite, bracts entire. This is not a well-known species, although a plant under this name is occasionally offered by specialist nurserymen. It has greyish pinnate leaves, with the leaflets themselves lobed, and loose racemes of pinkish-purple flowers 2–3cm long. Iran, Caucasus.

C. popovii Scale absent, leaves opposite, bracts entire. A dramatic species, suitable for the bulb frame or alpine house. The blue-grey or grey-green leaves are divided ternately two or three times with the lobes, especially the central larger one, obovate or nearly orbicular. The large flowers, often only a few per raceme, are held horizontally and are 4.0–4.5cm long, the spur curved a little at the tip; the colour is usually a deep purple on the upper and lower lips, paler lower down with a pink to white spur. When growing well one tuber can produce many stems, making a considerable patch of colour. The tubers do not divide up naturally, so seed is the main method of propagation. It is related to *C. ledebouriana* but the much longer, horizontal-spurred flowers distinguish it.

C. popovii is a native of the Pamir-Alai Mountains in Soviet Central Asia in rocky places.

C. rutifolia Scale absent, leaves opposite, bracts entire. An attractive species which requires alpine house or bulb frame cultivation since its tubers need a warm dryish period in summer. It is very variable throughout its wide range, especially in leaf division, and several subspecies have been named. Like its eastern relative *C. verticillaris* the leaf and flower stems run underground before emerging. The leaves are very grey-green, usually biternately divided but varying a great deal in the amount of division and shape of the lobes. The flowers may be solitary but there are usually several in a loose raceme and normally deep reddish purple on the lips of the petals, paler lower down, with a pink or whitish curved spur; they are 1.5–2.5cm long.

Four subspecies have been recognized, based on combinations of features. They are natives of rocky hillsides in full sun.

C. rutifolia subsp. *rutifolia* is confined to Cyprus. This has leaves with the central leaflet much longer than the lateral ones and rounded at the apex. The racemes have two to seven flowers with narrowly obovate bracts.

C. rutifolia subsp. *uniflora*, from Crete only, has only one or two flowers on each stem, with ovate bracts.

C. rutifolia subsp. *erdelii* is widespread in Turkey and Lebanon. Here, the leaves have the central and lateral leaflets more or less equal and the central one is acute. The racemes have two to seven flowers with narrowly obovate bracts.

C. rutifolia subsp. *kurdica* is in S.E. Turkey and N.E. Iraq and represents the variant with the most divisions to the leaves; they are three or four times ternately divided with very narrow linear or elliptic lobes, otherwise similar to subsp. *erdelii*. In these much dissected leaves it approaches *C. verticillaris* from Iran but there is a difference in the shape of the capsules and in the latter species the racemes do not overtop the leaves, whereas in *C. rutifolia* they clearly do so.

C. schanginii (C. longiflora) Scale present, leaves alternate, bracts entire. An interesting species which has only recently appeared in cultivation; it has so far proved very amenable to bulb frame or alpine house treatment. The leaves are much-divided into narrow grey-green segments, making it attractive in foliage. The racemes are fairly loose, carrying very long flowers – some 3–4cm in length – including the slender gradually tapering spur which is pale purple or whitish, while the petals are tipped darker purple. It is from the USSR, recorded over a wide area from the Altai to Tien Shan mountains. Among the species with a scale on the stem it is very distinct with its greatly elongated spur to the upper petal.

C. schanginii subsp. *ainii* is a beautiful variant with bright yellow upper and lower petals, brown inner petals and a long white spur, apparently not difficult to cultivate.

C. solida (C. halleri) Scale present, leaves alternate, bracts (all or just lower) dissected. This is one of the best known species, easy to grow in a wide range of situations and increasing well by tuber division or by seed. The slightly grey-green leaves are biternately divided with the lobes varying from rather narrow to broadly obovate. The racemes may be few-flowered and loose to many-flowered (up to 20) and dense, and the bracts on the racemes also vary in the amount of toothing; the lower ones are always lobed or toothed but the upper ones may be entire. In flower colour there is also a wide range, the most common being a dull purple, but anything from white through pinks and purples to a deep reddish-brick may be found. With this set of variables it is therefore possible to have many combinations all looking very different from each other. The flowers are about 1.5–2.5cm long with a blunt spur which is slightly curved near the tip.

It is a widespread species through much of Europe, east into the USSR and Turkey, growing in meadows or woodland. Attempts have been made to divide the species but there seems to be no satisfactory classification because intermediates can be found. The following subspecies and varieties have been recognized.

C. solida subsp. *solida* has all the bracts deeply cut, densely-flowered racemes and rather narrow oblong or oblanceolate leaf segments; its variety *densiflora* (*C. densiflora*) has leaves with the narrowest segments, linear-lanceolate in shape.

C. solida subsp. *laxa* from Sweden and Finland also has all the bracts deeply divided but has loosely-flowered racemes and the leaf segments are broadly obovate.

C. solida subsp. *slivenensis* is a Balkan variant in which the upper bracts are undivided, not even toothed; the racemes are densely-flowered and the leaf segments broadly obovate.

C. solida subsp. *brachyloba* has loosely-flowered racemes, the bracts of which are merely shallowly toothed; it is from Lebanon and S. Turkey.

C. solida subsp. *tauricola* from S. Turkey differs in having a narrow linear capsule (broad in other subspecies) and the pedicels remain straight in the fruiting stage, whereas in other variants the pedicels bend downwards.

C. solida subsp. *wettsteinii*, which comes from Mount Athos in Greece, has entire upper bracts but has loosely-flowered racemes and narrow oblong leaf segments.

In addition to these variants, other forms have been introduced to cultivation, most of them unnamed. One, however, because of its exceptional colouring, has been named and has become much sought after. It is *C. solida* 'George Baker', with flowers of a deep rich reddish-salmon. This was grown at Ingwersen's nursery for many years, from a tuber sent by Sir William Laurence in about 1930. In 1960, when I had the pleasure of working there, it was still there under the name of *C. transsilvanica* which presumably indicates an Eastern European origin. The name however has no botanical standing and the plant is certainly a form of *C. solida*. There is a var. *speciosa transsilvanica* from Romania but it does not refer solely to this red-flowered plant, being described as 'purple, rose, pale pink, white or variegated'. The Ingwersen form has now been propagated and distributed under the cultivar name of 'George Baker' and is a very desirable plant.

It appears that reddish and pinkish colour forms are rarely to be found mixed in colonies of the species and I have a beautiful pink form sent to me many years ago now by Jim Jermyn of Edrom Nurseries, who was at the time at Munich Botanic Garden, where it was also grown as '*transsilvanica*'. Seedlings of the various colour forms vary to some extent, so there is scope for raising an even greater range of attractive garden plants within *C. solida*.

C. pumila is related to *C. solida* but has only about three to eight purplish flowers per raceme and even the lowest are held on very short pedicels, 5mm or less long; in *C. solida* the lowest ones are normally at least 1cm long. It is less widespread than *C. solida*, in Northern, Central and Eastern Europe.

C. angustifolia is also similar in its overall characters to *C. solida* but the slender-spurred flowers are white to creamy-yellow and 2–3cm long; it differs in that the bracts normally have three divisions, while the upper ones may be entire. The leaves have narrow linear-lanceolate leaflets, so it is a slender, delicate-looking plant. To date I have only grown the white form, which is not unattractive, but a yellow one would be more desirable. It is a native of the Caucasus.

C. alexeenkoana is very closely related to *C. angustifolia*, but has a generally shorter flower about 2cm long with a thicker spur; the capsules are broader and shorter than in the latter species in which they are linear and only 2–3mm broad; it is also Caucasian.

C. paczoskii from the Ukraine is very like some forms of *C. solida*. It has only a few purple flowers in a loose raceme and differs botanically in having rather short pedicels, about 5–10mm long.

C. decipiens is a purple-flowered, very floriferous plant, sometimes available from nurseries. It is said to be the same as *C. pumila*, but the original specimen seems to me to represent a form of *C. solida*.

C. verticillaris   Scale absent, leaves opposite, bracts entire. This is unfortunately not in cultivation to my knowledge, although Paul Furse did introduce it in the 1960s. It is very closely related to the variable *C. rutifolia* and should perhaps be regarded as another variant of it, with extremely divided leaves. These are grey-green, usually tripinnate, with the many leaflets and lobes narrowly oblanceolate or linear. The flowers, carried in a loose raceme which scarcely overtops the leaves, are pinkish-purple, tipped darker, and about 2.0–3.5cm long, the spur often slightly curved upwards. Subsp. *grandiflora* has flowers up to 3.5cm long with a nearly straight spur. Subsp. *boissieri*, which I have seen on Mount Darreh Bid in Iran, also has larger flowers but the spur is much curved up and over like a scorpion's tail.

C. verticillaris is widespread in N. Iraq and W. Iran, in rocky places.

Crocus

A large genus of about 80 species, nearly all of which are attractive and worth growing, but quite a number of these are very rare in cultivation and may only be found in specialist collections.

Crocus are instantly recognizable by the wine-glass or goblet-shaped flowers with a long tube; they have only three stamens, which immediately distinguishes them from the similarly shaped *Colchicum* and *Sternbergia*, which have six stamens. The leaves too are distinctive, being very narrow with a whitish line along the centre. They are particularly useful in gardens, since they come in a fairly wide range of colours and flowering times from early autumn through to spring. The autumn ones may flower before the leaves appear or together with the leaves, while the spring ones all have the leaves emerging with the flowers.

Although I would obviously prefer everybody to buy my monograph of the genus (*The Crocus*, Batsford 1982) I realize that it is rather specialized so I have therefore provided a much shorter, more horticultural version in the following pages! The identification of the species is, like riding a bicycle, easy when you know how and I have attempted to simplify matters by dividing them into three: A, yellow-flowered; B, spring flowering other than yellow; C, autumn flowering. Where there is an overlap I have mentioned that particular species in more than one group.

Features to note which will aid identification are: type of corm tunic, colour of flower and whether or not the throat is yellow, colour of stamens (anthers) which may be yellow, whitish or blackish, whether the style is divided simply into three branches or more, and the absence or presence of leaves at flowering time. One point to remember is that most Crocus species are very variable, so it is possible to have a wide range of different looking plants all belonging to the same species because they have the same set of characteristics.

One very fortunate point from our point of view as identifiers is that Crocuses are very 'moral' and there are very few hybrids to worry about!

All the Crocuses mentioned require full sun and good drainage unless mentioned to the contrary. They are mostly natives of open stony places in the wild, so I have only commented upon the habitat when it differs from this.

A Yellow-flowered Crocus, Autumn or Spring

C. angustifolius (C. susianus) The Cloth of Gold Crocus, a plant known in cultivation since the seventeenth century. It has a coarsely netted corm tunic and yellow to orange flowers, which are marked externally with bronze stripes or suffusion, sometimes almost wholly bronze outside; in sun the segments roll back on themselves, revealing the gold interior. The stigma is three-lobed. Crimea, Ukraine and Armenian SSR.

C. ancyrensis from Turkey is similar but the orange-yellow flowers are normally unmarked on the outside and the segments are more rounded (acute in C. angustifolius).

C. chrysanthus A very well known yellow-flowered species which has given its name to a group of garden Crocuses in a wide range of colours, some varieties of which should be referred to the blue or white-flowered C. biflorus; there are also hybrids between the two such as 'Advance'. C. chrysanthus has a tough paper-like tunic with rings at its base. The late-winter or spring flowers vary from pale to deep yellow and may have bronze speckling or stripes on the outside; the stigma is three-lobed, often deep orange-red, and the anthers are yellow or rarely black. It is a native of the Balkans and Turkey.

Horticultural selections with larger flowers include 'E.A. Bowles', 'Uschak Orange' and 'Gypsy Girl', which is striped bronze.

C. danfordiae is like a diminutive version with the tiny flowers having perianth segments only 1.0–1.5cm long. The colour is usually very pale lemon with greyish speckling on the outside, but there are also whitish and pale blue forms. C. Turkey.

C. almehensis from N.E. Iran is very closely related to C. chrysanthus; it has much wider V-shaped leaves and orange-yellow flowers, strongly suffused bronze externally.

C. sieheanus from central-southern Turkey looks very like C. chrysanthus but differs in the corm tunic, which splits lengthways and has no rings at the base. The style is very long and prominent, overtopping the anthers considerably.

C. cvijicii A rare species in cultivation, but corms which I introduced in 1972 settled down well; it does not appear to be difficult to grow. Others have collected it and this attractive species is now well established in specialist collections. The corms have finely netted tunics. At flowering time in spring the leaves are very short, hardly visible. In cultivation the flowers have segments up to 4cm long, making it a very showy species with clear yellow flowers and a three-lobed orange stigma. Creamy forms occur in the wild. S. Yugoslavia and N. Greece in meadows near the snowline. It is a superb alpine house plant.

C. flavus (C. aureus, C. maesiacus) The most well known of the yellow spring Crocuses, especially the old large-flowered cultivar 'Dutch Yellow' ('Golden Yellow') which is actually a C. flavus hybrid. The true species is smaller-flowered and less vigorous. It has a papery corm tunic which splits lengthways into soft fibres and persists as a brown neck of old tunics at the apex of the corm. There are up to eight narrow erect leaves and up to four yellow to orange flowers, which are usually unmarked on the exterior and have a three-lobed stigma which does not overtop the stamens. Balkans and W. Turkey in scrubland and woods. The commonly cultivated 'Dutch Yellow' is very vigorous in grass or borders and increases well by corm division, although it produces no seeds.

Subsp. dissectus has the stigma divided into six or more slender branches.

C. gargaricus   A rare species in cultivation. Its corms have netted tunics and give rise to short stubby leaves and small bright orange unmarked flowers – which have rather rounded segments – giving them a solid appearance. Subsp. *gargaricus* from W. Turkey has very coarsely netted tunics and is non-stoloniferous, whereas subsp. *herbertii* from only one mountain in N.W. Turkey has finely netted tunics and increases into patches by means of stolons. The latter is easily cultivated outdoors and is becoming more plentiful in cultivation, but subsp. *gargaricus* seems less easy to please.

C. korolkowii   A bright spring-flowering species, not difficult to grow. It has yellow flowers which have a shiny, varnished appearance on the segments and which are marked externally with bronze or purplish stippling in the most frequently seen form. The corm tunics are finely fibrous, and it has a three-lobed orange style. Afghanistan, Pakistan and adjacent USSR.

C. olivieri   A smallish bright yellow- to orange-flowered spring Crocus, related to *C. flavus* but differing in having a few (1–4) broader spreading leaves (up to eight erect ones in *C. flavus*) and a divided stigma, into six or more slender branches. The corm tunic is papery, splitting lengthways. Balkans and Turkey.

Subsp. *balansae* has up to 15 divisions of the stigma and the outside of the perianth segments is striped or suffused bronze, sometimes almost completely. W. Turkey.

Subsp. *istanbulensis* differs from subsp. *olivieri* mainly in its corm tunic which is slightly netted at the apex. N.W. Turkey.

C. scardicus   A truly bicoloured spring Crocus with the flowers, mainly orange, but with the lower part of the segments and the tube purple. The very fine rigidly erect leaves have no white stripe along the centre. The small corms have a finely fibrous tunic. S. Yugoslavia and E. Albania.

This is not an easily cultivated species and seems to prefer cool growing conditions in a peaty-gritty soil with no dry dormant period in summer.

C. scharojanii (C. lazicus)   A rarely seen autumn-flowering species with the long slender orange-yellow flowers produced before the leaves appear. The corms have a thin netted tunic and sometimes produce stolons as a means of propagation. It grows in wet alpine meadow conditions in N.E. Turkey and the Caucasus and does best if given a peat-grit mixture which retains moisture. It should not be dried out excessively in summer.

C. vitellinus   This varies in flowering time from late autumn to early spring. Its corms have papery tunics splitting lengthways and the orange-yellow flowers, which appear with the leaves, have a stigma which is divided into a mass of slender branches. Although the flowers are usually unmarked, some forms have brownish-purple stripes on the exterior. S. Turkey, south to Lebanon. It is, I find, not very hardy and requires frame protection at least.

C. graveolens, from similar regions, differs in having usually five to eight very narrow greyish leaves and the flowers are normally bronze-striped on the outside. They often have a strong unpleasant smell; *C. vitellinus* usually has two to four wider green leaves and pleasantly fragrant flowers.

(B) Spring-flowering Crocus species (non-yellow)

C. abantensis   A fairly recently described species with very striking rich blue flowers with a yellow throat. The corm tunic is of netted fibres and it has five to ten very narrow leaves per corm. N.W. Turkey in alpine meadows. Rare, and best kept in a frame or alpine house.

C. alatavicus The most easterly occurring species, attractive for its white flowers, with a yellow throat marked on the outside with grey or purple stippling. The corm tunic consists of a mass of almost parallel fibres. It is unusual in having as many as eight to fifteen leaves per corm. Soviet Central Asia and adjacent China.

C. *michelsonii* is related but has fewer leaves (four to seven) and flowers shaded blue on the outside without a yellow throat. It is one of the loveliest of Crocuses but is not easy to grow and increase; best kept in a frame or alpine house. N.E. Iran and adjacent USSR.

C. aleppicus This is closely related to the autumnal C. *veneris* from Cyprus and is described after this species in the autumn group.

C. antalyensis As yet a very rare plant in cultivation, but apparently not difficult to grow. It has a papery corm tunic splitting lengthways and variable pale to deep lilac-blue flowers with a yellow throat, sometimes biscuit-coloured on the outside with a small amount of striping. W. Turkey.

C. baytopiorum A most exciting species, very rare in cultivation as yet but not difficult in an alpine house or frame. It has pale but brilliant blue flowers with delicate slightly darker veins, with no trace of yellow in the throat. The corm tunic is netted-fibrous. S.W. Turkey.

C. boulosii This is mentioned in the autumn-flowering section under C. *veneris*, its nearest relative.

C. biflorus One of the best known of the spring species and an excellent garden plant in its many forms and cultivars, which are often sold as C. *chrysanthus*. The corm tunic is papery or eggshell-like, splitting into rings at the base. It is extremely variable and there are many subspecies in addition to the named garden selections and hybrids with C. *chrysanthus*. They are mostly easy to cultivate.

Subsp. *biflorus*, the 'Scotch Crocus' – although it is not a British native. It has white or pale lilac-blue flowers with a yellow throat conspicuously striped purple or brownish outside. The stamens are yellow. Var. *argenteus* and var. *parkinsonii* are synonyms. Mainly Italy. Subsp. *stridii* from N.E. Greece is closely related and resembles it in most features but has more leaves per corm (up to eight, up to five in subsp. *biflorus*) which are long at flowering time. The stamens are sometimes blackish. Subsp. *artvinensis* from N.E. Turkey is little-known; it has flowers with a lilac-violet ground and only one bold stripe on the outside of each segment. Subsp. *adamii* has flowers with three to five conspicuous stripes on the outside, usually on a lilac ground; there are only three to four short leaves at flowering time. C. *tauricus* and C. *geghartii* are probably variants of this. Mainly Yugoslavia, Crimea, Caucasus. Subsp. *isauricus* is scarcely known in cultivation. The flowers are white or lilac, with three to five purple stripes outside and the stamens, although having yellow anthers, usually have a greyish stripe along the centre. S. Turkey. Subsp. *punctatus*, also from S. Turkey, has smallish pale lilac flowers minutely speckled on the outside.

Subsp. *melantherus* differs from the above subspecies in having blackish-purple anthers to the stamens. The flowers are produced in autumn and are white, strongly striped purple or brownish on the outside with a yellow throat. S. Greece, on the Peloponnese.

Subsp. *crewei* has similar colouring but is spring-flowering. W. Turkey. Subsp. *nubigena*, also spring-flowering, has more leaves per corm (usually 4–8) than subsp. *crewei* (usually 2–3); subsp. *pseudonubigena* from E. Turkey differs from subsp. *nubigena* mainly in having a glabrous style (densely covered with minute hairs in the latter); it is barely in cultivation. All these have blackish anthers.

Subsp. *pulchricolor* has blue flowers without any conspicuous stripes on the exterior, sometimes shaded darker blue or violet near the base of the segments outside; the throat is deep yellow and the anthers yellow. It is best known in the forms seen in nurseries and garden centres under the names of 'Bluebird' and 'Blue Pearl', usually sold as *C. chrysanthus* varieties. These are lovely and excellent garden plants. Subsp. *tauri* is bluish-lilac without prominent striping and differs mainly in having more and wider leaves per corm; it is not such an attractive plant. C. Turkey, and east to Iran and Iraq.

Subsp. *weldenii* differs from all the above variants in having no yellow zone in the throat. Its flowers are white, often suffused pale blue on the base of the segments outside and sometimes faintly suffused blue throughout; the stamens have yellow anthers. W. Yugoslavia. Subsp. *alexandri* is related to this and also lacks a yellow throat; the outside of the flower is stained deep violet-blue, making it a very striking plant. C. and S. Yugoslavia, adjacent Bulgaria. The commercial form sold as *C. chrysanthus* 'Ladykiller' is very similar.

The following species are related to *C. biflorus* and most have a similar corm tunic with rings at the base.

C. danfordiae This is also mentioned above with the yellow flowered group since it can have pale yellow, pale blue or whitish flowers. They are very small with segments only 1.0–1.5cm long (at least 2cm in *C. biflorus*) and have greyish stippling on the outside. C. Turkey.

C. cyprius is endemic to Cyprus and has smallish white or lilac-blue flowers with a yellow throat, heavily stained violet on the outside near the base of the segments and the tube. The stamens have deep orange filaments, whereas none of the *C. biflorus* variants have this feature. The anthers are yellow.

C. hartmannianus should be mentioned here, although its corm tunic splits lengthways, not into obvious rings. It is very similar and closely related to *C. cyprius* and differs mainly in these tunic features, but it also has blackish purple anthers. Very rare on Cyprus.

C. aerius (*C. biliottii*) is like a bluish form of *C. biflorus*, sometimes veined darker, with a yellow throat and yellow anthers; the corm tunic however splits lengthways, not into rings. N.E. Turkey. The name *C. aerius* has been used in commerce for blue *C. biflorus*.

C. pestalozzae is a delightful little Crocus, rare in cultivation but easy to grow and an ideal alpine house plant. The small flowers are clear blue or white with a yellow throat and there is a black spot at the base of each filament making it look, as E.A. Bowles said, as if grains of soil had fallen into the flower. N.W. Turkey.

C. jessoppiae is a small white Crocus of garden origin, probably a hybrid of *C. pestalozza*.

C. adanensis is barely known in cultivation. It has pale lilac flowers with a large white zone (occasionally pale yellow) in the throat; the corm tunic splits lengthways. S. Turkey.

C. leichtlinii can be mentioned here since it looks so much like some forms of *C. biflorus* when in flower. It has pale blue or greenish blue flowers with a yellow throat, and yellow stamens. The corm tunic is completely different, being very hard and tough like an eggshell and splitting into sharp triangular teeth. It requires bulb frame or alpine house cultivation. S. Turkey, in stony places which become hot and dry in summer.

C. cambessedesii This occasionally produces flowers in late winter but is mainly autumnal and will be found in that section.

C. candidus   A white-flowered species, unusual in often having only one broad leaf per corm. The flowers are white with a yellow throat, stippled greyish on the exterior. N.W. Turkey.

C. corsicus   This attractive little species is ideal for the rock garden. It is very variable but in its most frequently seen forms its flowers are bright lilac on the inside and striped on the outside, enlivened in the centre by intense orange or reddish style branches. The corm tunic is finely netted. Corsica.

C. etruscus   An easily grown species for sun or semi-shade. The corm tunics are coarsely netted-fibrous. It has fairly large flowers in lilac-blue with a pale yellow throat, and usually with a biscuit-coloured or silvery wash on the outside with a few purple stripes. N.W. Italy in light woodland.

It can be distinguished from the similar coloured *C. dalmaticus* by having only one papery bract sheathing the tube; two can be seen in *C. dalmaticus* and its ally *C. sieberi*.

C. kosaninii looks very like *C. etruscus* in its colouring but has normally only two leaves per corm (3–4 in *C. etruscus*) and a more finely netted corm tunic. S. Yugoslavia. It is proving to be a very easily cultivated Crocus.

C. fleischeri   A small species requiring a hot sunny situation with good drainage. The flowers are white with a yellow throat, sometimes marked brownish or purplish on the base of the segments outside. The stigma is particularly attractive, bright orange-red and divided into a mass of slender branches. It has an unusual silky corm tunic with the fibres interwoven. W. Turkey.

C. hyemalis   This is so early flowering as to almost qualify as an autumnal species, usually right in the middle of winter. Unfortunately it is rather tender and needs protection. The flowers are white with purple stripes on the outside and a yellow throat, and the stamens are blackish. It has a papery corm tunic splitting lengthways. Israel.

C. imperati   An excellent, brightly coloured large-flowered Crocus suitable for the rock garden. The flowers are rich violet on the inside and biscuit-coloured outside, with strong violet stripes; a very striking combination. It has a papery corm tunic which splits lengthways into fibres. W. Italy. There is also a white form.

Subsp. *suaveolens* is very similar and differs mainly in having only one bract sheathing the tube, whereas subsp. *imperati* has two. The cultivar 'De Jager' is a good colour and vigorous.

C. laevigatus   This is described in the autumn section since it mainly flowers then, but some forms flower in winter and others in early spring.

C. malyi   A very easily cultivated attractive species which was until recently extremely rare in cultivation. It has a rather fibrous corm tunic. The white flowers are long and elegant with a yellow throat, and have a slender bright orange style which is a conspicuous feature. There is often a small amount of brown or bluish staining on the exterior near the base of the segments. W. Yugoslavia, in grassy rocky places.

C. minimus   This small species makes up for its lack of size by having rich purple flowers strongly striped or suffused on the outside with even darker purple. Unlike its relative *C. corsicus* the corm tunic consists of vertical fibres, not netted. It is a native of Corsica and Sardinia and is easily cultivated in the rock garden.

C. nevadensis   A species rarely seen in cultivation and best grown in a frame or alpine house since it is not very vigorous. It has a fibrous corm tunic and rather long flowers with a creamy or pale lilac ground colour overlaid with darker veining and often a greenish suffusion; the throat may be white or pale yellow. It is a native of Spain, Morocco and Algeria.

C. carpetanus from Spain and Portugal is related but is quite different from all other Crocus species in its leaves which in cross-section are approximately half-moon shape, with a white stripe covering most of the upper surface. The flowers vary from white to pale lilac, with a white or faintly yellow throat, and the white or lilac stigma is expanded like a miniature cauliflower.

C. pelistericus   A very rare species, barely in cultivation. It has deep violet flowers with no yellow in the throat, a fibrous corm tunic and spiky leaves which have no white stripe on the upper surface; the only other species with such a leaf is the yellow *C. scardicus*. It is a native of S. Yugoslavia and N. Greece, in alpine meadows, and appears to require cool growing conditions with no prolonged period of dormancy in summer.

C. reticulatus   A small Crocus with white or lilac flowers strongly striped on the outside with dark purple, with a whitish or yellowish throat. The corm tunic is coarsely netted-fibrous. It is not a strong grower and seems best in an alpine house or frame. Eastern Europe, east to Turkey, the Crimea and Caucasus.

Subsp. *hittiticus* from S. Turkey has blackish-violet stamens (yellow in subsp. *reticulatus*).

C. sieberi   A well known and attractive variable species consisting of several subspecies, the best of which for the garden is subsp. *atticus*; all the variants have a yellow zone in the throat, a netted corm tunic and yellow stamens.

Subsp. *sieberi* from Crete has flowers with a white background, variously banded or suffused with purple on the outside. It is not very vigorous and is best in a frame or alpine house.

Subsp. *atticus* from mainland Greece, especially the Athens area, has lilac-blue flowers and is a strong grower for outdoor cultivation. These are some good vigorous cultivars such as 'Firefly' and 'Violet Queen', and a cross between it and subsp. *sieberi* called 'Hubert Edelsten', which has darker purple zones on a pale ground.

Subsp. *sublimis* is the most widespread variant in Greece, S. Yugoslavia and S. Bulgaria, but is not such a good garden plant as subsp. *atticus*. It usually has paler lilac flowers and differs mainly in its corm tunic which is finely fibrous (coarse in subsp. *atticus*).

Subsp. *nivalis*, like subsp. *sublimis*, has a finely fibrous corm tunic and differs slightly from it by having no hairs in the throat of the flowers; in subsp. *sublimis* there is a ring of minute hairs. It is not a vigorous plant. S. Peloponnese.

C. dalmaticus is very similar to *C. sieberi* in having netted corm tunics and lilac flowers with a yellow throat. The perianth segments are however normally biscuit coloured on the outside, with purple stripes. One very attractive form which I found in Yugoslavia has an almost gold-coloured exterior. It is an easily cultivated species. W. Yugoslavia.

C. veluchensis is not cultivated a great deal although it is not difficult. It is closely related to *C. sieberi* and has a finely netted corm tunic. The flowers vary from pale lilac to deep violet and lack any yellow in the throat. I also have an albino form. S. Yugoslavia, Albania, Bulgaria, Greece.

C. tommasinianus   This needs little introduction for it is frequently to be seen seeding itself around in gardens and providing a fine display at the first hint of spring. It is extremely variable in flower colour but all the forms have a long slender whitish perianth tube and lack any yellow in the throat. The colour ranges from pale silvery lilac to deeper lilac, purple and warm reddish- or pinkish-purple; some forms have darker tips to the pale segments and often there is a silvery or whitish wash on the exterior. An albino is also in cultivation. The garden form sold as 'Ruby Giant', a very fine deep purple colour, is probably a hybrid with *C. vernus*. Other named forms include 'Whitewell Purple', 'Barr's Purple', 'Taplow Ruby', 'Pictus', 'Albus'. The corm tunics are finely netted. It is a native of W. and S. Yugoslavia in light woodland.

C. vernus   This is the species from which most of the large Dutch white, purple, violet and striped Crocuses have been raised by selection and they now far exceed the wild forms in size and range of colour. There are many named varieties. Features of the species which all the variants have in common are a finely netted corm tunic and a white or coloured throat without any yellow zone. The flowers are more solid-looking than those of *C. tommasinianus*, which tend to be slender and more pointed in appearance.

Subsp. *vernus* often has large lilac, purple or violet flowers, and the orange-yellow stigma overtops the stamens. Widespread in the mountains of C. and E. Europe in meadows. *C. scepusiensis* and *C. heuffelianus* are names given to Eastern European variants which have large rounded flowers often with dark purple tips to the segments.

Subsp. *albiflorus* is the much smaller Spring Crocus of the Alps, which often has tiny white flowers with the stamens overtopping the stigma; it may also be purplish or striped in colour. It is found from the Pyrenees to Czechoslovakia through the chain of the Alps. *C. siculus* is a very similar plant from the mountains of Sicily.

C. versicolor   Although at one time in the nineteenth century this was a very popular Crocus with many selected forms it is now scarcely cultivated. The corm tunic is papery, splitting lengthways into many fibres. It has rather elegant longish flowers with a white or lilac-purple ground colour, with conspicuous darker stripes on the outside; the throat is usually very pale yellow. It is easily cultivated. S. France and adjacent N.W. Italy.

C   Autumn-flowering Crocus species (non-yellow)

C. banaticus (C. iridiflorus, C. byzantinus)   This is one of the most distinct and beautiful of all Crocus species. It is leafless at flowering time with long-tubed pale to deep lilac blue flowers, which are without yellow colouring in the throat; they have three large outer segments, much larger than the three inner ones which remain erect. It thus looks somewhat like a small Iris flower. The style is divided into a mass of whitish or lilac branches, over-topping the inner segments. It has a finely fibrous corm tunic. Romania, in rich meadows. Although rare in cultivation it is very easy to grow in a cool moist position, and this applies to the rare and equally lovely white form 'Albus'.

C. biflorus subsp. **melantherus**   Since this is a variant of the spring-flowering *C. biflorus* it will be found in section B under that species.

C. cambessedesii   A delightful miniature Crocus, which really needs to be grown in an alpine house because it is lost in the expanse of the garden. The corm tunic is papery, splitting lengthways and the very narrow thread-like leaves are well developed at flowering time. Although flowering time varies it usually starts in autumn, with the small purple flowers strongly striped on a paler ground externally and with no yellow zone in the throat; the segments are only about 1.5–2.0cm long. Majorca and Minorca.

C. cancellatus   An extremely variable and widespread species which is not very reliable in the open garden, preferring bulb frame or alpine house cultivation. It has a netted-fibrous tunic, lacks leaves at flowering time (occasionally the tips are showing) and has a stigma divided into six or more slender branches. There are several subspecies, only one of which is at all well known in cultivation, and even that is quite uncommon.

Subsp. *cancellatus* is sometimes sold as var. *cilicicus*. It usually has slender pale blue flowers striped darker violet on the outside and the throat is nearly white or slightly yellowish. S. Turkey.

Subsp. *damascenus* has a much more coarsely netted corm tunic than the above and the flowers are often very pale lilac. E. Turkey, Iran and Iraq south to Israel.

Subsp. *lycius* from S. Turkey is a colourful variant with whitish flowers, with a deep yellow throat and a mass of bright orange stigma branches.

Subsp. *mazziaricus* usually has large, rounded flowers in white or lilac with a definite yellow throat. Mainly in Greece.

Subsp. *pamphylicus* differs from all the other variants in having white stamens (yellow in other subspecies). The flowers are usually white with a yellow throat. S. Turkey.

C. hermoneus from Israel and Jordan is closely related to *C. cancellatus* and resembles subsp. *cancellatus* in flower; it differs mainly in having a rather papery corm tunic which splits lengthways, not netted-fibrous. It can only be grown satisfactorily in a bulb frame.

C. caspius   A most attractive species, not difficult to cultivate, but it may be killed in very severe winters if the ground freezes to a considerable depth. It has the leaves developed at flowering time. The flowers are white or a soft pinkish-lilac with a deep yellow throat and the corm has a papery tunic which splits lengthways. The style has only three divisions. It is a native of the Caspian region of N. Iran and adjacent USSR. The name 'Lilacinus' has been attached to the lilac forms.

C. goulimyi   A very successful and attractive autumn Crocus in gardens requiring only a sheltered sunny position. It flowers together with the leaves and has a very long slender perianth tube with rather rounded segments which often differ slightly in colour, the inner three often paler lilac-blue than the outer three; there is no yellow zone in the throat. The corm tunic is smooth and tough, splitting lengthways at the base into sharp teeth. S. Greece mainly in olive groves.

There is also a lovely white form in cultivation, equally vigorous, called 'Albus'.

C. hyemalis   This Israeli species is rare in cultivation. It flowers mostly in winter and is described in group B, the winter and spring species.

C. kotschyanus (C. zonatus)   An easily cultivated early autumn species flowering before the leaves appear. The flowers are pale lilac, delicately veined darker with a ring of yellow blotches in the throat, sometimes merging to give a yellow zone. It is one of the few species which has creamy-white stamens, not yellow. The corm has a thin papery-fibrous tunic and is sometimes rather flat and misshapen in subsp. *kotschyanus*; in some variants it stands on edge in the soil. It is a native of C. and S. Turkey south to Lebanon.

Subsp. *hakkariensis* differs in having wedge shaped perianth segments and rather pale markings in the throat. S.E. Turkey.

Subsp. *cappadocicus* has no hairs in the throat whereas the other subsp. given above have a tuft of minute hairs. C. Turkey.

Subsp. *suworowianus* is very similar in flower structure to subsp. *kotschyanus* but has creamy white flowers veined with purple lines. N.E. Turkey and Caucasus. It flowers in very early autumn, usually the first Crocus to appear after the summer rest.

Subsp. *kotschyanus* var. *leucopharynx* is a variety without any yellow markings in the throat, instead having a large white zone in the centre of the bluish-lavender flowers. It is a very vigorous plant, often sold as *C. karduchorum* which it is not. The wild origin is unknown.

C. karduchorum is a related species, very rare in the wild and in cultivation. It has lilac-blue flowers, finely veined darker, with no yellow throat markings. The stigma is the most attractive feature, a mass of thread-like white branches standing well above the white stamens unlike the above species which has yellow few-branched stigmas. S.E. Turkey in oak scrubland.

C. gilanicus is barely in cultivation and is not very striking. It has white flowers like *C. kotschyanus* subsp. *suworowianus*, but they have no yellow marks in the throat which is furnished with hairs (yellow-blotched and glabrous in the latter). W. Iran.

C. laevigatus   One of the better known and easier autumn Crocus, flowering with the leaves present; usually very late, sometimes into winter. It is very variable in the wild from white to lilac-violet with a deep yellow zone in the throat, but the form most often seen in cultivation known as 'Fontenayi' has fragrant flowers with a lilac-purple ground, strongly striped and feathered darker purple on the outside. The stamens have white anthers and the stigma is divided into many orange branches. *C. laevigatus* has a characteristic corm tunic which is smooth and eggshell-like, breaking vertically into sharp teeth at the base. Greece, Crete.

C. boryi is related to this but usually has larger white flowers which are a most attractive goblet shape, not opening out flat and starry like those of *C. laevigatus*. Its corm tunic is papery, splitting lengthways. It is a lovely species for the bulb frame or alpine house. W. and S. Greece, Crete.

C. tournefortii, like *C. boryi*, has a papery corm tunic but has large widely-opening lilac-blue flowers not, or only slightly, marked with darker veins on the outside. The flowers remain open on dull days and at night, unlike those of *C. laevigatus* and *C. boryi*. It is a lovely plant, particularly attractive for the mass of long orange stigma branches contrasting with the white anthers. Cyclades and in Crete, where it is sometimes white-flowered.

C. longiflorus   This has very fragrant flowers together with the leaves in mid to late autumn. They are pale to deep lilac with darker striping on the outside, often the stripes being on a yellowish or biscuit-coloured ground; the throat is yellow, the anthers yellow and the few-branched style orange-red, so it is a colourful flower and is not a difficult Crocus to grow. It has a finely fibrous corm tunic. S.W. Italy, Sicily, Malta.

C. medius   A bright late autumn Crocus, flowering before the leaves appear. The corm tunic is coarsely netted-fibrous. In the best forms the flowers are purple but it can be paler. The throat has no yellow zone, the stamens are yellow and the stigma is divided into many slender orange or reddish branches. N.W. Italy and adjacent S.E. France.

C. niveus   This is one of the largest-flowered Crocus species, fairly easy to grow in a sheltered sunny place but not yet common in cultivation. The leaves appear at flowering time. It can have enormous flowers and I have measured one individual with a perianth tube 18cm long and segments 6cm long – but it is usually somewhat smaller, either white or very pale lilac with a deep yellow throat, yellow stamens and three or more orange-red style branches. There are no markings on the exterior. It has a large corm with finely fibrous tunics. S. Greece, on the S. Peloponnese, often in olive groves.

C. nudiflorus An unusual species in that its corms, which have papery-fibrous tunics, produce stolons enabling it to produce patches. It is thus best grown in a place where it can be left undisturbed and is especially good in grass. The long-tubed flowers appear long before the leaves and are, in the best forms, deep purple, without any yellow in the throat. The stamens are yellow and the style dissected into many slender orange branches. It is a native of rich meadowland in S.W. France and E. Spain and is naturalized in parts of England.

C. ochroleucus A small species flowering in late autumn before the leaves appear or when they are very short. The flowers are pure creamy-white with a deep yellow throat, white anthers and a three-branched yellow stigma. The corm has a thin papery-fibrous tunic and increases freely by producing offsets. It is easy to grow and I find does well in grass. There is also a completely white form with no yellow in the throat. Israel, Lebanon, Syria.

C. robertianus A large-flowered species flowering before the leaves appear, rare in cultivation but apparently quite a strong grower. Its corms have coarsely netted-fibrous tunics. The flowers are lilac blue with a whitish or very pale yellow throat, yellow stamens and three frilly orange stigma branches which are a striking feature. It was first noted by Dr John Marr in 1967 and is named after his son who sadly died at an early age. Greece, on wooded hills in the Pindus Mountains.

C. sativus (C. orsinii, C. sativus var. **cashmirianus)** The Saffron Crocus. I have used this species to introduce a whole group of others which are little-known in cultivation but which all have the same basic set of features, notably a three-branched red style which is the source of the dye and flavouring agent, saffron. They have yellow anthers, corm tunics which are finely netted-fibrous and very slender leaves which appear with the flowers or immediately afterwards as soon as the flowers begin to fade.

C. sativus has large wide open lilac-purple flowers, veined darker purple, with no trace of yellow in the throat. It is sterile and increases only by corm division. To succeed with it in the garden I have found that very deep planting is required, 12–18cm, in rich soil which is in full sun and well drained. It is not known as a wild plant and is probably an ancient selection of the next species.

C. cartwrightianus is like a smaller version of *C. sativus* and differs only in size, with perianth segments about 1.5–3.0cm long (3.5–5.0cm in *C. sativus*) and length of style branches, 1.0–2.7cm as opposed to the 2.5–3.2cm of *C. sativus*. This lovely species often produces striking pure white forms which retain the yellow stamens and red style branches. It is best in a bulb frame or alpine house but will do well in a hot sunny position. Greece, mainly in the Athens area, the Cyclades, Lebanon and Jordan.

C. moabiticus is a very rare species, barely in cultivation, from Jordan. It is similar in its features to *C. cartwrightianus* but usually has flowers which are white with purple lines.

C. oreocreticus from the mountains of Crete has, like *C. cartwrightianus*, long red style-branches and purplish flowers without a yellow throat. It differs most obviously in having a glabrous throat (pubescent in the latter) and a buff-coloured or silvery wash over the exterior of the flower.

C. pallasii is a widespread and very variable member of this group, with much shorter style branches than in the above species; the style is divided into three well up in the flower above the base of the anthers, whereas in *C. sativus, C. cartwrightianus, C. moabiticus* and *C. oreocreticus* it is divided right down in the throat. *C. pallasii* has lilac flowers with no yellow in the throat, often veined darker. It occurs in the Crimea and Balkans, Turkey and Iran south to Israel. It is not difficult to grow in a bulb frame or sheltered sunny place.

Subsp. *turcicus* from E. Turkey often has rather narrow pointed segments.

Subsp. *dispathaceus* (*C. dispathaceus*) is a purplish or reddish-plum coloured variant with very narrow strap-like segments. S. Turkey, N. Syria. Very rare in cultivation.

Subsp. *haussknechtii* has club-shaped style branches and a corm tunic which has a very long neck. W. Iran, Jordan.

C. asumaniae is a very local species from S. Turkey with white or very pale lilac flowers, often with a faintly yellow throat. The style branches are long, 1.3–2.0cm, but the point of division is high up in the throat above the base of the anthers; the fibres of the corm tunic are not very netted, unlike all the other species in this group. It seems to be best suited to a bulb frame or alpine house.

C. thomasii may be compared with *C. pallasii* in having style branches arising from a point well above the base of the anthers, but it differs in having a yellow throat to the flower. The colour may be pale to deep lilac, not very veined, or rarely white. W. Yugoslavia (Adriatic) and S. Italy. It is quite a vigorous species for a sheltered sunny spot.

C. hadriaticus in its most frequently seen variants has white flowers with a deep yellow throat, thus easily distinguished from white forms of *C. hadriaticus* which are not yellow-throated. The main point of difference between the two is that the style divides higher up in *C. hadriaticus*, not down in the throat as in *C. cartwrightianus*. W. and S. Greece. This form with the yellow throat is sometimes seen in cultivation as var. *chrysobelonicus* or erroneously as *C. cartwrightianus* 'Albus'. A good clone of this has been selected and named by Michael Hoog after O.E.P. Wyatt. It is a vigorous plant, easily cultivated and increasing well.

Forma *parnassicus* from Mount Parnassus has no yellow zone in the throat, just a pure white flower.

Forma *lilacinus* from the S. Peloponnese is the name for variants with soft lilac flowers.

C. scharojanii (C. lazicus) This is described under group A, the yellow-flowered species, the only truly autumnal yellow Crocus, flowering before its leaves, although some forms of *C. vitellinus* also flower in autumn.

C. serotinus A variable western Mediterranean species which flowers with its leaves, or the leaves emerge immediately after the flowers have finished. Subsp. *salzmannii* (*C. salzmannii*, *C. asturicus*, *C. granatensis*) is the most frequently seen variant in gardens and is an excellent autumn Crocus for a sunny border or rock garden, or for planting in grass. Its corm tunics are papery splitting lengthways into soft fibres. The flowers are extremely variable from pale bluish-lilac to deep violet and may have a faint flush of yellow in the throat; one of the darkest forms is known commercially as *C. asturicus atropurpureus*. It also varies a lot in size of flower, and some forms I have from North Africa (one of them given to me by Beth Chatto) are among the largest-flowered Crocuses of all. It is a native of Gibraltar and N. Africa and is widespread in Spain.

Susp. *serotinus* is much more rare in cultivation and is not easy to cultivate outside. It has very coarsely netted corm tunics. S. Portugal.

Subsp. *clusii* (*C. clusii*), mainly from C. and N. Portugal, has very finely netted corm tunics but is otherwise similar to some forms of subsp. *salzmannii*.

C. speciosus   A very well known autumn Crocus, very easy to cultivate and good for naturalizing. It has long slender-tubed flowers produced before the leaves and these may be lilac-purple to deep purple-blue or white without any trace of yellow in the throat and with yellow anthers; the style is divided into many orange threads. There is normally some darker veining on the outside, or some darker stippling, except in the white form. The corm tunic is smooth, non-fibrous, with some rings at the base. In view of the popularity of this species some of the different forms have been given names, for example 'Oxonian' with deep purplish-blue flowers, 'Albus', white, 'Aitchisonii', a large pale lilac, 'Artabir', pale lilac with conspicuous veining. It is a native of N. Turkey, the Caucasus and N. Iran in woods and open hillsides.

Subsp. *ilgazensis* is much less interesting from the horticultural point of view; it has smaller flowers with a less showy style, not divided into so many branches. The corm tunic differs in being papery, splitting lengthways. N. Turkey.

Subsp. *xantholaimos* differs in having a pale yellow throat but is otherwise similar to subsp. *speciosus*. N. Turkey.

C. pulchellus is a close relative of *C. speciosus* and will hybridize with it in gardens. It has smaller, more goblet-shaped flowers (rather funnel-shaped in *C. speciosus*) which are in the bluer shades, usually a clear pale bluish-lilac. The throat is deep yellow and the anthers white, so it cannot be confused with *C. speciosus*. It is an equally good garden plant and is to my mind rather more attractive. S. Yugoslavia, Bulgaria, N. Greece, N.W. Turkey in meadows.

C. vallicola   A lovely early autumn species which is not as difficult to grow as was at one time believed. It has creamy white flowers with a zone of yellow blotches in the throat, white anthers and an inconspicuous style divided into three cream-to-yellow branches. The segments are usually slightly purple-veined and are drawn out at the tips into fine points, a characteristic feature of the species. The leaves appear much later. It has a thin membranous corm tunic with slender fibres. N.E. Turkey, Caucasus in moist alpine meadows. It succeeds best for me in a peaty-gritty soil which does not dry out excessively in summer.

C. autranii is closely related and has similar structural features but the flowers are mid to deep violet with a white zone in the centre. It is extremely rare in cultivation. Caucasus.

C. veneris   A small species, barely known in cultivation and of no great garden value. It has papery corm tunics, splitting lengthways slightly at the base and the flowers are produced at the same time as the leaves. They appear in late autumn or winter and are white with purple stripes on the outside, with a yellow throat, yellow anthers and a much-divided orange style; the segments are only about 1.5–2.5cm long. Cyprus.

C. aleppicus (*C. gaillardotii*) is equally rare and might be found in a few specialist collections. It is similar to *C. veneris* but has more leaves per corm, five to nine as opposed to three or four in *C. veneris* and it has a much more fibrous corm tunic. The anthers may be yellow or blackish. Israel, Jordan, Lebanon, Syria. It requires bulb frame or alpine house cultivation.

C. boulosii is just about in cultivation in one or two collections. It is apparently related to *C. veneris*, but flowers a little later, in January in the wild. It has five to eight leaves per corm, like *C. aleppicus*, but a papery corm tunic more like that of *C. veneris*. The flowers are white with segments about 2–3cm long. Libya, only in Cyrenaica.

C. vitellinus   This has forms which flower in spring and autumn but, since it has yellow flowers it is described in group A.

Cyclamen

This small and distinctive group of beautiful tuberous-rooted plants are extremely popular, so much so that a Cyclamen Society now flourishes. The selections of *C. persicum* are among our most important pot plants, especially for a winter display, while the hardier species are suitable for the alpine house and rock garden and can provide interest for almost every month of the year except mid-summer.

At a first glance the 18 species are all rather similar in that they have rounded to heart-shaped leaves and the characteristic Cyclamen flowers with swept back petals. However, on closer inspection there are plenty of features by which they can be recognized, and even within one species there can be found a fascinating range of variation in leaf shape and markings and flower colour, so much so that it is possible to have hundreds of distinct forms. Even the fruiting stages of Cyclamen show interesting distinctions, for the flower stalk coils like a watch spring in most species but in *C. persicum* remains straight; the majority coil from the top downwards but in *C. graecum* it starts coiling at the base.

Propagation is mainly achieved by seed which should preferably be sown as soon as it is collected, usually in early to mid summer, and kept watered from then on; after germination the young seedlings can be left for a whole growing season and then pricked out into boxes or pans when they are large enough to handle. Flowering time from seed varies from only one season with *C. persicum* to several years with some of the hardy species.

Cultivation of Cyclamen will mainly be mentioned below under each species, but a few general comments can be made. They do not like heavy, wet soils or fine compacted composts; they prefer a light open medium which has leafmould and grit incorporated and, since they are mainly natives of limestone regions, they thrive best in neutral to alkaline soil although light acid sandy soils with humus added seems to give good results, as shown by the lovely plantings of *C. hederifolium* at Wisley. During their dormant season, in mid to late summer, they are dried off to a certain extent, the degree depending upon the species. Much has been said about planting depth but I am sure that it is best to have the tubers covered by at least 2–3cm of loose open soil, except in the case of *C. persicum* which is best grown with the tuber sitting on the surface. When exposed to the elements, Cyclamen which are planted on the surface are subject to frost damage, overdrying and sun scorch in summer – and to physical damage.

Key to Cyclamen species

A   Autumn-flowering... B
      Winter and spring-flowering .... J
B   Cone of anthers projecting beyond mouth of flower .... *C. rohlfsianum*
      Cone of anthers hidden within tube C
C   Flowers with conspicuous swellings ('auricles') around the
        mouth.. D
      Flowers with no very conspicuous auricles........................... G
D   Flowers white with sharply defined crimson markings around the
        mouth.. *C. cyprium*
      Flowers pink or purplish, or if white then with no sharply defined
        red markings .... E
E   Tuber with thick fleshy roots from the bottom centre only; flower
        stem coiling in fruit from the base................................. *C. graecum*
      Tuber producing fine roots from almost anywhere but especially
        around the rim; flower stem coiling in fruit from the apex ..... F

F   Leaf and flower stem travelling horizontally underground before turning upwards to emerge.. *C. hederifolium*

      Leaf and flower stem erect from the tuber .... *C. africanum*

G   Flowers pink, reddish or white with no distinct darker red spot at the mouth .... H

      Flower white or pale pink with a distinct red spot at the mouth.. I

H   Flowers small with petals to 1cm long, white or pale pink, unscented.. *C. intaminatum*

      Flowers larger with petals 1.5–2cm long, pale to deep pink or reddish, very fragrant.. *C. purpurascens*

I   Flowers with petals toothed at apex; leaves with scalloped edge with horny points on the teeth .... *C. mirabile*

      Flowers with smooth-edged petals; leaves often rounded with entire margins.. *C. cilicium*

J   Flowers white with no pink markings at the mouth............... K

      Flowers pink, magenta or white with a darker zone at the mouth L

K   Leaves with rather obvious large teeth, often dark green with silvery zoning .... *C. creticum*

      Leaves entire or with shallow teeth, often silvery green all over .. *C. balearicum*

L   Flowers pale pink with precisely defined red marks at the mouth *C. libanoticum*

      Flowers various colours but if pale pink then mouth marked with a darker pink or carmine stain, not precisely outlined.......... M

M   Flowers with lobes more than twice as long as wide and twisted lengthways .... N

      Flowers with lobes as long or only slightly longer than wide ...... O

N   Leaf and flower stems creeping underground before emerging; flower stem coiled in fruit... *C. repandum*

      Leaf and flower stems erect from the tuber; flower stems not coiling in fruit.. *C. persicum*

O   Flowers longer than wide, produced in late spring; leaves heart-shaped with conspicuous teeth .... *C. pseudibericum*

      Flowers about as long as wide or wider than long, produced in winter or early spring; leaves orbicular or heart shaped, not usually with very conspicuous teeth .... P

P   Petals held almost horizontally and twisted in a propeller-like way; flowers musty-fragrant .... *C. trochopteranthum*

      Petals held more vertically, slightly twisted; flowers not fragrant Q

Q   Flowers lilac-pink with a dark stain at the mouth, very small with petals about 5mm long; leaves plain dull green .... *C. parviflorum*

      Flowers white, pink or carmine in various shades with a dark stain at the mouth, with petals more than 5mm long; leaves usually conspicuously silvery-zoned but if plain green then usually shiny .... *C. coum*

C. africanum   This is a poor garden plant since it is tender, requiring glasshouse cultivation, and is less attractive than its close relative *C. hederifolium*. Its general description is the same but the leaf and flower stems arise directly from the tuber instead of creeping underground before emerging. The leaves are generally larger than in *C. hederifolium*, brighter green and less well marked. North Africa, in scrub. Autumn-flowering.

It apparently hybridizes with *C. hederifolium* in cultivation, so the true plant is rarely seen.

C. balearicum A small, slightly tender species, but in sun or semi-shade in protected gardens and milder districts it is well worth growing for its white fragrant flowers in spring. The heart-shaped, scallop-margined leaves are heavily silvered all over the upper surface in the most commonly seen form. Balearic Islands in pinewoods and scrubland.

C. cilicium This delightful smallish autumnal species is easy to grow in sun or semi-shade and is hardy in all but very cold districts. The flowers are produced in autumn, white or pink with a dark carmine stain around the mouth; they have no auricles and are unscented; a pure white form is known. The leaves vary a great deal from orbicular to heart-shaped, with a wide range of silvery and greenish patterns. S. Turkey, especially the Cilician Taurus mountains in rocky ground beneath pines.

C. coum (C. hiemale, C. ibericum, C. orbiculatum,, C. vernum, 'C. atkinsii')
This is one of the most useful species, since it flowers in winter or very early spring and is very hardy. The flowers are somewhat 'dumpy' in shape, being about as long as wide, but are often a good strong carmine colour although it varies through to pale pinkish-lilac; the white form is especially attractive. All forms have a dark carmine stain around the mouth. The leaves are more or less orbicular, with variable silvery-green zones on the upper surface, sometimes almost wholly silvery, sometimes plain shiny green. Flowering from Christmas onwards for a long period. It grows wild in the mountains of Bulgaria, Turkey and Lebanon, usually in shaded places. In cultivation it does well in sun or partial shade.

   C. coum subsp. *caucasicum* (*C. abschasicum, C. adjaricum, C. caucasicum, C. circassicum, C. elegans*) has slightly larger pinkish-lilac flowers and heart-shaped leaves, rather scalloped at the margin. It is a native of the Caucasus and N. Iran. I have seen it growing in moss on trees in the Caspian woodlands, a beautiful plant but less hardy in cultivation than 'ordinary' *C. coum*.

C. creticum A smallish, tender species, best grown in an alpine house except in very mild districts. The flowers are normally white, occasionally flushed pink, and fragrant, produced in spring. The heart-shaped leaves are toothed at the margins and are most frequently dark green splashed with silvery markings. It is a native of Crete in open rocky places or under bushes.

C. cyprium A charming autumn-flowering species, but best kept in an alpine house. The white, very fragrant, flowers have swellings ('auricles') around the mouth and a ring of carmine markings. The leaves are angular, deep green with paler zoning. It grows wild in Cyprus in rocky places.

C. graecum A good autumn-flowering species with pale to deep pink (a rare white form is known) unscented flowers which have swellings around the mouth, and a darker carmine stain, very like those of *C. hederifolium*. The leaves vary enormously in markings from almost plain green to nearly wholly silvery-washed on the surface, but are normally green with silvery-green zones. The texture on the surface is satin-like. The tuber is distinctive in being rather globose with fleshy roots coming from the centre underside only, quite unlike the flattened tubers of *C. hederifolium*. It occurs wild in Greece and Turkey and the E. Mediterranean islands in rocky places, often in full sun. In cultivation its tubers require drying off and giving a good sun-baking in summer if they are to flower well; it is thus best grown in a deep pot, so that the strong roots can develop properly, in the alpine house.

C. hederifolium (C. neapolitanum) This is the best species for garden use, extremely hardy and easy to grow in sun or semi-shade and seeding itself freely when growing well. The flowers are produced just before the leaves expand, over a long period in early to mid autumn, and are pink with a darker stain around the mouth, which possesses swellings ('auricles'), or they may be pure white; some forms are deliciously fragrant. The leaves vary enormously in shape but are normally rather ivy-shaped and green with silvery-green zones; some forms have long, narrow, pointed leaves. It can be very long lived, the corms reaching 10cm in diameter. Apart from being charming in flower, its leaves remain attractive through winter until the following summer. It grows wild in the Mediterranean region from Italy to Turkey, usually in partial shade.

C. intaminatum A relative of *C. cilicium* (see above), this has smaller flowers in a slightly greyish-white or very pale pink, with no darker stain around the mouth. The normally orbicular leaves are plain green or with a zone of small greyish blotches. Although hardy, its small size makes it more suitable for the alpine house than outside. It is a native of W. Turkey.

C. libanoticum This is one of the most beautiful species, and best grown in the protection of an alpine house. The larger pale pink flowers are produced in spring and have very sharply defined red markings around the mouth; they have a distinctive rather musty fragrance. The large leaves are dull green with paler zoned patterns and are purplish beneath. It is rare in the mountains of Lebanon.

C. mirabile An autumn-flowering species very like *C. cilicium*; it is distinguished from it by having toothed edges to the petals and heart-shaped leaves with scalloped margins. The flowers are usually pale pink with a dark stain around the mouth. It occurs west of the region of *C. cilicium*, in S.W. Turkey in rocky places; it requires similar conditions in cultivation.

C. parviflorum As its name suggests this is small-flowered, the flowers only 5mm long in pale pinkish-lilac with dark stain at the mouth. The orbicular leaves are flat on the ground or only short-stalked and are plain dull green with no markings. It is a native of N.E. Turkey in woods and alpine turf where it never dries out completely. In cultivation it is best grown on a peat garden or, if in a pot, in a cool position.

C. persicum The species from which all the large-flowered florists' cyclamen have been raised through selection. The wild plant flowers naturally in winter or early spring and has strongly fragrant, long and slender flowers in pure white, white with a carmine mouth or various shades of pinkish carmine. The leaves are tremendously variable in their silvery markings; it is this extreme variation in leaf and flower which has made it such a success with plant breeders, also it is easy to grow and quick to flower from seed. Unfortunately it is very tender and requires at least a frost-free greenhouse and preferably some extra heat. *C. persicum* is a native of the eastern Mediterranean from the Aegean Islands eastwards in open rocky areas and in scrub. Unlike all other species its fruiting stems do not coil.

C. pseudibericum This is one of the most attractive species with large showy fragrant flowers in spring, usually in a rich purplish carmine with a very dark stain around the mouth and a white rim at entrance to the corolla tube. The leaves are heart-shaped with distinctly toothed margins and they are often beautifully marked with silver and green patterns. It grows wild in central and southern Turkey in woods and scrub; in cultivation it is fairly hardy and has grown well for me in a sunny part of the peat garden.

C. purpurascens (C. europaeum)   Although this has the best scent of all it is not so free-flowering as most cyclamen. The leaves are present through most of the year, rather rounded in shape and variable in colour from plain green to mottled with silver-green. The flowers appear from late summer to late autumn and are pale to deep carmine, sometimes reddish, and a white form is also known; they have no prominent swellings around the mouth like *C. hederifolium*. It is a native of mountain woods and rocky places in the eastern Alps from Italy to Yugoslavia and Czechoslovakia, probably also in the Caucasus.

   C. purpurascens is best in semi-shade in leafmould-rich soil, preferably alkaline.

C. repandum   The best of the spring species for garden use, easy to grow in semi-shade in a humus-rich soil. The leaves are almost triangular and often somewhat toothed, dark green with paler zoning in var. *repandum*. The fragrant flowers are produced in mid-late spring and are rich carmine, becoming darker towards the mouth in var. *repandum*, which is a native of Italy, Corsica and Yugoslavia. It is a plant of bushy places and shady banks.

   Var. *rhodense* from Rhodes has dark leaves splashed with silver and white flowers with a carmine-pink stain around the mouth. The 'Peloponnese form' known from the central and south Peloponnese in Greece also has silver-splashed leaves; the flowers are pink with a darker stain at the mouth.

   The Peloponnese and Rhodes variants are less hardy than var. *repandum* and are best grown in an alpine house.

C. rohlfsianum   Probably the most tender of all the species, and rather rare, so it is best grown in the safety of a frost-free greenhouse. It is autumn-flowering, rather like *C. hederifolium* in colour and shape but with the cone of anthers protruding from the mouth of the corolla; in *C. hederifolium* the anthers are enclosed in the tube. The leaves are large with a few coarse teeth, so that they are almost lobed in outline, and they are deep green with silver patterns. It occurs wild in Cyrenaica, Libya. *C. rohlfsianum* is one of the few cyclamen where vegetative propagation is a practical proposition. The large tubers produce separate growing points on the upper surface so that they can be cut up, each piece with a 'crown'; it is best to treat the cut surfaces with a fungicide and allow them to dry before replanting.

C. sp. Somalia   An exciting recent development in the Cyclamen world is the finding of a new species in Somalia by Mats Thulins. As yet it has not been named and I know nothing of its affinities.

C. trochopteranthum   This relative of *C. coum* has also been called '*C. alpinum*', but the latter name is poorly defined and may not refer to the same species. It is a spring-flowering species, the flowers varying from pinkish carmine to white, with a darker stain around the mouth and a distinctive musty fragrance; the name describes the twisted petals, like a ship's propeller. The leaves are rounded or slightly heart shaped with shallow toothing and variable silvery-green markings.

   It is hardy, but can be damaged in severe winters – so is best treated as an alpine house plant. It is a native of S.W. Turkey in rocky areas.

Cyclobothra

This name applies to a group of *Calochortus* from Mexico which is sometimes given the status of a genus. *C. lutea* is the most well-known species which, when regarded as a *Calochortus*, takes the name *C. barbatus*. I prefer to keep them together with their more northerly-occurring relatives, so they will be found under *Calochortus*. From a gardener's viewpoint they differ mostly in that they are winter-dormant, flowering in late summer, whereas the North American Calochortus are the reverse and are summer dormant after flowering in spring.

Cypella

An interesting South American genus with rather bizarre *Iris*-shaped flowers which are actually more like those of *Tigridia* to which it is related. Only one species, *C. herbertii*, is at all hardy and this has survived many years without protection in my garden. It is a summer-growing plant, dormant in winter so that in very cold areas the bulbs can be lifted and stored. Seeds are produced freely and these take only two or three years to produce flowering bulbs.

The best site for *C. herbertii* is in a sheltered sunny border – but not too hot and dry – so an adequate amount of water must be available for its summer growth period. Flowering is in late summer.

C. herbertii   A loosely scaled reddish bulb produces erect linear-lanceolate pleated leaves and a much-branched wiry stem, 15–50cm in height, bearing many short-lived flowers in succession. These are 4–6cm in diameter, mustard yellow with three large

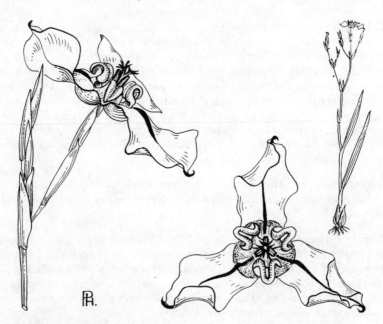

CYPELLA HERBERTII

outer perianth segments and three curiously inrolled and convoluted inner ones which
are spotted with purple. It is a native of Argentina and Uruguay.

Subsp. *brevicristata* is a smaller plant, slightly more attractive in the form I have grown
since the flowers are a bright canary yellow and the whole habit is more slender.
C. gracilis is like a dwarf, narrow-leaved form of *C. herbertii*.

Other species, like the beautiful yellow *C. peruviana* and violet *C. herrerae* (now in the
genus *Hexperoxiphion*) are sadly too tender for outdoor cultivation.

Cyrtanthus

Only a few species in this predominantly South African genus are at all hardy and even
these need a sheltered position in light soil and may be killed in severe winters.
C. purpureus (*Vallota speciosa*) is the best known of the tender species and this is an
exceptionally fine pot plant for the window sill.

Propagation is either by seed or by division of established clumps.

C. brevifolius (Anoiganthus luteus, A. brevifolius)   This is rather Sternbergia-
like in having funnel-shaped yellow flowers 2–3cm long. However, unlike Sternbergia,
they are carried in umbels of up to 20, on stems 5–20cm in height. The linear leaves
appear with the flowers in summer and then the bulbs become dormant for the winter. It
is a native of southern Africa in the E. Cape, Natal, Transvaal and Lesotho, usually in
humus-rich soil near streams.

C. gracilis from Tanzania is very similar.

C. mackenii   I have found this surprisingly hardy, growing and flowering in a border
by the greenhouse without protection for ten years, although scarcely increasing at all. It
has four to ten fragrant tubular flowers in an umbel on a 15–25cm scape and these are
about 5cm long with a slightly curved tube. Var. *mackenii* has white flowers, while var.
cooperi is cream or yellow; there are also several cultivars with pink, white or yellow
flowers. It is a native of the eastern Cape and Natal and is summer-flowering.

C. macowanii   This too has survived and flowered in the same open sunny bed as
C. mackenii. The six to eight tubular flowers are pale to deep red and 3.5–4.0cm long, also
with a curved tube and are carried in umbels on 10–20cm scapes.

C. macowanii and *C. obrienii* (which is probably just a variant of it), are natives of the
mountains of the eastern Cape and the Drakensberg.

Dicentra

Graceful plants related to *Corydalis* and belonging to the same offshoot of the Poppy
family, the Fumariaceae. The flowers have two spurred petals, not one as in Corydalis,
and this has led to the common name of Dutchman's Breeches since in certain species the
two spurs are slightly inflated like traditional Dutch trousers. The most striking species
for gardens are the larger herbaceous one such as *D. formosa* and *D. spectabilis*, which are
superb, but there are a few dwarf tuberous ones which have their place among
enthusiastic plantsmen.

They can be increased by division of the tubers when they have multiplied into a clump, but in certain cases, such as *D. peregrina*, seeds sown while fresh is the best method of propagation.

D. canadensis   Small rounded tubers produce one basal leaf, which is grey-green and finely cut, and 10–20cm stems just overtopping the leaves and carrying in mid spring short racemes of four to ten white flowers, each about 2cm long. It is a native of woods in eastern North America and in cultivation prefers a humus-rich semi-shaded position.

D. cucullaria   This is very similar to *D. canadensis* but has longer narrower spurs to the flowers which, since the spurs are reflexed, have an overall triangular appearance. It is widespread in North America. In cultivation it makes a lovely alpine house plant for mid spring with its graceful ferny grey leaves and white flowers, but is also perfectly at home in a cool position on the rock garden or peat garden.

D. pauciflora   A tempting miniature species which, however, is very tricky to cultivate. It has a small elongated tuber and produces in summer dissected greyish leaves and a 5–10cm tall inflorescence, which carries one to three pale pinkish-purple flowers about 2.0–2.5cm long. It grows in shaded gravelly places in California. I did succeed with this for a while in a leafmould and grit mixture in semi-shade.

D. peregrina (D. pusilla)   Although this is undoubtedly one of the gems of the genus it is rather tricky to grow, even in the alpine house or frame. The rootstock is a short erect rhizome producing several much-dissected blue-grey leaves, overtopped in summer by short racemes of pink flowers; these have swollen reflexed spurs and are about 2cm long. It is a native of eastern Siberia and Japan, on sandy gravelly slopes at up to 2000m. Some successful growers keep it in almost pure gravel, sand or pumice dust, water it almost daily, and feed it regularly with liquid fertilizer. This has been hybridized with the Californian *D. nevadensis* (which is rather like the commonly cultivated herbaceous *D. formosa*). The result, *D.* 'Tsuneshiga Rokujo', is an attractive grey-leaved plant, larger and looser than *D. peregrina*, with pink lyre-shaped flowers 2cm in length.

D. uniflora   An interesting little species but very tricky in cultivation. It grows only about 5cm in height with one dissected basal leaf about 2cm across, and in spring produces solitary lilac, pink or white short-spurred flowers about 1.5cm long. It occurs wild in western North America from British Columbia south to California at up to 2500m on rocky or gravelly slopes.

Dichelostemma

These American bulbs are relatives of *Brodiaea* and *Triteleia* and a general discussion about the differences between these will be found p.19, under *Brodiaea*.

D. ida-maia (Brodiaea coccinea, Brevoortia ida-maia)   The curious name commemorates a girl called Ida May Burke, daughter of a Californian stage-coach driver. It is a striking species, 20–30cm tall, known as the Californian Firecracker because of the umbel of several pendent crimson flowers tipped with green; they are tubular, the tube about 2–3cm long, with short perianth segments flared outwards. The linear leaves have a keel on the underside. It is a native of California and Oregon and is not very hardy, although I have grown and flowered it successfully in Surrey in a sheltered spot against a warm fence. It flowers in late spring.

D. venustum is similar to this but has rose-red flowers with a shorter tube 17mm or less long. It is a rare plant in N.W. California.

D. pulchellum (Brodiaea capitata)   This handsome species has lilac-blue flowers in a tight dense umbel about 4–5cm in diameter, subtended by broad violet spathes; each flower is about 1.5cm long and the same across at the mouth. It grows wild in Oregon and California, in pinewoods or grassy places at low altitudes, so is probably best cultivated in a bulb frame for protection in cold districts.

D. multiflorum (*Brodiaea parviflora*) also from Oregon and California, is similar but the flowers are somewhat constricted at the throat and the tube is 8–10mm long (5–8mm in *D. pulchellum*).

D. congestum occurs widely in the States of Washington, Oregon and California and is also similar to *D. pulchellum*, but the flowers are not carried in a perfect umbel; their pedicels join together at the base and so the inflorescence is really a congested raceme. With Roy Davidson I saw a large patch of this on the rocky gorge sides of the Clackamas river in Oregon, a most striking plant with rich violet blue flowers.

D. lacuna-vernalis, which occurs in spring pools in California (hence the odd name), is related to *D. pulchella* but has only one to three flowers in the umbel and up to six stems per bulb.

D. volubile (Brodiaea volubilis)   An unusual species which has a twining flower stem requiring a dwarf shrub for support. It produces tightly-flowered umbels up to 8cm in diameter of tubular pinkish-mauve flowers in spring. Being rather tender it is best given a sheltered position on the sunny side of a shrub which it can use for protection and physical support. It is a Californian native.

Eminium

A small genus of Aroids related to *Biarum* (see p. 15) but differing in having the leaves lobed at the base; in *Biarum* they are entire with no lobes or arrow-shaped base. The spathes are very similar, produced at ground level, usually velvety purple or blackish, but appear in spring in *Eminium* and mainly late summer or autumn in *Biarum*. They are natives of areas with hot dry summers and are best grown in a bulb frame where the tubers can be planted deeply and given a warm dry rest period in summer. Beautiful to the eyes of an enthusiast!

E. albertii   This has rather narrow leaves with pointed basal lobes, almost withering away by flowering time in spring or early summer. The broad dark purple-red spathe lies almost flat on the ground, leaving the similarly coloured pencil-like spadix standing erect. It is a native of Soviet Central Asia.

E. intortum   This has rather short broad leaves with two basal lobes and conspicuous veins which separate at the base away from the midrib at an angle, instead of running parallel alongside it. The evil smelling purple-brown spathes are smooth and velvet-like with a blackish spadix. Syria, S. Turkey, in rather hot dry areas.

E. rauwolffii   This is like *E. intortum* but the leaves have veins which run parallel to the midrib at the base before diverging. The purple spathes are about 10–15cm long and up to 5cm wide, and the dark cylindrical spadix up to 7cm long. Var. *kotschyi* has a more conical shaped spadix. Syria, S. Turkey.

E. spiculatum   This has the leaves more dissected, not just with two basal lobes. The dark purple to almost blackish spathe can be as much as 20cm in length and 10cm wide, but often less, and the spadix about 10cm; unlike the previous two species the spathe is rough inside, covered with minute protuberances. It is widespread from Egypt east to Syria, Iraq and S. Turkey and is variable, with several varieties described.

Eranthis

The Winter Aconite is a must for gardeners since it is one of the first yellow-flowered bulbs of the year and associates well in semi-shade with all the whites of Snowdrops and Snowflakes. It is ideal for naturalizing beneath shrubs in places where there is little disturbance of the soil and they can be left to increase at will. *Eranthis* seem to be particularly good on alkaline soils and are good companions for Hellebores in this respect.

E. hyemalis   The common Winter Aconite, growing to 10cm in height, with erect solitary yellow cup-shaped flowers 2.5cm in diameter, carried stemless on a dissected leaf-like bract (involucre) acting as a ruff. It is a native of woods in Europe and is naturalized in Britain; var. *bulgaricus* has its leaves and bracts rather more divided and hence it approaches *E. cilicica* in this respect.

E. cilicica   A delightful plant but less easy to grow than *E. hyemalis*, probably requiring slightly more sun and drying out in summer to some extent. The leaves and bracts are often tinged with a bronze colour and are much more dissected than in *E. hyemalis*. The flower is a bright shiny golden-yellow and like *E. hyemalis* it is stemless on the bract leaves. It comes from shady rocky places in the Cilician Taurus mountains in S. Turkey.

When grown together these two species hybridize to produce very vigorous sterile plants with large flowers. A particularly good form has been given the name of *E. × tubergenii* 'Guinea Gold', this having bright golden flowers surrounded by a bronzy ruff. It is better on the rock garden than under shrubs and is a fine plant for a sunny spot where an early splash of colour is required.

E. pinnatifida (E. keiskei)   This is similar in habit to other species but has smaller white flowers about 2cm in diameter. Each of the leaf lobes is again pinnately divided, hence the name. It is a delightful little species for the alpine house. It does well with me in a raised peaty bed where it flowers in early spring. A native of Japan in mountain woods.

E. longistipitata   This is perhaps more of interest than beauty for it has smaller yellow flowers than *E. hyemalis* and is less easy to grow. However, it has particular affection for me since I saw it in Uzbekistan, pushing its much-dissected leaves and yellow flowers out of cool rock crevices. It differs most obviously from *E. hyemalis* in its bract leaves being dissected and in the flowers being carried on a stalk above the ruff of bracts – in *E. hyemalis* and *E. cilicica* they are sessile. It is a native of Central Asia.

E. sibirica (*E. uncinata*) from Siberia is very similar to this but has the bract leaves less finely divided. *E. sibirica* var. *glandulosa* has yellowish glandular hairs on the pedicels but in var. *sibirica* they are glabrous.

    E. stellata from eastern USSR and N. China is also similar to *E. longistipitata* but, like *E. sibirica*, has the bract leaves less finely divided; the pedicels are white-hairy, not glandular, so in this respect it differs from *E. sibirica*.

Erythronium

A delightful group of spring-flowering plants, nearly all of which are worthy of cultivation in partially shaded sites in humus-rich soil. They are characterized by having pendent flowers with reflexed perianth segments carried on leafless stems over two broad basal leaves which may be plain green or beautifully mottled. The majority of species occur wild in North America, especially in the western United States, but *E. dens-canis* the Dog's Tooth Violet is European and Asiatic with variants of it occurring eastwards through the USSR to Japan. Dog's Tooth refers to the bulb, which is normally elongated and pointed rather like a large canine fang, but in the United States there are far more attractive names, referring to the habitat or mottled leaves, such as Avalanche Lily, Glacier Lily, Trout Lily and Fawn Lily.

    As already noted, they are plants for a cool position where they will not become sunbaked in summer, although on the other hand they must not be too wet whilst in their dormant state and a position where the roots of summer-growing shrubs and trees extract most of the surplus moisture is ideal. Raised peat beds provide the right sort of conditions and here their beauty can be better appreciated but the more vigorous ones are perfect for planting between shrubs and under trees in a semi-woodland setting.

    When dormant in summer the bulbs can be lifted and divided but at no time should they be over-dried. Propagation is also successful by seed which is normally produced quite freely, but this will take three or four years to produce flowering-sized bulbs.

    All Erythroniums flower in spring, following on from the early bulbs such as Crocus.

Key to Erythronium species

A	Leaves mottled..	B
	Leaves plain green..	M
B	Stigma clearly divided into 3	C
	Stigma entire, or only very obscurly 3-lobed	I
C	Filaments widely expanded in lower half	D
	Filaments narrow or slightly flattened	E
D	Flowers pink	*revolutum*
	Flowers white or cream	*oregonum*
E	Anthers white or cream	F
	Anthers yellow or purplish	G
F	Flower stem solitary per bulb	*californicum*
	Flower stems in mature vigorous plants more than one per bulb ...	*multiscapoideum*
G	Flowers white with a yellow centre	H
	Flowers various colours, but if white, with a ring of dark marks near centre	*dens-canis*
H	Perianth segments 3.5–4.0cm long with a dilated base	*helenae*
	Perianth segments less than 3.5cm not dilated at base.............	*albidum*

I   Perianth segments up to 1.2cm long .... *propullans*
    Perianth segments over 2cm long .... J
J   Flowers white or yellow sometimes pinkish outside .... K
    Flowers lavender.. *hendersonii*
K   Flowers yellow; anthers yellow, brown or purplish .... *americanum* (incl.
                                                                            rostratum &
                                                                            umbilicatum)
    Flowers white or cream; anthers whitish........................... L
L   Perianth segments about 2cm long, not lobed at base .... *howellii*
    Perianth segments 2.5–4.0cm long, each with 2 lobes at base..... *citrinum*
M   Stigma with three free lobes .... N
    Stigma entire or very obscurely lobed .... Q
N   Flowers yellow .... *grandiflorum*
    Flowers white, sometimes with pinkish outside.................... O
O   Anthers white... *idahoense*
    Anthers yellow... P
P   Leaves of flowering specimens abruptly narrowed at base .... *montanum*
    Leaves of flowering specimens gradually narrowed at base .... *albidum*
Q   Flowers white or cream .... R
    Flowers yellow .... S
R   Anthers yellow; perianth segments swollen at base .... *klamathense*
    Anthers white, perianth segments not swollen at base............. *purpurascens*
S   Anthers red, perianth segments with no appendage at base ...... *nudopetalum*
    Anthers yellow, perianth segments with appendage at base ...... *tuolumnense*

E. albidum   Leaves narrower than in most species, up to 3.5cm wide, attractively mottled. Flowers solitary, white inside with a yellow centre, usually bluish or pinkish on the exterior. Var. *mesochoreum* (*E. mesochoreum*) is very similar but has unmottled leaves. East-central North America from southern Canada to Texas in woods and valleys. Not as easy and free-flowering as most of the western U.S. species.

E. americanum   This species has beautifully mottled leaves, sometimes forming a ground cover since this species spreads rapidly by stolons. It is unfortunately shy of flowering. The flowers are solitary, yellow with a purplish or brownish suffusion outside and darker-spotted inside, with yellow, purplish or brown anthers. It is a woodland plant from Eastern North America, from southern Canada to Kansas and Florida. Not difficult to establish in moist semi-shaded situations.

   E. americanum subsp. *harperi* (*E. harperi*) from Alabama and Tennessee differs in the shape of its capsule, in subsp. *americanum* it is rounded or truncate at the apex while in subsp. *harperi* it has a minute point.

   E. rostratrum is closely related and similar to *E. americanum* but has its capsule extended into a long beak at the apex; the perianth segments are somewhat dilated at the base and have distinct basal lobes whereas in *E. americanum* the segments are not dilated and not, or only slightly, lobed. Alabama, Tennessee and possibly several other adjacent eastern States.

   E. umbilicatum is also similar to *E. americanum* but the apex of the capsule has a dip, not rounded, pointed or beaked as in the above two species; the stem bends after flowering so that the capsule touches the ground. The segments have no basal lobes so it differs from *E. rostratum* in this respect. Susp. *umbilicatum* has bulbs which do not produce stolons. This occurs widely from Virginia south to Florida. Subsp. *monostolum* from N. Carolina has bulbs which produce one stolon each.

E. californicum Leaves mottled with brownish-green. Flowers usually one to three per stem, creamy-white with a ring of ill-defined orange-brown markings near the centre; stigma three-lobed; anthers white. California, in humus-rich woodland soil to 1000m. A good garden plant, flowering freely.

E. citrinum Similar to *E. californicum*, but has swellings at the base of each perianth segment and the stigma is not three-lobed at the apex. S. Oregon and N. California, in oak and pine woods.

E. dens-canis The European Dog's Tooth Violet which occurs also in Asia. The elliptical leaves are beautifully mottled with brownish- and bluish-green ground colours. Flowers usually solitary, variable in colour, but in the range of rose, pinkish-lilac and carmine with a white, yellow or brownish centre surrounded by purple or brown marks; there is also a white form. The anthers are purplish or bluish.

E. caucasicum from the Caspian region of Iran and the Caucasus has creamy coloured flowers.

E. sibiricum from the USSR has large flowers with yellow anthers.

E. japonicum from Japan is one of the best and largest variants with rich violet flowers with a dark centre.

E. dens-canis and its forms is an excellent garden plant, satisfactory in partially shaded sites in humus-rich soil or in grass. In the wild it occurs mostly in deciduous woodlands.

E. giganteum A confused name which has been applied to *E. grandiflorum* and *E. oregonum*.

E. grandiflorum A rare species in cultivation since it is not easy to grow, although I now have a successful patch in a cold, shaded part of the peat garden. It has unmottled green leaves and one to six large yellow flowers which differ from other yellow, plain green leaved species in having a trilobed stigma. In western North America it is widespread in meadows and light conifer woods at altitudes up to 3000m in the Rockies, the Cascades and the Olympics in Washington State where, thanks to Mr Brian Mulligan and his wife, I have been able to enthuse over great drifts of this lovely plant. The anther colour varies from very dark blackish-red to yellow or white and some varieties have been named using this feature: var. *grandiflorum*, red anthers; var. *pallidum*, white anthers; var. *chrysandrum*, yellow anthers. Occasionally they occur in mixed populations. The two latter varieties have also been named *E. parviflorum* by some authors.

E. helenae An attractive species, thriving on a raised bank of the peat garden and a particular favourite of mine. It is like *E. californicum* in overall appearance, but the yellow centre is sharply defined and it has yellow anthers. California, on wooded slopes of the Coast Range.

E. hendersonii One of the most beautiful species and not difficult in partial shade, where it will dry out in summer. Leaves marked with paler bands. Flowers up to ten, lilac with a deep purple centre; anthers bluish. S.W. Oregon and N.W. California, on open slopes up to 1500m.

E. howellii   This is like *E. californicum* and *E. citrinum* in overall appearance, but differs from the first in having an undivided stigma and from the latter in its segments not being lobed at the base. S.W. Oregon, in rocky situations. I have no experience of its cultivation.

E. idahoense   A rare species in cultivation, related to *E. grandiflorum* but with white flowers with a green centre. The leaves are plain green, the anthers white and the stigma three-lobed. E. Washington State and W. Idaho in yellow-pine woods.

E. klamathense   Another rarity in cultivation, although apparently not difficult to grow in the peat garden. It has plain green leaves. Flowers usually solitary, white or cream with a large yellow centre, a more or less entire stigma and yellow anthers. Pinewoods of the Siskyou and Cascade Mountains in S.W. Oregon and N.W. California.

E. mesochoreum   See **E. albidum**

E. montanum   The beautiful Avalanche Lily is a difficult species to accommodate in cultivation. It has plain green broad leaves abruptly narrowed at the base and one to three pure white flowers with a small yellow centre; anthers yellow. In the United States and Canada it occurs in meadows near the snow line at up to 2500m in the Olympic and Cascade Mountains. It also occurs at lower altitudes on Vancouver Island, and it is possible that plants from this area will be rather easier to cultivate. There can be few more graceful small bulbs than this beautiful plant, especially seen in its natural surroundings, and thanks to Roy Davidson of Seattle I have now had the opportunity to see it on Mount Hood in Oregon.

E. elegans is a new species related to this, described in 1985 from Oregon growing on open grassy slopes and edges of bogs at just below 1000m. The leaves vary in colour from plain green to slightly mottled and are rarely completely mottled. The one to two (rarely four) flowers are white or pale pink, with a yellow centre with swollen appendages at the base of each segment; the filaments are narrow or slightly expanded and the anthers are yellow. The style is deeply three-lobed.

It is suggested that *E. elegans* is related to *E. montanum* but there has been some hybridization with *E. revolutum* in the past, giving for example the pinkish flower colour in some specimens.

E. multiscapoideum (E. hartwegii)   The name was given to this because of its ability to produce more than one stem per bulb, although this effect is actually caused by one stem branching low down between the leaves. Apart from this it is very like *E. californicum* with white, yellow-centred flowers, mottled leaves and white anthers. The bulbs are said to produce stolons which also makes it distinct from all similar species, but I have not yet observed this feature and cannot comment. Like its relative it is a good and handsome garden plant. California, on wooded slopes of the Sierra Nevada.

E. nudopetalum   A rare species both in cultivation and in the wild. It has plain green leaves and small solitary bright yellow flowers which are veined greenish; style not three-lobed; anthers reddish. Unlike *E. tuolumnense* there are no swollen appendages at the base of the segments. Idaho, in conifer woods near the snow line.

E. oregonum   An easily cultivated species, free-flowering and increasing well. It has mottled leaves and one to five flowers, which are creamy white with a ring of zigzag brownish marks around a yellow centre; stigma three-lobed; anthers yellow on flattened ribbon-like filaments. N. Oregon, Washington State and Vancouver Island in fir woods.

Var. *leucandrum* has white anthers.

E. parviflorum   See **E. grandiflorum**

E. propullans   A small-flowered but interesting little species. It has narrow, mottled leaves and a solitary pink flower only 1.0–1.2cm long. The stem produces a stolon which results in a new bulb at its tip. Minnesota, in maple woods.

E. purpurascens   A rare species in cultivation, distinctive in usually having up to eight smallish flowers in a raceme, although weak ones may have one or two. It has bright green leaves and white flowers with a yellow centre, ageing to pink or purple, hence the name; style not three-lobed; anthers white. California in the S. Cascade and Sierra Nevada range, growing near the snow line.

E. revolutum   A well known and attractive species of easy cultivation. The leaves are beautifully mottled. It has one to three large flowers, deep pink with a yellow centre, a three-lobed stigma and yellow anthers. A widely distributed species in California northwards to Vancouver Island, growing in woods and damp places to about 1000m.

Var. *johnstonii* is the name given to a particularly good pink form.

E. tuolumnense   The easiest of the yellow-flowered species in cultivation; increasing well. It has pale green leaves, unmottled, and one to four bright yellow flowers with yellow anthers; stigma entire. California, in Tuolumne County at about 500m in woods.

Hybrids   There has been a certain amount of crossing in the genus and some of the results have provided good garden plants. 'White Beauty' is the most popular of these, a vigorous white-flowered form with mottled leaves, resembling *E. oregonum*. 'Jeanette Brickell' is another lovely white hybrid, free-flowering and increasing well. 'Pink Beauty' is a good pink, probably a form or hybrid of *E. revolutum*. 'Pagoda' and 'Kondo' are hybrids between *E. tuolumnense* and one of the white-flowered species, both having pale yellow flowers with slightly mottled leaves. Mr John Walker of Kent has also produced some fine hybrids involving *E. oregonum, E. tuolumnense* and 'White Beauty'.

Eucomis

An interesting group of South African bulbs, mostly summer-growing and dormant in winter, so that they are hardy in the cooler climates. I have grown several species successfully out in the open garden for many years. They also make interesting subjects for growing in large pots or tubs on the patio. The large bulbs produce rosettes of strap-shaped basal leaves and stout densely-flowered racemes of rather fleshy flowers, which open out flattish and starry. Overtopping these is a tuft of small leaves at the top of the inflorescence, hence the common name of Pineapple Flower. Most species are fairly large and require plenty of room, preferably planted in a sunny position against a sunny wall or fence, but where they will get plenty of moisture in summer.

E. autumnalis (E. undulata)   This has wavy-edged leaves 5–12cm wide and stout stems, usually 20–30cm in height, carrying many white or pale greenish flowers about 1.5–2.5cm in diameter. Subsp. *amaryllidifolia* has narrower leaves not more than 4cm wide. South Africa, in the eastern (summer rainfall) regions northwards to Zimbabwe and Malawi. It flowers in late summer.

E. bicolor   One of the best-known species in cultivation with undulate-edged leaves 8–10cm wide and densely flowered racemes usually about 20–30cm in height carrying green flowers with purple margins, each 2–3cm in diameter; the pedicels are pendulous on the mature flowers. The lower part of the stem is often purple-blotched or streaked. Late summer. It is a native of Natal, and in the wild varies considerably in flower colour from pale green to purple, sometimes with a dark purple centre.

E. clavata   This is sometimes called *E. autumnalis* subsp. *clavata*. It has ovate-lanceolate leaves 6–13cm wide and racemes of whitish flowers, each about 2.5–3.5cm in diameter. The name describes the shape of the flower stem, narrow as it emerges from the bulb and thickening into a club shape. Eastern regions of Southern Africa and Botswana.

E. comosa (E. punctata)   A well-known species, more colourful than most. It has lanceolate leaves purple-spotted underneath and purple-spotted or striped flower stems 30–70cm in height, carrying many pale green flowers with a darker purple ovary forming a conspicuous eye in the centre; they are about 2.5cm across. There are now some selections of this, perhaps hybrids with another species, which have pinkish or purplish flowers, some of them also with purplish foliage. They seem to be very hardy and are attractive late summer garden plants. E. Cape and Natal.

E. humilis   A dwarf species from the Natal Drakensberg. The leaves are small and attractively spotted and blotched purple. The short dense racemes carry wholly green flowers which are held on slightly pendulous pedicels. The stamens have purple filaments, giving a dark eye to the flower.

E. pallidiflora   A robust species with long broad leaves about 10–12cm wide, crinkly at the margins. The many-flowered racemes reach 45–75cm in height with pale greenish flowers 2.5–3.0cm in diameter. Summer flowering, lasting through into autumn.

E. pole-evansii   This is the giant of the group, up to 2m in height with leaves 10–18cm wide. The flowers are greenish white and it looks like a larger version of *E. pallidiflora*, not for the smaller garden!

E. regia   This differs from the rest in being a winter-growing species, flowering in spring and is thus not a satisfactory plant outdoors for countries with frosty winters. It has broad leaves and stout but shortish racemes of pale green flowers.

E. schijffii   A species I have only just obtained, thanks to Bill Small of Natal. It is the smallest species, only 4–10cm in height, with dark purple flowers in late summer. The leaves lie flat on the ground. Drakensberg Mountains of Natal.

E. vandermerwei   A smallish species 15–25cm in height with undulate leaves. Both leaves and flower stems are heavily spotted and suffused purple and the flowers, which are carried in a fairly loose raceme, are green with purplish edges to the segments; the stamens have green filaments. Transvaal.

E. montana is somewhat similar but has purple filaments to the stamens.

E. zambesiaca   The form of this which is in cultivation is an attractive small plant only about 15–25 cm in height, with dense racemes of white flowers, and leaves which are not too gross – so it is quite suitable for the smaller garden.

Fritillaria

The 'Frits' are enjoying great popularity at present and a large proportion of the known species have been introduced into cultivation, although most of these are in the hands of specialist growers and surprisingly few are offered in the nursery trade.

Fritillaries need little description for they are well known to most gardeners, if only through the gorgeous Crown Imperial, *F. imperialis*, and the more humble British native Snakeshead Fritillary, *F. meleagris*. There are approximately 125 species distributed throughout Europe, North Africa, temperate Asia and North America. They nearly all have pendent flowers, although one or two of the American ones, for example *F. falcata*, are upward-facing; they have six more or less equal perianth segments but in colour the outer three may differ noticeably from the inner three, often having more conspicuous markings. The shape and arrangement of the flowers differs widely, but there are some obvious affinities, such as the group with umbellate flowers like *F. imperialis*, the type with long racemes of small flowers, of which *F. persica* is the only member, and those with flattish flowers with deep nectaries forming 'humps' on the backs of the segments, which is the characteristic shape of *F. gibbosa* and *F. bucharica* and their relatives (Rhinopetalum). The main bulk of the species can be, for convenience, divided into those with broad bells with a rounded or squared base, in contrast to those with generally smaller conical bells, narrowing more gradually at the base; within the latter group it is useful to note for identification purposes whether or not the stigma is entire (undivided) or separated into three distinct lobes. In addition to these floral differences there is great variation between the species in their general stature, from dwarfs of only a few centimetres to tall plants a metre high. The leaves may be arranged alternately up the stem, or sometimes in pairs (opposite), or mixed alternate and opposite, or they may be in whorls; some species have tendrils on the tips to cling on to adjacent vegetation.

The cultivation of Fritillaries varies widely and it is difficult to generalize. They are however all autumn-spring growers, that is their bulbs begin to root in autumn and the plants continue to grow slowly through winter, until they emerge to flower in spring. By early summer they have died down again and at this period require only a little moisture. They therefore require well-drained sites which dry out to some extent in summer but are not necessarily hot and sunbaked, such as, for example, the Tulips enjoy. The majority of species are best grown in the alpine house or bulb frame, partly so that conditions can be controlled and for protection from hard frosts in early spring, and partly because they are so uncommon; few people will have enough of them to risk planting out in the open! I do not, however, want to give the impression that they are very difficult to cultivate; on the whole they are fairly easy and a number of species are perfectly happy in the open garden without protection.

In making the following list of species I am indebted to Martyn Rix and Roger Macfarlane for their extensive work on the genus and to various people who have

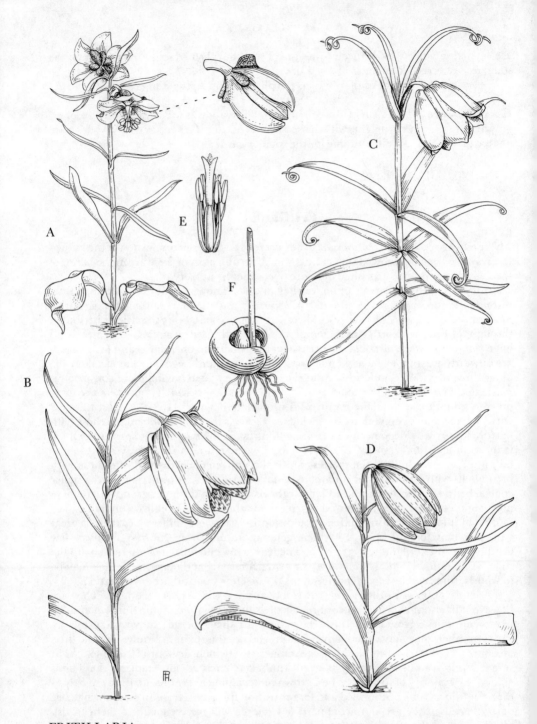

FRITILLARIA

(A) F. gibbosa, *an example of the Rhinopetalum group* (B) F. tubiformis, *typical of the type with broad squared 'shoulders'* (C) F. verticillata *with its whorled or opposite leaves, tendril-like at the tips* (D) F. ehrhartii, *one of the smaller species with conical bells* (E) *Style and stamens of* Fritillaria *showing a 3-lobed stigma* (F) *A typical* Fritillaria *bulb* supplied information (and bulbs!) over the years, notably Paul Furse, Wayne Roderick, Vic Horton and Ole Sønderhousen.

Although this is primarily a book on the smaller bulbs, for completeness in this popular group I have included the taller ones as well. Rather than a completely alphabetical list I have made a few informal groups in order to clarify them slightly, but within these they are in A–Z order; the American ones are grouped separately since, on the whole, they seem to be fairly unrelated to the rest.

The groups are as follows:

(1) *F. imperialis* and its allies (Petilium) (p. 77)
(2) *F. persica* and its forms (Theresia) (p. 78)
(3) *F. gibbosa* and its allies (Rhinopetalum) (p. 78)
(4) *F. sewerzowii* (Korolkowia) (p. 79)
(5) American Species (p. 79)
(6) European and Asiatic Species (p. 82)
(7) Some little known, mainly Chinese, species

In the following descriptions the nectaries are mentioned; these are glistening glands to be found inside the flower on the basal part of each perianth segment, sometimes elongated along the centre to about half way.

(1) *F. imperialis and its allies*

F. imperialis   The Crown Imperial is the most superb species; indeed it is probably one of the most handsome of all bulbous plants, so stately that it has been popular as a garden plant for over 400 years and the subject of numerous botanical illustrations. The stiff stems can reach a metre or more and carry alternate or whorled glossy leaves on the lower part – then there is a leafless portion up to the umbel of flowers which is overtopped by a further tuft of narrow leaf-like bracts. The flowers are pendent bells up to 6cm long and 5cm wide, with large white nectaries at the base containing a drop of nectar. The usual colour of the flowers in the wild is brick-orange but various selections have been made, including reddish ones, e.g. 'Rubra' and yellow, 'Lutea'. The yellows are particularly showy in the garden and are my personal favourites. All have a characteristic 'foxy' smell from the bulbs and especially the young shoots when they emerge in mid spring. Flowering. Wild in S.E. Turkey, east through Iran to the W. Himalaya, on rocky hillsides.

Crown Imperials are best grown in well-drained soil in a sunny position which dries out in summer; the bulbs should be planted at least 20cm deep and left undisturbed as long as they thrive; feed annually in autumn and spring with a potash-rich fertilizer.

F. chitralensis   A shorter plant, reaching 30cm, which has only one to three smaller bells in clear yellow; it does not have the foxy smell. This is a delightful species which comes from E. Afghanistan and the western Himalaya. I have not yet tried it outside of the bulb frame.

F. eduardii from Soviet Central Asia is similar in overall appearance to *F. imperialis* but the orange flowers are much more widely open, the perianth segments flaring outwards.

F. raddeana (F. askabadensis)   Although belonging to the same group and having the same overall appearance as *F. imperialis*, this charming species is quite distinct in being more slender throughout with smaller flowers in a soft greenish-yellow or straw

colour. It is a native of N.E. Iran and adjacent USSR and is a good garden plant for a
sunny position.

(2) *F. persica* and its forms

F. persica (F. libanotica, F. eggeri)   This is one of the tallest species, reaching 1.5
metres at most, with many narrow, alternate greyish leaves, often somewhat twisted
lengthways. A long raceme carries up to 25 smallish conical flowers 1–2cm long, varying
from blackish-plum to brownish or a greenish or yellowish straw colour, often with a
greyish 'bloom'. The form known as 'Adiyaman' is a good blackish colour, named after a
town in Turkey; some of the pale variants I have seen in Iran are scarcely worth
growing.

   F. persica is a native of S. Turkey, east to Iran and south to Israel and Jordan. It is an
easy plant to grow in a sunny, well drained position, flowering in mid-late spring.

(3) *F. gibbosa* and its allies

I have chosen *F. gibbosa* to represent this, the Rhinopetalum group, since it is the most
widespread species and probably the most beautiful. The flowers of Rhinopetalum are
characterized by deeply sunken nectaries at the base of each perianth segment, which
show through on the outside of the flower as hump-like projections; these six humps are
equal in some species, unequal in others.

   They are all highly treasured plants, best cultivated in an alpine house or bulb frame
since they mostly come from areas which become hot and dry in summer. *F. bucharica* is
the easiest to cultivate and has grown successfully in a sunny, well-drained position.

   The flowering time of all species is in early-mid spring.

F. bucharica   This is usually about 10–20cm high, sometimes more, carrying ovate-
lanceolate grey-green leaves and a short dense raceme of up to ten flowers 1.5–2.5cm in
diameter; these are a silvery white with a hint of green, tending to be cup-shaped, rather
than flattish as they are in *F. gibbosa*. It is a native of N. Afghanistan and the adjacent
mountains of Soviet Central Asia, growing in open hillsides of heavy, sticky soil which
dries out in summer.

F. gibbosa   A very variable species 5–15cm in height with greyish leaves and usually
only one to five flowers, but well-grown specimens may have more. These are flattish
with the uppermost nectary deeper than the rest, hence the 'hump' on the outside is more
pronounced. The colour varies from pale pink to a deep brick-red or apricot, usually
with a darker tessellated pattern. It is native in Iran and Afghanistan, growing in open
stony or sandy places which become very hot in summer.

   This is a tantalizing species, very beautiful yet difficult to keep for long. Some fine
colour forms were introduced in the 1960s by Paul Furse but these, sadly, did not persist
for long in cultivation – but those sent more recently by John Ingham are faring rather
better with some growers and are being propagated by seed.

F. ariana   From Afghanistan; similar to *F. gibbosa*, but has no tessellation on the
flowers.

F. karelinii   Differs from *F. gibbosa* mainly in the shape of its capsules, which are
smooth with no wings at the corners; those of *F. gibbosa* are conspicuously winged. Soviet
Central Asia.

1   *Allium akaka*
in E. Turkey

2   *Allium mirum*

3   *Amana edulis*
(Tulipa edulis)

4 *Anemone petiolulosa*
in Uzbekistan

5 *Arisaema sikokianum*

6 *Arisarum vulgare*

7   *Arum dioscoridis*
in S.W. Turkey

8   *Bellevalia hyacinthoides*
(Strangweia spicata)

9   *Biarum davisii* in Crete

10 *Bloomeria crocea*

11 *Brodiaea californica*

12 *Calochortus amoenus*

13 *Calochortus macrocarpus* in Washington State

14 *Calochortus tolmiei*

15 *Chionodoxa luciliae* 'Alba' *(C. gigantea* 'Alba'*)*

16 *Colchicum cupanii* in Crete

17 *Colchicum doerfleri*

18 *Colchicum luteum* in Uzbekistan

19 *Colchicum macrophyllum* in Crete

20 *Commelina dianthifolia*

21 *Cooperia drummondii* in Mexico

22 *Corydalis aitchisonii*

23 *Corydalis bracteata*

24 *Corydalis cashmeriana*

25 *Corydalis ledebouriana* and *Tulipa bifloriformis* in Uzbekistan

26 *Corydalis popovii*

27 *Crocus alatavicus* in Uzbekistan

28 *Crocus banaticus*

29 *Crocus cvijicii*
in N. Greece

30 *Crocus sieberi*
f. tricolor

31 *Crocus tournefortii*

32 *Cyclamen pseudibericum*

33 *Cyclamen purpurascens (C. europaeum)* in N. Yugoslavia

34 *Dicentra cucullaria*

35 *Dichelostemma congestum* in Oregon

36 *Eranthis longistipitata* in Uzbekistan

37 *Erythronium grandiflorum* in the Olympic Mountains, Washington

38 *Erythronium helenae*

39 *Eucomis zambesiaca*

40 *Fritillaria chlorantha* in Iran

41 *Fritillaria cirrhosa* in Sikkim

42 *Fritillaria affinis (F. lanceolata)* on Saddle Mountain, Oregon

43 *Fritillaria michailovskyi*

44 *Fritillaria minima* in E. Turkey

45 *Fritillaria sewerzowii*

46 *Fritillaria stenanthera*
in Uzbekistan

47 *Gagea villosa*

48 *Galanthus rizehensis*

49 *Gymnospermium albertii*

50 *Gynandriris sisyrinchium*

51 *Habranthus martinezii*

52 *Hermodactylus tuberosus*
(Iris tuberosa) in Yugoslavia

53 *Hyacinthella pallens*
(H. dalmatica)

54 *Hyacinthus transcaspicus*

55 *Iris albomarginata*

56 *Iris narbutii*

57 *Iris nicolai*

58 *Iris vicaria*

59 *Iris warleyensis*
in Uzbekistan

60 *Iris willmottiana*

61 *Iris histrio*

62 *Iris kolpakowskiana*

63 *Iris reticulata* 'Alba'

64 *Ixiolirion tataricum*

65 *Leontice armenaica
(L. minor)* in Iran

66 *Leucojum
trichophyllum*

67 *Lloydia flavonutans* in Sikkim

68 *Merendera trigyna*

69 *Moraea stricta (M. trita)*

70 *Muscari caucasicum (Leopoldia caucasica)*

71 *Muscari pseudomuscari (M. chalusicum)*

72 *Narcissus asturiensis (N. minimus)*

73 *Narcissus romieuxii (N. bulbocodium var. romieuxii)*

74 *Narcissus pseudonarcissus* subsp. *alpestris*

75 *Narcissus serotinus* in Crete

76 *Ornithogalum lanceolatum*

77 *Oxalis* 'Ione Hecker'

78 *Oxalis laciniata*

79 *Oxalis purpurea* 'Ken Aslet'

80 *Puschkinia scilloides* in E. Turkey

81 *Rhodohypoxis milloides*

82 *Romulea linaresii*
in W. Turkey

83 *Roscoea auriculata*
in Sikkim

84 *Scilla scilloides*
(S. chinensis)

85 *Sternbergia candida*
in S. Turkey

86 *Sternbergia sicula*
in Crete

87 *Tapeinanthus humilis*
(Narcissus humilis)

88 *Tecophilaea cyanocrocus*

89 *Trillium ovatum* on Mount Hood, Oregon

90 *Trillium rivale*

91 *Triteleia ixioides*

92 *Tulipa humilis* in E. Turkey

93 *Tulipa montana* and *var. chrysantha* in Iran

94 *Tulipa urumiensis*

95 *Tulipa vvedenskyi*
in Tashkent

96 *Zephyranthes
candida*

F. stenanthera   At one time this was scarcely known in cultivation but during the last ten years it has been introduced and is to be found in specialist bulb collections. It is in overall stature like *F. gibbosa* but the flowers are more bell-shaped, with the segments flaring outwards slightly at the mouth. The colour is variable and some forms in cultivation are a poor muddy pinkish-purple, but some of those I saw in the mountains near Tashkent were a beautiful clear pink; there is little or no tessellation on the flower. Soviet Central Asia, on open hillsides.

(4) *F. sewerzowii*

An isolated species, sometimes placed in a separate genus *Korolkowia*. It is a striking plant, best grown in an alpine house or bulb frame since, although hardy, it tends to emerge early in the spring and may get caught by frost. If it is to be tried outdoors, a well drained sunny spot with protection from the north and east by an evergreen shrub seems to give the best chance of success.

F. sewerzowii   The stout 10–25cm stems bear broad, very grey-green, lanceolate leaves all the way up the stem, the upper ones becoming bracts and each subtending one flower; the raceme carries up to ten, rarely more, bell-shaped flowers with the segments flared outwards, and these may be a clear greenish colour or dull purple overlaid with a greyish 'bloom'. Some forms I saw in the mountains of Uzbekistan were purple outside and bright green within, a delightful combination. It is a widespread species in Soviet Central Asia, in the Tien Shan and Pamir-Alai ranges, flowering in mid spring on rocky hillsides.

(5) The American Species

On the whole these are comparatively unrelated to the European and Asiatic species so there is little need for comparison. However, one species, *F. camschatcensis*, is native in eastern Asia and North America. The small yellow *F. pudica* does resemble some of the little Turkish species such as *F. minima*, but this seems to be purely superficial.

The American Fritillaries occur in a wide range of habitats, so it is difficult to generalize about their cultivation requirements, although all require a dryish dormant period in summer after they have flowered and died down. They all seem to grow reasonably well in an alpine house or bulb frame in loam-based composts. Those which occur in heavy soils (adobe clay) in the wild, such as *F. pluriflora*, *F. striata*, *F. biflora* and *F. liliacea*, all did exceptionally well in a bulb frame I once had which was built up over clay soil; the bulbs pulled themselves down out of the prepared compost into the sticky clay underneath!

F. affinis (F. lanceolata, F. mutica, F. ojaiensis)   A very variable species, 15–120cm in height with whorls of lanceolate leaves. The one to several flowers are widely bell-shaped with squared 'shoulders', up to 4cm long and up to 2.5cm wide, varying considerably in size and number, so that plants with few large flowers look very different from those with a raceme of small flowers. The colour too may be anything from green to deep purple, usually with tessellation but sometimes without. It is a widespread species in western North America from Alaska south to California, usually at low altitudes in or near woodland. Var. *tristulis* is a goood dark form, sent to me by Wayne Roderick some years ago. Var. *gracilis* (*F. phaeanthera* of Purdy) has smallish wider flowers with narrow greyish leaves.

The bulbs of *F. affinis* have a solid central flattish core surrounded by many 'rice grain' bulblets which take several years to grow on to flowering size.

F. viridia from California is similar to some variants of *F. lanceolata*, with small green flowers, but the bulb is quite different, consisting of a few large scales with no rice grain bulblets.

F. agrestis   See under **F. biflora**

F. atropurpure (F. adamantina, F. gracillima)   This is a very variable Fritillary, from 10–50cm in height, with the leaves not in whorls but narrow and scattered up the stem, with a rather erect disposition. The 4–15 small (1–2cm long) widely opening, nodding flowers have rather narrow pointed segments and are mottled yellow and purple. It is a widespread western American species in pine or fir woodland, or in open sagebrush, at up to 3000m altitude. The bulb has many 'rice grain' bulblets.

F. pinetorum from the southern Sierra Nevada is closely related to *F. atropurpurea* and similar but has the flowers facing outwards, not nodding.

F. biflora   Known as Mission Bells, is one of the easiest of the American species to cultivate. It has a bulb consisting of a few large scales without 'rice grain' bulblets and is usually deep in the soil. The rather broad shiny green leaves are clustered together at the base of the stem, which can reach about 40cm but usually only 15–20cm in cultivation. One to six nodding, bell-shaped, unpleasantly scented flowers are produced, about 2.0–3.5cm long, and they are deep shiny purple-brown, usually with some green shading. It is a native of California in fields at altitudes up to 1000m.

F. agrestis is very similar but the flowers are of a greenish-yellow colour, spotted purplish within; it is also a native of California.

F. roderickii, (*F. biflora* var. *ineziana*) is similar in general appearance to *F. biflora* but is a more striking species from coastal California with brown flowers with a conspicuous white patch on each of the segments, which do not flare outwards at the tips as in *F. biflora*.

F. brandegei   This rarely cultivated species is of the type which has a bulb with many bulblets surrounding it. The leaves are produced in whorls and the flowers are purple with a yellow centre; an unusual feature is the entire style, not three-lobed. It is Californian, growing in oak-pine woods.

F. camschatcensis   The Black Sarana, which is the one species to occur both in North America and Asia. It has a bulb with 'rice grain' bulblets and also sometimes sends out short stolon-like growths. It has stems 10–70cm in height with whorled glossy leaves and one to eight pendent widely bell-shaped flowers 2–3cm long, which are usually dark purple-brown but may be almost black or occasionally yellowish. It is a native of north-west Canada and America, Kamchatka, the Kuriles and Japan. Unlike most Fritillaries it grows in damp places and should be given a position in partial shade which does not become hot and dry in summer. It flowers later than most species, in late spring or early summer.

F. eastwoodiae   See under **F. micrantha**

F. falcata   One of the really dwarf species only 5–10cm in height with broad, curved, grey leaves and solitary flattish flowers 2–3cm in diameter facing upwards, with a whitish or yellowish ground, speckled with reddish-brown. It is a rare Californian native in exposed screes, and in cultivation it must be given a soil with good drainage in a bulb frame or alpine house.

F. gentneri   See under **F. recurva**

F. glauca   Like *F. falcata*, this is a dwarf plant reaching about 10–15cm, with a few broad grey leaves. The one or two flowers are pendent yellow open bells, slightly marked with brown and about 1.5–2.0cm long; the segments are not overlapping. A brownish form is also known. It is a native of California and Oregon in screes up to 2500m. It performed best for me potted into a gritty soil mix.

F. grayana   See under **F. biflora**

F. lanceolata   See **F. affinis**

F. micrantha   A horticulturally dull species, since the flowers are small. It has whorls of leaves and a raceme of up to 12 pendent, widely bell-shaped purple flowers, only 1–2cm long; the segments do not recurve at their tips. It is of the type whose bulb has 'rice grain' bulblets. California, in light woodland.

   F. eastwoodiae (*F. phaeanthera* of Eastwood), also Californian and having small (1–1.5cm long) purplish or reddish pendent flowers, differs from *F. micrantha* in that they are narrowly bell-shaped and have recurving tips. It is intermediate between this and *F. recurva*.

F. liliacea   An attractive and easily-grown species in the alpine house or bulb frame. It usually grows to 15–25cm with semi-erect shiny green leaves clustered near the base of the stem. The one to three pendent conical flowers are creamy with a hint of green, about 2cm in length. It grows wild at low altitudes in clay soil near the Californian coast and is becoming rather rare.

F. phaeanthera   See *F. eastwoodiae*, under **F. micrantha**

F. pinetorum   See under **F. atropurpurea**

F. pluriflora   One of the gems of the American species with 15–40cm stems carrying light grey-green lanceolate leaves clustered mostly towards the base and one to twelve rather conical bells, often facing outwards rather than pendent, about 2.5–3.5cm long; the segments are not recurved at the tips. The colour is normally a lovely clear pink but Wayne Roderick has also seen white and deep pinkish-red forms. It is a native of heavy clay soils in California which dry out and become sunbaked in summer. This has grown well for me in long pots and planted deeply in a bulb frame; the bulbs are not of the 'rice grain' type but have a few elongated scales.

   F. striata is closely related but has pendent, sweetly scented, paler pink flowers with recurved tips to the segments. California.

F. pudica   One of my own favourites among the North American species, only 5–15cm (rarely to 30cm) in height, with a few narrowly linear erect leaves and one or two clear yellow or orange-yellow pendent conical bells 1.5–2.5cm long; in some forms the flowers rapidly change to a reddish colour as they age. It is native to a very wide area of western North America, from British Columbia and Alberta south to New Mexico, growing in open situations at up to 2000m in gritty or sandy soils, drying out in summer. This is not a difficult species to grow in the alpine house or bulb frame, although some people find it so. I suspect that plants from the various parts of its wide distribution differ in their tolerance to cultivation since those sent to me from Alberta seem to be much more vigorous than those from California. *F. pudica* increases by 'rice grain' bulblets.

F. purdyi   a stocky species usually 10–35cm in height with the lanceolate wavy leaves more or less whorled in a basal cluster. The one to five pendent flowers are widely bell-shaped, 1.5–2.0cm in length, and have a whitish or greenish ground colour heavily mottled with dark maroon. It grows over a wide altitude range from 500 to 2000m in California, in rocky places which have heavy soil drying out in summer. The bulbs have a few fleshy scales with no bulblets. It requires bulb frame or alpine house treatment.

F. recurva   Quite the most startling of *Fritillaria* species, unfortunately difficult to cultivate well. The 20–80cm stems bear whorls of narrow leaves and one to six tubular bell-shaped orange-scarlet flowers 2.5–3.5cm long with conspicuously recurved tips to the segments; there is usually some yellowish flecking in the flower. Some variation exists in the depth of colour, and a more reddish form with segments not reflexed was described as var. *coccinea*.

F. *recurva* is a native of California and southern Oregon at 700–2000m altitude in, or on the margins of, light woodland. The bulbs produce rice grain bulblets. Although tricky to grow it is not impossible and I have flowered it both in pots and in the bulb frame. Sir Cedric Morris used to grow it unprotected in his Suffolk garden and I well remember many years ago being amazed to see a clump of several tall flowering plants apparently in perfect health growing by the pathside.

F. *gentneri* is a relative with larger, slightly more open bells without recurved tips to the segments. S. Oregon.

F. roderickii   See *F. grayana*, under **F. biflora**

F. striata   See under **F. pluriflora**

F. viridia   See under **F. affinis**

(6) The European and Asiatic Species

These all flower in mid spring after the first of the early bulbs (*Scilla, Crocus*) are finished.

F. acmopetala   10–45cm tall with about seven alternate narrowly linear grey-green leaves and one to three flowers; these are pendent broad bells about 2.5–4.0cm long, 2–3cm wide, with the segments recurved at the tips, green usually with a reddish-brown stain on the inner segments, sometimes tipped brown; nectary dark green, ovate; style three-lobed. Eastern Mediterranean region, often in fields. Can be grown in an open sunny position.

Subsp. *wendelboi* from S. Turkey has fewer (usually only four) wider leaves (1–3cm) and the flowers are squared at the shoulders of the bell, not rounded.

F. alburyana (F. erzurumica)   An exciting species but difficult to cultivate well. It is 5–10cm tall with a few alternate, lanceolate grey leaves and one or two flattish or shallowly cup-shaped pink flowers which are slightly tessellated and 4–5cm in diameter when fully open; style three-lobed. It is a native of the mountains of E. Turkey, flowering in June as the snow recedes. In cultivation it requires a cold winter followed by a sudden warm spring to elongate the stem.

F. alfredae   See under **F. bithynica**

F. amabilis   See under **F. japonica**

F. armena   A dwarf species, 5–15cm in height, with glabrous stems carrying alternate lanceolate grey-green leaves and usually one (rarely to three) narrow bell-shaped flowers, dark plum coloured inside and out, and covered on the outside with a grape-like 'bloom', about 1.0–2.5cm long. The papillose style is shortly three-lobed. It is a native of E. Turkish mountains, flowering near the snowline. A good alpine house or bulb frame species.

F. caucasica is similar but is often more robust, to 20cm with flowers up to 3.5cm long; the filaments are glabrous or very slightly papillose whereas in F. armena they are densely papillose. There is a slight difference in flower shape between the two, F. armena having rather straight-sided bells, while those of F. caucasica are often bulging outwards in the middle, giving a more tubby appearance. E. Turkey, Caucasus and N.W. Iran. It is a more showy plant than F. armena.

F. pinardii (F. alpina, F. fleischeri, F. syriaca) is similar to F. armena but the flowers are not dark inside, usually yellowish or greenish; the outside may be purple to a 'gunmetal' colour. It is a widespread and variable species in Turkey, Transcaucasia, N.W. Iran, Syria and Lebanon on stony hillsides.

F. zagrica is like F. armena but usually shorter, to 12cm and has dark chocolate-purple coloured flowers with a yellow tip to the segments, sometimes running along the centre as a stripe. It is a most attractive dwarf Fritillary, reminding me of happy days plant hunting in the mountains of W. Iran; it also occurs in S.E. Turkey. Unfortunately it is rare in cultivation.

F. minuta (F. carduchorum). In overall size and stature this is like F. armena but has reddish-brown or orange flowers and bright shiny green, not greyish, leaves. It is an attractive little species, suitable for the alpine house or frame. E. Turkey, on stony slopes.

F. assyriaca (F. canaliculata – the plant formerly cultivated as 'F. assyriaca' with greyish-purple flowers, tipped with yellow is **F. uva-vulpis**)   A rather slender-looking species to 20cm with alternate, linear grey-green leaves and one to four narrow bell-shaped flowers, with the tips of the segments recurved, 1.0–2.5cm long; the colour is variable, usually brownish or purplish, with a grey 'bloom', yellowish on the inside. Style undivided, papillose. C. Turkey to W. Iran, often in fields or open hillsides.

Subsp. melananthera from S. Turkey has black anthers and the flower is green and black striped within.

F. elwesii (F. sieheana) is similar in appearance but usually taller, up to 50cm, and has longer (2–3cm) purplish flowers striped green. The style is three-lobed and densely papillose. A rather attractive plant which will grow in an open sunny situation if it dries out in summer. S. Turkey.

F. fleischeriana from W. Turkey is similar to but shorter (5–15cm) than F. elwesii; it also has dark brownish-purple flowers striped green, but they are smaller, 1–2cm long.

F. latakiensis is very like *F. elwesii* but has a nearly, or completely, glabrous style. S. Turkey and N. Syria.

F. aurea (F. bornmülleri)   This is one of the most attractive of the dwarf species, only 5–15cm in height with a few grey lanceolate leaves and solitary pendent flowers which are large in relation to the size of the plant. The broad bells are 2–4cm long and are bright yellow tessellated with brown. The style is three-lobed. It occurs in central and southern Turkey on open hillsides. *F. aurea* is an easy plant to grow in a bulb frame or alpine house, increasing by small bulblets.

F. latifolia, of which *F. nobilis* is a dwarf form, is closely related but has brownish-purple flowers, strongly tessellated; the large bells can be up to 5cm long and are carried on stems varying from 5–35cm in height. The more vigorous, taller forms can be cultivated in the open garden but the dwarf ones, in which the stems are so short that the bells often rest on the ground, are best given the protection of an alpine house or frame.

F. collina (*F. lutea*) from the Caucasus is like *F. latifolia* but has narrow grey leaves and yellow, brown-tessellated flowers. The perianth segments are pointed and the inner three have a fringed margin; in *F. aurea* and *F. latifolia* the segments are more rounded and not fringed.

F. lagodechiana is related but has the upper leaves whorled; the flowers are yellow-green. Georgian SSR.

F. bithynica (F. citrina, F. dasyphylla, F. pineticola, F. schliemannii)   One of a number of smallish green or yellow-flowered species which are mentioned below with their distinguishing features. It is a variable dwarf green Fritillary, easy to grow and increasing well by bulblets. The stems reach 5–20cm in height with oblanceolate grey-green leaves, the upper three of which are usually in a whorl and the two broader lower ones opposite. The one or two flowers are conical-bell shaped, about 2.0–2.5cm long, yellowish-green with a grey 'bloom' on the outside; the style is glabrous and undivided at the apex. It is a native of the Aegean Islands and W. Turkey in stony soils, often in scrub.

F. subalpina from central-south Turkey is very similar but has broader leaves, the lowest of which are alternate, not opposite.

F. carica from south-west Turkey is of similar stature but has the grey-green leaves all alternate, not with a lower pair or a whorl of three at the top and the narrowly bell-shaped flowers are more yellow, only 1.5–2.0cm long; the papillose style is either three-lobed or undivided. A charming plant for the alpine house. Subsp. *serpenticola*, discovered by Ole Sønderhousen in south-west Turkey, is a dwarf plant with broad leaves and conical flowers, certainly distinct from subsp. *carica*.

F. conica from scrub-covered hillsides on the Peloponnese has shiny green leaves, the lowest two broadest and opposite, the others alternate with no whorl at the top. The conical yellow flowers are produced on stems 10–25cm tall and are 1–2cm long with a three-lobed style which is glabrous. Of the small yellow Fritillaries I think this is perhaps the most attractive and distinct, for its bells are really cone-shaped.

F. minima from E. Turkey is a splendid sight on its rocky native mountain slopes but has not yet, for me at least, been quite so accommodating in cultivation as the other yellow species mentioned above. It is a very dwarf plant, only 5–10cm, with deep shiny green leaves, all alternate, and the clear yellow flowers are narrowly bell-shaped and about 1–2cm long; the style is papillose, three-lobed at the apex. At the late flowering stage the colour changes to reddish.

F. sibthorpiana is a very rare species from S.W. Turkey in rocky places. It has taller stems, 20–30cm in height, but they carry only two or three alternate grey-green leaves (4–12 in the other species mentioned). The solitary yellow narrow bells are about 2cm long and have a papillose, more or less undivided, style. The true plant is seldom seen in cultivation but sometimes *F. carica* masquerades under the name.

F. rhodia is a very slender species from Rhodes up to 30cm in height with linear-lanceolate, alternate, grey-green leaves and 1–2cm long flowers of a yellowish-green; they are narrowly bell-shaped but the segments flare out at the tips. The style is glabrous and undivided.

F. forbesii is very similar to *F. rhodia* in its slender appearance; the papillose style is, however, either entire or has three short lobes. It is a native of rocky places in south-west Turkey at low altitudes.

F. euboeica from Euboea in Greece is only 5–10cm in height with grey-green leaves. The small bell-shaped bright yellow flowers are 1.5–2.5cm long and have a glabrous style divided slightly into three at the apex. It thus is most closely related to *F. conica* but has a less conical flower, is shorter and has a brown nectary (green in *F. conica*).

F. viridiflora is related to *F. bithynica* but is often more robust, to 25cm, with larger green flowers 3.0–3.5cm long. It is a native of farther east in Turkey, restricted to the Gaziantep area, and is very rare in cultivation.

F. alfredae subsp. *alfredae* is a slender species with stems to about 25cm carrying narrow grey-green leaves, the upper in a whorl of three; there is usually one narrow bell-shaped green flower 1–2cm long, glaucous on the outside; the papillose style is almost entire or slightly three-lobed. It is a rarely seen species from Lebanon. In Turkey occurs its subsp. *glaucoviridis* (*F. glaucoviridis*), which is better known in cultivation. It is more robust, up to 35cm, and has broader leaves. The one to three flowers are up to 3cm long. S. Turkey, in scrub and oak woods. It is an attractive plant for the bulb frame or alpine house. In subsp. *platyptera* the lower leaves are linear or linear-lanceolate and the upper three are rather longer, about 5–6cm, than in subsp. *glaucoviridis* (2.5–4.0). It occurs only in the extreme south of Turkey (Yayladağ) and adjacent N. Syria.

F. chlorantha is another dwarf green-flowered species, one of the most exciting plants I saw on the Bowles Scholarship expedition to Iran in 1965, growing on rocky slopes. It is only 5–10cm high with shiny green alternate leaves, the lowest of which are broad, up to 5cm wide and set almost at ground level. The one or two green flowers are narrowly bell-shaped, about 1.5–2.5cm long, with a three-lobed style. It is related to the purple *F. zagrica* and was, I think, on the mountain Shuturunkuh, hybridizing with it. In cultivation the stem unfortunately elongates a little.

F. camschatcensis   See above under American species, p. 80.

F. caucasica   See under **F. armena**

F. chlorantha   See under **F. bithynica**

F. cirrhosa   One of the few Himalayan Fritillaries. A tall slender species to 60cm in height with linear-lanceolate leaves in whorls, the upper ones with tendrils for clinging to adjacent vegetation for support. The one to four large pendent wide bells, 3.5–5.0cm long, are often greenish-yellow tessellated brown, or they may have an overall purplish appearance; the style has three branches. It is a native of the central and eastern Himalaya and China, often growing in *Rhododendron* scrub. Although not a difficult plant to grow in a cool humus-rich position, it has a tendency to emerge early and is liable to be caught by spring frosts.

Var. *dingriensis* from Xizang province in China has shorter flowers.

Var. *jilongensis* has narrower perianth segments than is usual, also from Xizang province.

Var. *brevistigma* is a very slender variant with leaves less than 3mm wide; the style branches are very short. Gansu province.

F. roylei is like a robust version of *F. cirrhosa*, with many more leaves on the stem, and these are not tendril-like. In distribution it tends to be in the western end of the Himalaya, especially in Kashmir.

F. collina   See under **F. aurea**

F. conica   See under **F. bithynica**

F. crassifolia (F. ophioglossifolia)   A common species in Turkey and Iran, in one or other of its subspecies. Subsp. *crassifolia* is usually 5–10cm tall with alternate grey-green lanceolate leaves and one or two wide pendent bells about 2.0–3.5cm long and 2.0–2.5cm wide; they are most frequently greenish with conspicuous brownish tessellation, sometimes with a green stripe along the centre of each segment; the style is three-lobed and glabrous. It is an inhabitant of limestone screes in E. Turkey; cultivation is not difficult in a frame or alpine house.

Subsp. *kurdica* (*F. grossheimiana*, *F. kurdica*, *F. karadaghensis*) is more widespread, in E. Turkey, W. Iran and N. Iraq on open hillsides. It is very variable in the amount of tessellation on the flowers so that they may have an overall green or purple appearance. The main feature chosen by Martyn Rix to distinguish this from subsp. *crassifolia* is the length to width ratio of the lower leaves: 2.5–3.0 times as long as wide in subsp. *crassifolia* and 4–7 times in subsp. *kurdica*. It is easily cultivated in a frame or alpine house. I am particularly fond of the forms with grey twisted leaves.

Subsp. *hakkarensis* from S.E. Turkey (Hakkari) and adjacent N. Iraq has smaller flowers about 1.5cm long and shiny green, rather than grey-green leaves. It is rarely seen in cultivation.

Subsp. *poluninii* was collected by Oleg Polunin on his Iraq expedition of 1958 but was not described until 1974. It is a smaller plant than its relatives with rather wide open bells only 1.3cm long with narrow, pointed segments giving a less substantial flower. It is very rare in cultivation.

F. kotschyana looks very similar to *F. crassifolia* ssp. *kurdica* in overall appearance but is usually taller, 10–20cm. The broadly bell-shaped flowers are about 3.0–3.5cm long and are often heavily tessellated brown-purple. The main difference from *F. crassifolia* is in the nectary shape: ovate or lanceolate and less than half as long as the perianth segments in *F. kotschyana*; linear and more than half as long as the segments in *F. crassifolia*. It is a native of N. Iran, in the Elburz mountains where I have seen it on rocky hillsides above 2000m. In the adjacent Talysh mountains in the USSR is found subsp. *grandiflora* (*F. grandiflora*) which has flowers about 4–5cm long on stems 35–50cm in height. Unfortunately, it has never been rediscovered since the original collection in 1915.

F. hermonis is another relative of this group, with short lanceolate nectaries like *F. kotschyana*, thus distinguishing it from *F. crassifolia*. From *F. kotschyana* it differs in having a papillose style (glabrous in *F. kotschyana*). In overall appearance however, with its broad, strongly tessellated bells it is much the same. In subsp. *hermonis* the flowers are about 1.5–2.0cm long on stems only 3–5cm in height; it is endemic to Mount Hermon in Lebanon, and is very rare in cultivation. More frequently seen is subsp. *amana*, a striking Fritillary which has been cultivated for many years in a good form with long bells collected by E.K. Balls in 1934. It is taller than subsp. *hermonis*, 10–35cm in height, and has larger flowers 2.5–4.0cm long; these are often green with only slight tessellation, covered with a delicate 'bloom'. Subsp. *amana* is more widespread in the wild, from S. Turkey south into Syria and Lebanon.

F. olivieri is also related to *F. kotschyana* and *F. hermonis* in having flowers with short, lanceolate nectaries. It is a tall plant, 15–40cm, with narrow green (not greyish) leaves and the flowers are seldom conspicuously tessellated but usually have broad green bands along the centre of each segment, edged brown. The broad bells are 2.5–3.5cm long usually with the segments recurved at their tips. I have seen it in boggy meadows near streams in Iran and this is its usual habitat, consequently it is not a difficult plant to cultivate, although rather rare. It is an endemic of W. Iran.

F. whittallii is another Middle Eastern Fritillary in this group, rarely seen in cultivation. It is 10–20cm tall with narrow leaves and green, heavily brownish-tessellated bells about 2.5–3.0cm long; in this case the nectaries are short and broadly ovate, so in this it more closely resembles *F. kotschyana* and *F. hermonis* than *F. crassifolia*. It is confined to S.W. Turkey, growing in rocky places.

F. dagana   See under **F. thunbergii**

F. davisii   See under **F. graeca**

F. drenovskii   A slender species up to 30cm, usually much less in cultivation. The leaves are linear and grey-green, scattered up the stem. There are one to three conical, pendent flowers, about 1.5–2.0cm long, brownish-purple on the outside, yellowish-green within. The style is entire. There seem to be at least two forms in cultivation, one with several dark flowers on a tall stem, the other much shorter with usually solitary paler flowers. It is a native of N.E. Greece and adjacent Bulgaria. Bulb frame or alpine house.

F. rixii, named after Martyn Rix, is a recently described species, very similar in habit but with yellow flowers; it is from Euboea in Greece.

F. ehrhartii   An attractive dwarf Fritillary 5–15cm tall with alternate, lanceolate, grey leaves and one or two conical flowers 1.5–2.5cm long in deep purple, tipped with yellow on the segments and greenish on the inside; the style is entire. It is found in a few Aegean Islands and Euboea, mainly on non-limestone formations at low altitudes.

F. elwesii   See under **F. assyriaca**

F. epirotica   See under **F. graeca**

F. euboeica   See under **F. bithynica**

F. fleischeriana   See under **F. assyriaca**

F. forbesii   See under **F. bithynica**

F. glaucoviridis   See under **F. bithynica**

F. graeca (F. guicciardii)   A well-known smallish Fritillary, easy to grow in a bulb frame or alpine house, and also in sunny well-drained spots on the rock garden. It is variable, 5–20cm tall with lanceolate, alternate, grey-green leaves, the lower ones rather broad, and one to four wide bells 1.5–2.5cm long, 1.5–2.0cm wide; these are usually brownish-purple tessellated on a green ground, with a smart green stripe along the centre of each segment; the style is three-lobed. It occurs on mountains in the south of Greece.

Subsp. *thessala* (*F. ionica*, *F. thessala*, *F. thessalica*) is a more robust plant, easy to grow in the open garden. It can reach 30cm and is noticeably different in its leaf arrangement since the upper three are in a whorl around the flowers, which are larger at 3–4cm long, usually greenish and only slightly brown-tessellated. It has a more northern distribution in N. Greece, S. Yugoslavia and Albania, usually in woods or scrubland.

F. pontica, also an excellent plant for outdoor cultivation, is very like *F. graeca* subsp. *thessala* with similar stature, leaves and flower size but the green flowers are not at all tessellated but often have a warm brownish suffusion, especially on the apex and margins of the segments. It occurs in the same region as *F. graeca* subsp. *thessala* but extends into N.W. Turkey, usually in woods.

F. gussichae (*F. graeca* var. *gussichae*) should, I think, never have been classed as a variety of *F. graeca*, since it is very distinct and is more like *F. pontica* in overall appearance and in having untessellated green flowers. The very grey-green leaves are rather broad and clasp the stem; they are alternate, not with an upper whorl of three. It is a native of S. Bulgaria, where I have seen it in bushy situations, and in adjacent S. Yugoslavia and N. Greece. *F. skorpilii* is probably based on a weak specimen of this.

F. davisii is very similar to some forms of *F. graeca* subsp. *graeca* but has shiny-green leaves and the purple-brown strongly chequered flowers do not have conspicuous green stripes. Although not a spectacular 'Frit' this has a particular appeal for me since I brought it into cultivation in 1966 after a glorious month spent by myself roaming the Mani peninsular in southern Greece where it grows in olive groves and on rocky hills. It is named after Dr Peter H. Davis who discovered it in 1940.

F. epirotica from N. Greece is a dwarf mountain species 10cm or less in height; it has narrow twisted grey leaves and dark brownish-purple flowers with no green stripes.

F. gussichae   See under **F. graeca**

F. hermonis   See under **F. crassifolia**

F. involucrata   This could perhaps be compared with *F. pontica* or *F. graeca* subsp. *thessala* (above) since it has an upper whorl of three leaves but as these are very much narrower, linear or linear lanceolate, it is better linked with *F. messanensis*. It is 15–25cm in height with usually solitary widely bell-shaped flowers up to 4cm long and 3cm wide, which are more or less straight-sided, not with flared tips. They are normally pale green with slight brown chequering, giving an overall soft green appearance or even yellowish-green; the style is three-lobed. It occurs in the Maritime Alps of S. France and adjacent Italy in grassy places on limestone. It can be grown outdoors in well-drained spots.

F. messanensis (*F. oranensis*, *F. sphaciotica*) is a similarly tall slender Fritillary to 45cm with linear leaves, the upper three whorled. The flowers are bell-shaped but normally with the segments flared outwards and they are green, strongly tessellated purple-brown. It is a native of the Mediterranean region in N. Africa, Italy and Greece in rocky places and in scrub. It is not difficult to grow in a well-drained position.

F. messanensis subsp. *gracilis* (*F. gracilis*, *F. illyrica*, *F. neglecta*) is generally smaller with brownish-purple non-tessellated flowers and shiny green leaves. W. and S. Yugoslavia and Albania.

F. messanensis var. *atlantica* from the Atlas Mountains has, according to Martyn Rix, shorter, very grey leaves, but I have not seen this.

F. japonica   One of the delightful Japanese Fritillaries, very rare in cultivation. It is a small, delicate-looking species 5–10cm in height with narrow linear-lanceolate, often brownish-tinged leaves, the upper three of which are in a whorl. The one or two flowers are widely bell-shaped, 2.0–2.5cm long, white, very slightly tessellated purplish-brown. It is a native of lightly shaded places.

F. japonica var. *koidzumiana* (*F. koidzumiana*) has perianth segments with a hair-like fringe around the margin. They are both rare plants in Japan and seldom seen in cultivation but can be grown satisfactorily in a peat garden, for they appear to prefer cool conditions like so many Japanese plants.

F. amabilis is a related Japanese species with pale, almost white flowers but they are narrowly campanulate and nearly tubular (not tessellated) and about 1.5–2.0cm long.

F. sikkokiana differs from *F. amabilis* in having purple anthers (white in *F. amabilis*).

F. ayakoana is near to *F. amabilis* but is said to differ in the shape of the perianth segments.

F. muraiana and *F. kaiensis* both seem to be very similar to *F. japonica*.

F. kotschyana   See under **F. crassifolia**

F. kurdica   See under **F. crassifolia**

F. latakiensis   See under **F. assyriaca**

F. latifolia   See under **F. aurea**

F. lusitanica (F. hispanica, F. stenophylla)   An extremely variable species, 10–50cm in height with narrow linear or linear-lanceolate leaves, all alternate with no upper whorl of three like species such as *F. messanensis* and *F. involucrata*. The one to three flowers are widely bell-shaped, 2–4cm long, 2.5–3.0cm wide, and variable from brown to green with slight to conspicuous tessellation; the style is three-lobed. A distinctive feature is the long narrow linear nectary. It is a widespread species in Spain and Portugal in a wide range of habitats. The taller forms are easy to cultivate in a sunny well-drained position.

F. macedonica   See under **F. tubiformis**

F. maximowiczii   See under **F. thunbergii**

F. meleagris   The much-loved Snakeshead Fritillary which, next to *F. imperialis*, is the most well-known species in cultivation. It is our British native species from water meadows and is consequently easy to grow in rough grass, peat beds, damp borders or between shrubs. It grows to 15–30cm in height with alternate narrow linear leaves and usually has solitary broad bells 3.0–4.5cm long and almost as much wide. These may be purple or pinkish-purple, strongly tessellated darker, or pure white; sometimes these albinos are tessellated greenish or purple. Cultivar names have been given to some variants and these are occasionally offered by nurseries. Apart from Britain, *F. meleagris* occurs in much of Europe.

F. meleagris subsp. *burnatii* has shorter leaves, less than 8cm long; the flowers are purple. It occurs in alpine meadows in W. Switzerland and adjacent parts of Italy and France.

F. meleagroides   See under **F. montana**

F. messanensis   See under **F. involucrata**

F. michailovskyi   A very striking Fritillary, not difficult to grow and now being produced in some quantity in Dutch nurseries. It is a stocky species, 10–25cm with alternate, lanceolate, grey leaves and one to four broad pendent bells 2–3cm long and 2cm wide; these are brownish-purple in the lower part and bright yellow in about the upper third of each segment; the style is three-lobed. This dramatic bicoloured appearance makes it very distinct, the only other Fritillary with colour approaching this is *F. reuteri* (see below).

F. michailovskyi is a native of N.E. Turkey growing in alpine turf near the snowline. It is a species for which I have a particular affection since it was rediscovered and brought into cultivation from the 1965 expedition which I undertook with John and Helen Tomlinson and Margaret Briggs. Margaret, who is now my wife, found a colony on the Sarikamis Pass and we immediately sent a specimen to Paul Furse, who identified it as a 'missing' species, not seen since the original dried collection of 1914 and never introduced in the living state. Other collections have been made and it is now known from several localities. This lovely species forms the subject of our jacket illustration.

F. reuteri is similar in its bicoloured purple and yellow flowers but is taller and more slender with green leaves and up to eight smaller flowers 1.5–2.5cm long; the style is papillose. It is a native of Iran, growing in moist fields and in consequence is not a difficult plant to cultivate. John Ingham has recorded a pure yellow form amid the 'ordinary' bicoloured ones.

F. minima   See under **F. bithynica**

F. minuta   See under **F. armena**

F. montana (F. 'nigra', F. 'orientalis', F. 'tenella')   A slender species 15–50cm in height, with narrow linear leaves, the basal ones opposite and the upper ones often whorled, not tendril-like at the apex. The one to three flowers are broad bells about 2–3cm long, 1.5–2.5cm wide, heavily tessellated deep brown or blackish-purple so as to appear very dark; the style is three-lobed. It is a native of bushy places in Italy, S. France, N. Greece and Yugoslavia, and is not a difficult plant to cultivate, growing well for many years in my garden in a semi-shaded position.

F. meleagroides from the USSR is similar but the leaves are all alternate; it grows in damp meadows.

F. ruthenica is very similar to *F. montana* but the leaves are tendril-like at the tips. European USSR.

F. orientalis (*F. tenella*) is like *F. montana* in growth features but has larger flowers 3.0–4.5cm long; it comes from the Caucasus.

F. obliqua   A distinctive Fritillary, except from *F. tuntasia* (below); it has 10–20cm stems bearing alternate grey-green lanceolate leaves. The one to three pendent flowers are conical in shape, blackish-purple with a grey 'bloom' and about 2–3cm long and 1.5–2.0cm wide; the style is three-lobed. It is a Greek species, now very rare in the

Athens region. It is not difficult to grow and will succeed in a sunny, well drained position.

F. tuntasia is like a larger version of this with stems to 30cm carrying many more leaves, which are often twisted longitudinally. The flowers are however slightly smaller, at 1.5–2.5cm long, and there may be up to six per stem. It is known only from the Greek islands of Kythnos and Serifos.

F. olgae   See under **F. thunbergii**

F. olivieri   See under **F. crassifolia**

F. orientalis   See under **F. montana**

F. pallidiflora   A splendid species, very hardy and suitable for growing outdoors in a well-drained sunny position. It is 15–50cm in height with broad opposite or alternate grey leaves and one to four large squarish pendent bells in pale yellow, spotted reddish inside, about 4cm long and 3cm wide; the style is trifid. It is a native of Soviet Central Asia in the Ala Tau and Tien Shan at up to 3000m.

F. lixianensis is related but has narrower leaves 0.5–1cm wide; the flowers are a strong purple, not tessellated. Sichuan province of China.

F. pinardii   See under **F. armena**

F. pontica   See under **F. graeca**

F. pyrenaica (F. nigra)   An easily-grown Fritillary for open borders or between shrubs, forming clumps when doing well. It is up to 30cm in height with alternate lanceolate grey-green leaves and one or two unpleasantly-scented broad pendent tessellated bells of a very dark blackish-brown, shiny greenish-yellow on the inside; they are about 3.0–3.5cm long and 2.5–3.0cm wide, with the perianth segments recurved at the tips. The style is three-lobed. There is also a 'Giant form' in cultivation, very vigorous with large dark flowers having more segments than the usual six. Var. *lutescens* is a beautiful pure yellow form. It is a native of the Pyrenees in meadows and woods.

F. regelii   See under **F. thunbergii**

F. reuteri   See under **F. michailovskyi**

F. rhodocanakis   A distinctive little species, 10–15cm in height, with scattered lanceolate leaves and smallish but broad semi-pendent bells about 2.5cm long, widely flared at the mouth, purplish maroon and untessellated in the basal half to two thirds, yellow in the upper part; the style is trifid. I have also seen a form which is greenish-yellow throughout. It is endemic to the Greek island of Hydra (Idhra) on rocky hillsides.

F. roylei   See under **F. cirrhosa**

F. ruthenica   See under **F. montana**

F. sibthorpiana   See under **F. bithynica**

F. straussii   A distinctive Middle-Eastern Fritillary about 10–15cm tall with the lanceolate shiny green leaves in whorls or pairs. There are one or two broadly bell-shaped flowers, green with brownish tessellation, about 2.5–3.0cm long, rather flared at the mouth; the style is three-lobed. The leaf arrangement is reminiscent of *F. camschatcensis*. It is a native of W. Iran and S.E. Turkey. A bulb frame or pot cultivation suits it best.

F. stribrnyi   A rare plant, missing for many years but now rediscovered and introduced to cultivation. It is slender, 10–40cm in height, with narrow linear or lanceolate grey-green alternate leaves, the upper in a whorl of three. The one to three flowers are 2–3cm long and narrowly bell-shaped, wholly purple or green with purple edges to the segments, covered with a grey 'bloom'; the style is entire. It occurs in European Turkey and S. Bulgaria in bushy places but is rare in both countries.

F. thunbergii (F. verticillata var. **thunbergii)**   A tall slender plant up to a metre when growing well, but usually about 40–60cm. The leaves are narrowly linear, the lowest opposite, usually whorled higher up, and the topmost ones with tendril-like tips. Up to six widely conical flowers, about 2.5–3.5cm long, are produced in a raceme and these are cream-coloured and slightly flecked or tessellated green; the style is three-lobed. It occurs in China and Japan in scrub and light woods. Although easy to cultivate in the open garden in slight shade it is often not free flowering; the bulbs need planting deeply (15 cm).

F. verticillata, from E. Siberia and N. China, is very similar but has larger flowers and the leaves are more widely spaced on the stem.

F. ussuriensis also has whorled leaves on tall stems but the larger flowers are dark brownish-purple. Far eastern USSR. Probably not in cultivation.

F. regelii from Soviet Central Asia in the Pamir-Alai has stems to 40cm with the upper and lower narrowly lanceolate leaves paired, the rest alternate. The flower is usually solitary, brownish-purple and glaucous on the outside, about 3cm long. Not known to be in cultivation.

F. olgae, also from the Pamir-Alai, is apparently closely related to *F. regelii*, but the flowers are greenish-yellow, tipped purple and tessellated; it is a tall leafy plant to 60cm.

F. walujewii (F. ferganensis) is now to be found in cultivation and is most attractive. The very narrow leaves on 30–50cm stems are opposite or whorled, the upper with tendrils at their tips. There are up to three bells 3–4cm long, 2–3cm wide and, although variable, they are usually pinkish-purple in overall appearance, tessellated and faintly suffused green. Thanks to the organizing efforts of Mrs E.D. ('Tinge') Horsfall I have had the pleasure of seeing this in the wild, on rocky hillsides in the Pamir-Alai range in Central Asia; it also occurs in the Tien Shan and Ala Tau, into adjacent China.

F. dagana is related to *F. thunbergii* but is distinctive in having only one whorl of very narrow leaves on the slender stems. The flowers are deep purple-brown and tessellated. E. Siberia.

F. maximowiczii, also Siberian, seems scarcely distinguishable from *F. dagana*; it has acute perianth segments whereas those of *F. dagana* are obtuse. Neither are in cultivation to my knowledge, although I once grew *F. maximowiczii* for a few years, rather unsuccessfully.

F. tubiformis (F. delphinensis)   A lovely plant, easy to cultivate in an open sunny position. It is 10–25cm in height, with alternate narrowly lanceolate grey-green leaves and large squarish solitary purple flowers, tessellated and covered with a grey 'bloom' on the outside, 3–5cm long and 2.5–4.0cm in diameter; the style is three-lobed. It is a native of the Maritime Alps of France and Italy, in grassy places.

F. tubiformis subsp. *moggridgei* from roughly the same area is a delightful variant with yellow flowers, lightly tessellated brown.

F. macedonica is very similar to *F. tubiformis*, but the lower leaves are opposite and the upper ones are in a whorl of three; the flower is dark purple-brown, strongly tessellated. It is a native of alpine meadows in E. Albania and S.W. Yugoslavia and has not yet been introduced to cultivation. It is possibly a link between *F. tubiformis* and the Caucasian and Turkish *F. latifolia*.

F. tuntasia   See under **F. obliqua**

F. ussuriensis   See under **F. thunbergii**

F. uva-vulpis   This is well known in cultivation and was known as *F. assyriaca* until Martyn Rix showed that two species were involved and defined them. This is an easily-grown species, very satisfactory as an alpine-house plant, but also for an open well-drained spot on the rock garden. Increase is very rapid by the production of offsets. It is 10–30cm in height with erect shiny green, alternate, lanceolate leaves and one or two narrowly bell-shaped flowers 1.5–2.5cm long in a metallic purple colour, overlaid with a grey 'bloom' and tipped yellow; the style is undivided. It occurs wild in S.E. Turkey, N. Iraq and W. Iran, often in fields.

F. verticillata   See under **F. thunbergii**

F. viridiflora   See under **F. bithynica**

F. walujewii   See under **F. thunbergii**

F. whittallii   See under **F. crassifolia**

F. zagrica   See under **F. armena**

(7) Some little-known, mainly Chinese species

These I have not seen in the living or dried state and can only repeat brief details from their descriptions.

F. anhuiensis   Described as having a many-scaled bulb. The height is usually 10–15cm with long, rather widely lanceolate leaves, mostly opposite but the upper may be alternate or whorled. There is one flower (rarely two), a wide bell 4.0–5.5cm long, dark purple blotched white or whitish tessellated purple. It is from Anhui (Anhwei) province of China.

F. bhutanica   From Bhutan, 3–6cm in height, with three or four alternate elliptical olive green leaves and erect or suberect bells 2.5–3.0cm long in olive-brown, green on the inside. Near to *F. delavayi* but with smaller flowers.

F. bolensis   Very like *F. pallidiflora*, and said to differ in having elliptical leaves 1.5–3.5cm broad and pale yellow flowers spotted purple. These features seem to be within the range of variation of *F. pallidiflora*. It is from Xinjiang (Sinkiang) province of China.

F. chuanganensis   A recently described species related to *F. cirrhosa*. It has one to five flowers in a raceme with two to four bract leaves, and the lower leaves are paired or whorled. Sichuan (Szechwan) and Gansu (Kansu) provinces.

F. crassicaulis   Described as having the general appearance of *F. pallidiflora*. The leaves are wide, the lower two opposite and there is a whorl of three at the apex, subtending the solitary flower which is large, pale and tessellated darker. *F. zhufuensis* is related but has the lower leaves in a whorl of three and the flowers are non-tessellated. Xizang province.

F. dajinensis   A slender species 20–50cm in height with very narrowly linear leaves, the lower ones opposite, the upper alternate. The solitary flower is a narrow bell, almost conical, about 2.0–2.5cm long, greenish-yellow suffused brownish and striped brown on the inside, not tessellated. It is from Sichuan (Szechwan) province of China.

F. davidii   This has a many-scaled bulb like that of *F. camschatcensis* but is a slender plant up to 30cm with leafless stems and only a whorl of three smallish bract-leaves beneath the solitary flower. This is a 3–4cm long wide bell with a yellowish ground, marked with purple. The style is three-lobed. It is from Moupin in China.

F. delavayi   From Yunnan in China. The 30cm stems have alternate, ovate-lanceolate leaves and large rounded bell-shaped flowers in greenish-yellow, tessellated brown. The perianth segments remain attached right through to the fruiting stage. *F. delavayi* var. *banmaensis* has untessellated flowers. Quinghai (Tsinghai) province.

   F. xizangensis is related, a stocky plant 10–30cm tall with one flower and a few broad elliptic leaves. The flower is 2–2.5cm long, pale purple, spotted and tessellated. Xizang province.

F. duilongdeqingensis   From Xizang Province, related to *F. cirrhosa*. It has narrow bell-shaped flowers, yellow-green and tessellated, and the stems bear ten to fifteen leaves.

F. fusca   A dwarf Tibetan species only 3–6cm tall with two opposite (sometimes a third) small elliptic leaves and a solitary greenish-grey bell-shaped flower, blackish on the inside, about 1.5–2.0cm long.

F. gansuensis   A new species from Gansu (Kansu) province, China. It has conical bells only 2cm long, greenish-yellow spotted purple. The leaves are tendril-like at the apex.

F. glabra   Like *F. cirrhosa*, but has stamens with glabrous filaments. It was first described from Shaanxi (Shensi) province in China as *F. cirrhosa* forma *glabra* and is currently also known as *F. chuanganensis* var. *glabra*.

F. hupehensis   A tall species, up to 50cm with whorls of leaves, the upper of which have tendrils at their tips. The 4.0–4.5cm long bells are strongly tessellated. It is from Hubei (Hupei) province of China and presumably related to *F. cirrhosa*.

   F. huangshanensis is said to be related to *F. hupehensis* but has pale yellow flowers, tessellated or netted with purple. Jiangsu (Kiangsu). *F. austroanhuiensis* is also related to *F. hupehensis* but has smaller flowers, and the leaves are very strongly tendriliform.

F. monantha Appears to be rather like *F. hupehensis* and, in turn, therefore similar to *F. cirrhosa*. The tips of the leaves are not tendril-like and the flower is a large bell 4.5–5.0cm long, purple-tessellated. Var. *tonglingensis* is a yellow-flowered variant. China.

F. omeiensis is named after Mount Omei in China. It is said to be related to *F. cirrhosa* but has wider leaves without tendril-like tips. The large flower, about 5cm long, is held on a pedicel well above the upper whorl of three leaves.

    F. qingchuanensis is related to this but has two flowers and a pair of upper leaves. Sichuan (Szechwan) province.

F. przewalskii from Gansu (Kansu) province in China is said to differ in its capsule shape from *F. cirrhosa*. It has yellowish flowers and rather few narrow leaves on the stem.

    Var. *longistigma* has large flowers up to 5cm long, dark purple and spotted. Sichuan (Szechwan).

    Var. *tessellata* from Gansu has very prominently tessellated flowers.

    Var. *discolor* has the outer perianth segments pale purple with yellow spots while the inner are spotted purple. Gansu (Kansu).

    Forma *emacula* has unspotted flowers. Sichuan (Szechwan).

F. sichuanica Obviously from Sichuan (Szechwan) province. This looks rather like *F. cirrhosa*. It is described as 20–32cm tall with narrow opposite lower leaves, the upper ones alternate. The solitary broad bells are usually 2.5–3.0cm long, yellowish-green with purple blotches or slight tessellation.

F. sinica Reported as being like *F. omeiensis* (and therefore *F. cirrhosa*) but has dark purple, tessellated flowers and differently shaped perianth segments. The linear leaves are not tendril-like. It is from Sichuan (Szechwan) province in China.

F. taipaiensis Another relative of *F. cirrhosa*, but with differently shaped and unequal perianth segments, the inner three narrow and the outer three obovate and rounded at the apex. The solitary flowers are about 3–4cm long and yellowish green, not tessellated. It is from Shaanxi (Shensi) province of China. Two varieties, *ningxiaensis* and *wanyuanensis*, have been described, differing slightly in flower shape and colour.

    F. pingwuensis is apparently related to this but has the outer perianth segments purple and the inner yellow with purple spots. Sichuan (Szechwan) and Gansu (Kansu) provinces.

F. unibracteata From China, a small plant about 15–20cm in height with rather few opposite leaves, not tendril-like, and the upper one is solitary, not a whorl of three as in several of these Chinese species. The flower is 2.5–3.0cm long, very dark purple and obscurely tessellated.

F. wuyangensis A new species from Henan (Honan) province in China, described as being 20–50cm in height with the leaves in whorls. The one or two flowers are broadly bell-shaped, 3.0–4.5cm long, and yellow-green tessellated purple. The bulb appears to have many small scales.

F. xinyuanensis From Xinjiang (Sinkiang) province in China, said to be related to

F. walujewii (see under *F. thunbergii* above) but has pale yellow flowers scarely spotted or tessellated.

F. yuminensis From Xinjiang (Sinkiang) province of China, related to *F. verticillata* but is described as having pink or blue (!) flowers, not tessellated, about 2cm long. The leaves have tendril-like tips.

F. yuzhongensis A recently described species from Gansu (Kansu) province, China. It is like *F. cirrhosa* with greenish, purple-tessellated flowers but they are smaller, about 2.0–2.5cm long.

Gagea

A large genus with many species, distributed in Europe and Western Asia, which are very difficult to distinguish from each other. They are all small plants, mostly less than 10cm in height with starry (usually yellow) flowers in spring and are of no great ornamental value, although in the wild they can be most attractive when growing in large drifts in the mountains. They have tiny bulbs producing narrow basal leaves and one to several flowers, often in an umbel, facing upwards. Only a few species are likely to be encountered in cultivation and these only rarely. They are best grown on the rock garden, in a peaty-gritty soil which will not dry out too much in summer. *G. graeca*, however, which differs in having white flowers, is better grown in an alpine house or bulb frame.

G. fistulosa (G. liotardii) This has semi-cylindrical bright green hollow basal leaves, one or two per bulb, and 5–10cm stems carrying umbels of up to six yellow starry flowers about 2–3cm in diameter. Widespread from Southern Europe eastwards to Iran in moist meadows.

G. graeca An attractive delicate species with flat but very narrow basal leaves and small panicles of pendent white, purple-veined flowers which remain more or less bell-shaped, not opening out and starry as in other species. It is less than 10cm in height. Greece, S. Turkey in dryish rocky places.

G. lutea Has one flat, narrowly lanceolate leaf per bulb and 5–10cm stems with umbels of up to seven flat starry greenish-yellow flowers about 3cm in diameter. It is attractive when massed and is not at all difficult to grow in a cool position. Widespread in Europe, in woods and meadows.

G. peduncularis Differs from the other yellow-flowered species mentioned here in that the flowers are not in an umbel but in panicles. The narrowly linear basal leaves are solid, overtopping the flower stem which is usually less than 10cm in height. The yellow flowers are flat and starry, about 1.5–3.0cm in diameter. S. Europe, Turkey, N. Africa, on dryish hillsides.

G. pratensis has one flat linear-lanceolate leaf per bulb and umbels of up to four flat, starry, yellow flowers, each about 2–3cm across. Widespread in Europe east to Turkey in mountain meadows.

G. villosa (G. arvensis) An easy species, increasing by bulblets, and suitable for the rock garden. It is less than 10cm in height with two narrowly linear solid leaves per bulb. The umbels can carry up to 15 flowers which are yellow, flat and starry, about 1.5–2.0cm in diameter. Widespread in the mountains of Europe to N. Africa, east to Iran.

Galanthus

The beautiful and much-loved Snowdrops are easy enough to recognize as a genus but the species are less well-defined and it takes a practised eye to sort them out. Almost certainly too many have been given names and this is at least part of the problem. Coupled with this lack of distinctiveness is the fact that certain species hybridize freely and there are now countless garden variants, many with names, and it is becoming almost impossible to identify any unknown Snowdrop with any degree of certainty.

Galanthus are all instantly recognizable by their solitary pendent white flowers with three large outer segments and three small inner ones forming a cup; the latter three are each provided with green markings near the apex, sometimes also at the base. The leaves are basal, usually only two per bulb, and their colour and form is important in distinguishing between the species. Some are greyish-green, others bright green or with a grey stripe along the centre; most are flattish but some have a downward fold along each margin (plicate). Most Snowdrops are about 7–12cm in height but there are shorter and taller forms to be found.

Snowdrops are best in cool growing conditions with plenty of moisture available in winter and spring, drying out to some extent in summer but never sunbaked. They do extremely well on heavy alkaline soils but can be grown quite satisfactorily on lighter acid soils, especially if plenty of humus is incorporated to help in the retention of moisture. *G. reginae-olgae* is better if given a sunnier position with fairly good drainage.

Most species flower in late winter or early spring but *G. reginae-olgae* flowers in autumn and some forms of *G. caucasicus* are very early as well, often in the early winter months. They are best lifted and divided in spring after flowering while the leaves are still green, replanting as soon as possible. Most specialist bulb nurseries now deal with them in this way since dried bulbs do not settle in nearly as well. The leaves are often quite small at flowering time, expanding later, and the widths given are those at maturity.

I am indebted to Chris Brickell for his taxonomic work on this genus.

G. allenii A robust plant, rather rare in cultivation. It has broad flattish leaves up to 2cm wide, deep dull green with a very slight overlay of grey. The almond-scented flowers are about 2cm long with broadly obovate outer segments and the inner three marked with green near the apex only. Caucasus and adjacent N.W. Iran. This is almost certainly the plant which I and my colleagues on the Bowles Scholarship expedition to Iran saw in 1963 in the Talysh Mountains. It is very close to *G. latifolius* which has bright green leaves.

G. caucasicus This has broad flattish grey-green leaves up to 2cm wide, sometimes becoming slightly wider towards the apex. The large, 2cm long flowers have green markings only near the apex of the inner segments and are normally produced in late winter or early spring but there are late autumn to winter-flowering forms known as var. *hiemalis*. Caucasus in meadows and woods.

G. alpinus, also Caucasian, is smaller-flowered with short broad leaves and rather rounded outer perianth segments.

G. bortkewitschianus is closely related to both these. It has the leaves strongly hooded at the apex. Caucasus.

G. elwesii (G. graecus of Boiss., not of gardens; **G. maximus)**   The so-called Giant Snowdrop, which is imported every year in thousands from Turkey. It has bold grey-green leaves up to 3cm wide, oblanceolate and hooded at the apex. The flowers are very variable but mostly large and rather elongate, 2–3cm long, with green marks at the base and apex of each inner segment; these marks are sometimes joined to make a continuous green stripe. W. Turkey, N.E. Greece and E. Bulgaria in rocky shaded places.

G. fosteri   A rare species in cultivation, appearing to thrive best in a sheltered position where it will dry out in summer. It has bright green leaves about 2cm wide and sizeable flowers 2.0–2.5cm long with strong green marks at the base and apex of each inner segment. Rather uncommon in the mountains of Turkey and Lebanon.

G. gracilis (G. graecus of gardens*)*   A distinctive little Snowdrop with narrow grey-green leaves up to 1cm wide and twisted lengthways. The smallish flowers are 1.5–2.5cm long and have green markings at the base and apex of the inner segments. W. Turkey, Greece, Bulgaria. It is related to *G. elwesii* and has also been described as *C. elwesii* subsp. *minor*.

G. ikariae   (G. latifolius,   G. ikariae subsp.   **latifolius,   G. platyphyllus, G. woronowii)**   An easily recognized Snowdrop with its wide (up to 3cm) bright green leaves with no trace of grey 'bloom', and medium-sized flowers, 1.5–2.5cm long, which have green markings only at the apex of the inner segments. It is a widespread plant in the E. Aegean islands, N.E. Turkey and the Caucasus in woods and rocky places.

G. krasnowii is closely related and is probably only a variant which has the inner perianth segments without a notch at the apex (notched in *G. ikariae*).

G. nivalis   The Common Snowdrop which is the most frequently cultivated and probably the most variable. It is one of the smallest, with linear grey-green flattish leaves 1cm or less wide and flowers 1.5–2.0cm long but up to nearly 3cm in some of the selections. They have green marks near the apex of the inner segments. It is widespread in European woodlands.

Subsp. *cilicicus (G. cilicicus)* from S. Turkey is very similar but has very long leaves at flowering time and it tends to flower earlier in winter.

Subsp. *imperati* from Italy represents large-flowered forms near the upper range of the measurements given, rather elegant in shape, being elongated.

There are also many gardens forms too numerous to mention, but the following are often cultivated and excellent plants, fairly distinct in their features.

'Scharlockii' has two long spathes extended above the flowers like a pair of ears.

'Viridapicis' has strong green markings at the tips of the outer segments as well as the inner.

'Lutescens' and 'Flavescens'; small-flowered plants, not very strong growing, which have yellow marks on the inner segments instead of green. The ovary is also yellowish.

'Atkinsii' is a tall plant with 15–25cm stems and is thus useful for picking. The flowers are long and elegant in shape.

'Magnet' is rather distinct in having the flowers held out away from the stem on long slender pedicels.

'Sam Arnott' is another robust variety, with large rather rounded flowers of great substance.

'Flore Pleno' is the double-flowered Snowdrop, not to everyone's liking, but vigorous and quickly increasing to form large clumps. There are several other double forms as well, some with neater flowers with tight double centres.

G. plicatus   A robust species with dark green leaves overlaid with a glaucous bloom and with a pale stripe along the centre, up to 2cm wide with a crease along each side just in from the margin which is folded downwards, especially in the young stages. The flowers have green marks near the apex of the inner segments only and are about 2–3cm long. It is a native of woods in the Crimea and Romania.

Subsp. *byzantinus* (*G. byzantinus*) from woods in N.W. Turkey is very similar but has green marks at the base and apex of the inner segments; occasionally I have seen plants in Turkey with these green marks joined into a continuous band.

G. reginae-olgae (G. nivalis subsp. **reginae-olgae, G. olgae, G. corcyrensis)** This is very similar to *G. nivalis* in general size and appearance, with narrow leaves and flowers with only one green blotch on the inner segments. It differs mainly in that the leaves are dull green with a pale greyish stripe along the centre; in *G. nivalis* they are wholly grey-green. The flowering time varies from autumn through to spring, the earliest ones flowering before the leaves emerge, the later ones with well-developed leaves. In order to distinguish them the following names have been given, but there is some overlap in their characters. Subsp. *reginae olgae* is used for the early ones, flowering from mid autumn onwards; these come from S. and N.W. Greece, S.W. Turkey and Sicily. The later ones in late winter and spring are known as subsp. *vernalis*.

I find that *G. reginae-olgae* requires a warmer sunnier position than most Snowdrops since it is a native of dryish woodland at fairly low altitudes.

G. rizehensis (G. transcaucasicus)   This is seldom cultivated. It is a small species with narrow linear dark dull green leaves 1cm or less wide and flowers 1.5–2.0cm long; these have green marks near the apex of the inner segments only. N. Turkey, Caucasus, N. Iran in woods and scrub.

G. lagodechianus (*G. cabardensis*, *G. ketzkhovellii*, *G. kemulariae*) is very similar but has brighter green glossy leaves. Caucasus.

Gymnospermium

It seems extraordinary to include a member of the Berberis family in a book on bulbs, but *Gymnospermium* is in fact a herbaceous plant with a large tuber, flowering in spring and dying down in summer, behaving just like any other bulbous plant from western and central Asia, which is where all the species are distributed. They have rather attractive lobed leaves and racemes of yellow flowers rather like those of Mahonia or Berberis. Since they require drying out during their dormant period in summer they must be grown in a well-drained sunny position or in a bulb frame. A few species are in cultivation, by far the best of which are *G. altaicum* and *G. albertii*, which are sometimes placed in the related genus *Leontice*.

G. albertii (Leontice albertii)   This produces one or more stems per tuber, usually about 15cm at flowering time with three stalked stem leaves, each of which is lobed, with five leaflets. These are usually poorly developed at flowering time, rolled lengthways and bronze-tinged, but expand later and become pale green. The raceme of flowers is pendent at first, densely flowered, each flower up to 2.5cm in diameter when fully opened out, but they are more frequently seen in the bell-shaped stage, bright yellow with a coppery red exterior. It is a native of rocky hillsides in Soviet Central Asia and is a very hardy plant, easily raised from seed. I have successfully grown it in an open, well drained position, and it makes a fine plant for the unheated greenhouse.

G. altaicum is very similar but the ovary is stalkless whereas in G. albertii it is carried on a short stalk. As a garden plant it is of equal value.

G. odessanum from Crimea, Romania, east to western Siberia has slightly longer stamens.

G. smirnowii has sessile (unstalked) stem leaves. Caucasus.

G. darwasicum also has sessile stem leaves but they have only three or four leaflets. Soviet Central Asia and Afghanistan.

G. sylvaticum Like G. albertii, this has a stalked ovary but the leaves have only three leaflets. Afghanistan, and adjacent USSR.

G. microrhynchum has three-lobed leaves and the lowest of the stipules, adjacent to the leaf stalk, is also three-lobed, whereas it is entire in the other species. N.E. China, Korea.

Gynandriris

A close relative of *Iris* with short-lived flowers having the typical *Iris* shape. The genus has an interesting distribution; two species in the Mediterranean and W. Asia and several in South Africa with no connecting links. The South African representatives, such as *G. setifolia*, are winter growers and are not hardy, and the northern hemisphere ones, although fairly hardy, require a good baking in their summer dormant period in order to get them to flower. They thus require bulb frame cultivation where they are perhaps no more than of interest value since the small flowers pass so quickly.

G. sisyrinchium (Iris sisyrinchium)   The Barbary Nut has a corm covered by a netted tunic. The two basal leaves are narrowly linear and V-shaped, produced well before the flower stem, which appears in spring and reaches a height of 10–40cm. There are several flowers produced in succession from transparent papery bracts and these are about 3–4cm in diameter, like small Irises, varying from pale lavender to violet with a white or yellow patch in the centre of the three outer segments ('falls'). They open in the afternoon or evening and each lasts out that day, a few hours only. It is a very common Mediterranean plant and occurs eastwards to Soviet Central Asia and Pakistan, in fields and stony places.

G. monophylla is a very small plant, about 5cm in height, with one basal leaf coiled on the ground and the pale slaty-blue flowers are only 2.0–2.5cm in diameter. It is less widespread in Greece, Crete and North Africa.

Habranthus

A genus in the Amaryllidaceae, similar in overall appearance to *Zephyranthes* but having the flowers held at an angle slightly above the horizontal and the stamens unequal; in Zephyranthes the six stamens are equal in length and position and the flowers are erect. *Habranthus* are related to *Hippeastrum* (Amaryllis of commerce) but are on the whole much smaller plants, with only one flower per stem.

Habranthus are mostly tender bulbs and I have therefore excluded the majority, but there are a few species which may succeed in sheltered places.

H. robustus This is not hardy in most districts but worth a try in a very sheltered sunny border. It has solitary pale pink, widely funnel-shaped flowers about 5–6cm long in summer, produced on 10–15cm stems while the plant is leafless. It is a native of Brazil.

H. brachyandrus is similar in shape but has large red or carmine flowers 7.5–10cm long on stems up to 30cm long. Brazil and Paraguay.

H. martinezii is a lovely plant having very pale pinkish flowers with a darker centre, produced freely in autumn. It is very easy to grow if the bulbs are dried out in summer and is therefore best in an alpine house or frame.

H. tubispathus (H. andersonii, Zephyranthes andersonii) This produces flowers at irregular intervals during the late summer and autumn months, mostly while the leaves are absent; the leaves are narrowly linear. 10–20cm stems carry solitary funnel-shaped flowers which are held at an oblique angle to the stem; they are normally yellow with a coppery exterior and about 3cm long and 2cm wide at the mouth, with only a very short perianth tube. It is a native of temperate South America, especially Argentina and Uruguay.

This is an interesting little summer to autumn bulb, unexpectedly hardy and has survived for many years in a sunny border alongside the greenhouse; it seeds freely and these do not take long to produce flowering bulbs. A plant which I grow as var. *roseus* is a pinkish form, perhaps a hybrid.

H. texanus from Texas is very similar but has slightly smaller flowers.

Hermodactylus

A close relative of *Iris*, well worth growing in a hot sunny position for its green and blackish flowers. It differs from *Iris* mainly in having creeping underground finger-like tubers which, incidentally, enable it to build up into sizeable colonies; the construction of its ovary is different, having just one locule, not three as in *Iris*.

It is a winter-growing plant, so the tubers are planted in autumn; after flowering in spring it dies down and requires a hot dry dormant period. One of the best colonies I have seen was on a sunbaked chalky slope in the garden of Sir Frederick Stern at Highdown.

H. tuberosus (Iris tuberosa) The Snake's Head or Widow Iris has long narrow grey leaves, square in cross-section like those of *Iris reticulata*, and 20–40cm stems bearing solitary flowers in spring. These are of the usual *Iris* shape, about 4–5cm in diameter, in a curious shade of translucent green with velvety blackish-brown on the reflexed blade of the three outer segments (falls). It is sometimes seen as a cut flower in winter or early spring, an unusual subject for flower arrangers and nicely scented. It is a native of the Mediterranean region in dryish rocky places.

Hyacinthella

A smallish genus with 16 species, mostly Turkish. They are interesting little bulbous plants, usually with two or three basal leaves and short racemes of pale to deep blue or violet flowers, not very showy but attractive for the alpine house. They mainly occur in dryish rocky habitats and require a warm dormant period in summer if they are to thrive, hence they do not do well out-doors in cool damper climates. They have in the past been included in *Hyacinthus* but are quite distinct and obviously should be treated as a separate group. The leaves have prominent fibre strands and the bulb tunics often have powdery white crystals attached to them. The flowers have the segments joined into a tube with six short lobes and the dark blue-violet anthers are held just within the tube. They are natives of rocky hillsides, hot and dry in summer.

A full account of the species by Karin Persson and Per Wendelbo can be found in Candollea 36: 513–541 (1981).

The following species are the most likely to be encountered in cultivation.

H. dalmatica   See **H. pallens**

H. glabrescens (H. hispida var. **glabrescens, H. lineata** var. **glabrescens)**   This has glabrous leaves, greyish-green and up to 2cm wide, and rather loosely-flowered racemes. The tubular flowers are on fairly long pedicels and are a deep violet blue, about 5mm long. It is a native of central-southern Turkey, especially in the Taurus Mountains.

H. heldreichii   This is rather like *H. glabrescens* in having deep violet blue flowers, but they are more or less sessile on the stem, or at most on extremely short pedicels. The leaves are often slightly undulating. It is also Turkish, from the south-west to central-south.

H. hispida   Another of the dark, blue-flowered species. This has the leaves conspicuously covered on both surfaces and margins with white hairs and they are often rather undulate. The racemes are rather loose and the flowers are on distinct pedicels. It occurs in central-southern Turkey.

H. leucophaea   This has rather narrow linear-lanceolate leaves standing more or less upright and racemes of stalked flowers which are very pale blue. It is a native of Eastern Europe from Yugoslavia and Bulgaria to Poland and USSR.

H. lineata   Another dark-flowered species, deep blue or violet, but this has leaves with long hairs on the margins and sometimes on the lower surface as well. The flowers are carried on distinct pedicels in a rather loose raceme. It is mainly from W. Turkey.

H. nervosa   A pale-blue flowered species with the tubular flowers sessile in a fairly dense spike-like raceme; they are up to 1cm long. The leaves have a rough or minutely hairy margin and are often undulating. It is widely distributed in S.E. Turkey, Syria, Iraq, Jordan, Israel and Lebanon.

H. pallens (H. dalmatica)   One of the best known species, since it is sometimes offered by specialist bulb nurseries, usually as *H. dalmatica*. This has pale blue flowers, which are bell-shaped and rather short, 5mm or less, carried on distinct pedicels in fairly dense racemes. The leaves are linear-lanceolate, with rough, but not hairy margins, and they are often arched. It is, as its synonym suggests, a Yugoslavian species from rocky places near the coast.

Hyacinthus

Apart from the well-known *H. orientalis*, the species from which all our large garden varieties of hyacinths are derived, there are two others which are little-known in cultivation. All the other species which have been referred to the genus in the past are now transferred elsewhere, to *Muscari*, *Bellevalia*, *Brimeura* and *Hyacinthella*.

H. litwinowii   A little-known plant in cultivation which does well in a bulb frame but is untried in the open garden. It is about 10cm tall when in flower, with a rosette of strap-shaped or lanceolate leaves 1.5–2.0cm wide. The loose racemes bear two to five flowers which are tubular, about 2cm long with spreading or recurved lobes, pale blue with a darker stripe along each segment. The anthers are held within the tube. It grows wild in E. Iran at up to 3000m on rocky slopes.

H. orientalis   The wild Hyacinth is a rather different-looking plant from the very large, densely-flowered single and double garden forms which have been selected over a period of nearly 500 years, from Ottoman times onwards. The wild species has several basal linear or strap-like leaves only 5–10mm wide and loose racemes of very fragrant flowers on stems 10–30cm in height. These are each about 2–3cm long with a cylindrical tube and reflexing lobes and have the anthers carried well down inside the tube, much farther down than in *H. litwinowii*. The colour is normally mid-blue but white or pinkish forms may rarely be found, certainly never in a range of colours like the garden varieties. The nearest forms to the wild ones are the Roman and Cynthella types, which have smallish flowers in loose racemes. It is a native of S. Turkey and adjacent Syria on rocky slopes.

  H. orientalis subsp. *chionophilus* has wider leaves 1.0–1.5cm wide and the lobes of the perianth are about the same length as the tube; in subsp. *orientalis* they are shorter than the tube.

H. transcaspicus   Very rare in cultivation and requiring a bulb-frame. It differs from both the above in having a shorter flower with the stamens protruding from the mouth of the tube, and the shorter lobes stand out rather than reflex. It occurs in E. Iran and was one of the interesting introductions of Paul and Polly Furse in the 1960s.

Hypoxis

A large genus, mostly tropical and seldom cultivated, since they are on the whole not very showy and scarcely worth greenhouse space. A few are hardy and worth growing for interest's sake; they flower in summer.

H. hirsuta   This is 10–20cm in height with narrowly linear hairy leaves only 2–5mm wide and loose-branched inflorescences of several yellow flowers, green on the outside; each is about 1.5cm in diameter. It is a native of sandy pinewoods in central North America. In cultivation it will grow well in a sand-peat mixture on a peat garden.

H. hygrometrica   A small species less than 10cm in height with erect, very narrow awl-like hairy leaves and solitary yellow starry flowers 1.0–1.5cm in diameter, green on the outside. It grows wild in E. Australia and Tasmania and appears to be best treated as an alpine-house plant.

H. parvula An interesting little plant which I have only grown in the last few years from a collection made by B.L. Burtt. The form I know is about 10cm when in flower with rosettes of arching lanceolate hairy leaves about 1cm wide overtopped by slender hairy stems carrying one or two flat white flowers backed with green, about 1.5–2.0cm in diameter; the stamens are protruding as a yellow eye in the centre. The species often has yellow flowers, the more usual colour in the genus. It is a native of mountain meadows in the eastern part of southern Africa in Lesotho and eastern Cape.

I also have two hybrids between this white form and *Rhodohypoxis baurii*, both collected by B.L. Burtt and proving to be excellent little plants. One is white flowered, much like *H. parvula*, but the other has deep pink flowers, the colour of some *R. baurii* forms but with an eye of yellow stamens and the broader leaves of *H. parvula*. I have not yet tested their hardiness but they are certainly vigorous growers in pans of sandy-peaty soil.

Ipheion

A small genus of dwarf South American bulbs, mostly of garden value. They are distantly related to *Allium* but have only one upward-facing flower per stem, very rarely two in an umbel, and are also allied to *Nothoscordum* and probably *Brodiaea*. One species, *I. uniflorum*, has been popular for over a century but the others are scarcely known in cultivation. There has been much playing on the nomenclatural merry-go-round with this genus and the species may be found in literature under *Brodiaea*, *Milla*, *Triteleia*, *Tristagma* or *Ipheion*.

I. uniflorum is a hardy bulb, suitable for a sunny or semi-shaded position where it will produce leaves in winter and flower in mid-late spring, then die down for the summer. The other species that I have tried grow well in pots in a cold frame and seem fairly hardy but I have not yet experimented with them outside.

I will describe the commonly cultivated species first to 'set the scene'.

I. uniflorum The whitish bulbs produce small offsets and smell of onions. In spring there are several narrowly linear (up to 7mm wide) pale green, slightly glaucous leaves per bulb, so that a clump of bulbs appears very leafy. These are overtopped by the flower stems, which are usually about 15cm but they can be much taller, carrying one (rarely two) upright flattish flowers about 3–4cm in diameter with a tube 1.0–1.5cm long. The two spathes enclosing the flower in bud are joined into a tube which is usually bilobed at its apex. There are several colour forms in cultivation. The most commonly seen is pale blue but there are darker violet-blue ones such as 'Wisley Blue', 'Violacea' and 'Froyle Mill'. 'Album' is a white form and 'Rolf Fiedler' has large flowers in clear pale blue with a white throat. In the wild it is reported as being very variable in colour from white through blue to pink. It is a native of Argentina and Uruguay.

I. vittatum from Uruguay is very similar in overall appearance with white flowers with a purplish stripe on each segment. The leaves and flower stems are hairy (glabrous in *I. uniflorum*) and the two spathes are joined into a tube only near the base, so are free for most of their length.

I. tweedianum is like a diminutive *I. uniflorum* with glabrous leaves only 1–4mm wide and stems 5 or 6cm in height. It has white, dark-striped flowers. It is also very similar to *I. vittatum* but the spathe is long-tubular and the stem and leaves are glabrous. Argentina, Uruguay.

I. sellowianum This is a most attractive species, growing well in a cool glasshouse with me and well worth trying outside. It is about the same size as *I. uniflorum* but has narrower leaves, and the flowers which are about 3.5cm in diameter are bright yellow, speckled green and purplish outside. The flower stems are glabrous. Uruguay.

I. dialystemon is a similar yellow-flowered species to *I. sellowianum* in overall appearance but is the only species to have the stamens free from each other; in the remainder they are joined together at their bases. I have Alberto Castillo to thank for introducing this attractive plant. Argentina, Uruguay.

I. sessile (*Brodiaea recurvifolia*) is a tiny plant only 3–4cm in height with spreading or prostrate narrow leaves up to 3mm wide. The flowers are stemless and are carried aloft by the perianth tube which is about 1.5–2.5cm long. They are white, striped purple, about 2cm across. Uruguay.

Milla sessiliflora from Chile is said to be a synonym of this but it does look rather different, with even narrower erect leaves and smaller flowers.

To date I have been unable to obtain living bulbs of either.

I. setaceum This has very narrow thread-like leaves only about 1mm wide and 6–10cm flower stems which are glabrous. The 1.5–2.0cm diameter flowers are said to be white, although in specimens I have seen they appear to be yellow. The two spathes are joined only at the base so, if the flowers are white, this feature and the narrow leaves would distinguish it from *I. uniflorum* and *I. tweedianum*. If they are yellow it is nearest to *I. sellowianum* but the smaller flowers and very narrow leaves make it distinct. Argentina.

I. hirtellum looks very like *I. setaceum* but has hairy flower stems. The flowers are definitely a strong yellow colour. Uruguay.

Iris

There are only two groups of *Iris* in this large genus which really concern us here in having bulbous rootstocks and a fairly small stature; these are the well-known Reticulata Irises (subgenus *Hermodactyloides*) and the Juno Irises (subgenus *Scorpiris*), which are not cultivated to any great extent but are a fascinating group and a challenge to the enthusiast.

Since these two groups are very different from each other I will deal with them separately.

Subgenus Hermodactyloides – the Reticulata Irises

This very popular group of spring-flowering plants from western Asia contains some of the most attractive and valuable small bulbs for the garden. They are easy to grow, mostly very hardy and of neat sturdy appearance which makes them very suitable for the rock garden, bulb frame or alpine house. The best for outdoor cultivation are *I. reticulata* and *I. histrioides* and their selections and hybrids, *I. danfordiae* and *I. winogradowii*. The others are best given protection which either guards against excess cold in winter or excess rain whilst they are dormant in summer. The bulbs must be ripened if they are to flower well, so it follows that an open sunny position is necessary, with good drainage, so that the site becomes warm and dryish in summer.

Most species increase by producing offsets which can be detached at replanting time; alternatively they can be left undisturbed to build up into clumps. It is advisable, when growing a collection of different species and forms, to treat the dormant bulbs in autumn with a systemic fungicide to guard against 'Ink Disease', a serious complaint which can decimate Reticulatas in a very short time.

The characteristics of these Irises are the dwarf habit, not more than 15cm in height at flowering time, the netted tunics to the bulbs, the long narrow greyish leaves which are usually almost square in cross section and short at flowering time, and the long tube to the flowers. They all flower in early spring. These features will not be repeated below in the separate descriptions unless there are exceptions to the generalizations.

I. bakeriana   The form of this which is in cultivation has whitish falls with a deep violet apex and conspicuous violet spots and blotches around the central ridge; the standards and styles are bluish-lilac. There is no yellow colour in the centre of the falls. In wild forms in Iran, however, I have seen a wide range of colours from pale blue to purplish, with or without yellow markings. The main distinguishing feature, which makes it unique among the Reticulatas, is the nearly cylindrical leaf with eight ribs; all its relatives have the four-ribbed square-sectioned leaves.

It is a native of S.E. Turkey, N. Iraq and W. Iran on stony hillsides.

I. danfordiae (I. bornmülleri)   A popular little species for its bright yellow flowers very early in spring. The falls are spotted green in the centre where there is a deeper yellow-orange ridge. It is distinctive in that the standards have all but disappeared and are represented by tiny bristles. It is a native of Turkey in widely scattered localities in the mountains, flowering near the snowline.

I. danfordiae bulbs are very cheap to obtain. For a good display it is best to replace them every year, for the species is notorious for splitting up its bulbs after flowering into many small ones. However, I have succeeded in getting groups of bulbs to go on flowering year after year by planting them deeply, at least 10cm, and by feeding with a low-nitrogen, high potash fertilizer in autumn and early spring.

I. histrio   A lovely species, but not as successful in the open garden as *I. histrioides*, and best kept in a bulb frame or alpine house. It has large flowers 6–8cm across in pale blue, covered on the blade of the falls with darker blue blotches around a central yellow ridge. It is very early, flowering in late winter, and is a native of S. Turkey south to Lebanon in rocky places.

Var. *aintabensis* from the Gaziantep (Aintab) area of S. Turkey is smaller in flower but is much easier to grow and a much more satisfactory outdoor plant, for a well drained sunny position. The falls are less prominently blotched than in var. *histrio*.

I. histrioides   One of the best of all Reticulatas, producing its large well-formed flowers year after year in the open garden and remaining undamaged by the severest of weather in late winter or early spring. They are 6–7cm across, in a rich mid to deep blue, with a yellow ridge in the centre of the falls surrounded by a paler, blue-spotted area. There is variation in the depth of colour and markings and several cultivars have been named, for example 'Major', 'Lady Beatrix Stanley' and 'Angel's Tears'. There are also some hybrids with *I. reticulata* and *I. winogradowii* (see below). *I. histrioides* occurs in mountain turf on one mountain in N. Turkey.

I. hyrcana   This is probably only a variant of *I. reticulata* but is interesting in that the flowers have very clear colours, a feature which is impossible to convey in words but rather obvious when one sees the plants side by side. Although the form in cultivation has pale clear blue flowers I have seen it in Iran in shades of darker blue and reddish purple.

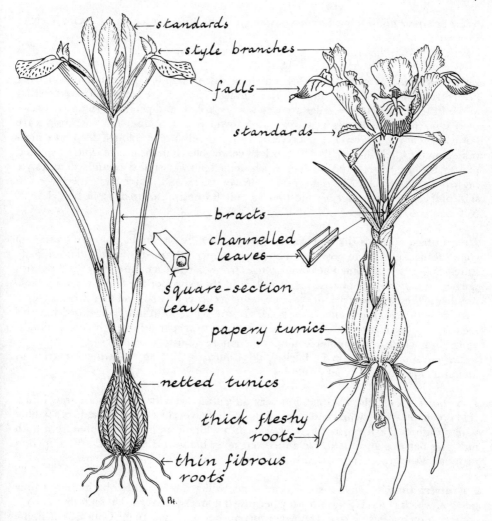

IRIS

Comparison of two groups of bulbous Iris. *Left: Subgenus Hermodactyloides, the Reticulata Iris group. Right: Subgenus Scorpiris, the Juno Iris group*

It appears to occur only in the north-west region of Iran and adjacent USSR, in the Talysh Mountains.

It is best grown in a frame or alpine house.

I. kolpakowskiana   A very distinct Reticulata since it has three or four narrow channelled leaves, not quadrangular ones. The flower has a pale lilac-blue ground colour with a deep reddish-purple blade to the falls which have an orange-yellow ridge in the centre, hence it is quite a colourful little species. It occurs farther east than the other species, in the Tien Shan Mountains, where I have seen it on hillsides in some very wet sticky clay, although this will dry out in summer. In cultivation it grows well in a frame or alpine house – but I am now trying it in the open garden, and it seems likely to succeed.

I. winkleri from the same area appears to be very similar.

I. pamphylica   A curious species, not long discovered but unfortunately proving rather tricky to grow. Unlike all other Reticulatas its flowers are carried on a stem so that in the fruiting stage the capsules are well above ground and pendent. In other species there is no stem (the flowers are carried aloft by the perianth tube) and the capsules are borne erect at ground level. The flower is a strange mixture of colours, deep brownish-purple on the blade of the falls with a bright yellow blotch in the centre which is spotted purple; the lower part of the falls is greenish, veined purple, while the standards and style branches are light blue. To date this has proved tricky and I have had little success in spite of trying a wide range of conditions; a bulb frame appears to offer the best chance. S. Turkey, in rocky places.

I. reticulata   This is the best known species, cheaply obtainable in a wide range of colour forms and easy to grow in an open, sunny, well-drained situation so it is ideally suited to the rock garden. The colour ranges from pale to deep blue, violet and reddish purple, usually with a bold stripe of yellow in the centre of the falls. A considerable number of these garden variants have been given cultivar names and there are also some hybrids with *I. bakeriana* and *I. histrioides*. A pure white form has been raised but this seems rather less vigorous and I have not been able to keep it although there is an almost white form which is in commerce and is much more robust.

I. reticulata occurs wild in E. Turkey, the Caucasus, N. Iraq and widely in Iran, in mountain meadows and rocky hillsides.

I. vartanii   A delightful species but very difficult to keep for long. I once grew it in a cold greenhouse for a while and enjoyed its lovely flowers in a delicate shade of sky blue with a slightly greyish cast. There used to be a white form freely available from bulb nurseries but this appears to have died out now. Being the most southerly-occurring member of the group, in Israel, it is undoubtedly rather tender.

I. winogradowii   This superb species is becoming more readily obtainable as time goes on, which is good to see, not only because it is an excellent garden plant but also for conservation reasons, since it is known from only one mountain in the Caucasus in alpine meadows. In the shape and large size of its flower it is very similar to *I. histrioides* but the colour is primrose-yellow throughout with some green spotting in the centre and lower part of the falls.

It grows well in the open garden and prefers situations which are not too hot and dry, so a bulb frame is not the best place for it, in fact it seems quite happy in a peat garden.

The close relationship with *I. histrioides* is borne out by the fact that the two will hybridize and there are at least two good hybrids which are becoming known in cultivation. *I.* 'Katharine Hodgkin' has yellow flowers, blue-veined and slightly suffused with pale blue. 'Frank Elder' usually has rather more blue so that it appears to be very pale blue with a hint of yellow; however, they both vary in colour a little from year to year, perhaps depending upon the temperature, and sometimes they are almost indistinguishable.

Subgenus Scorpiris – the Juno Irises

This exciting and large group contains many species which are scarcely known in gardens, except through a few specialist collections. This is partly because they are rare and difficult to obtain and partly because the majority of them are very tricky to grow and need careful attention in a bulb frame or alpine house. However, there are few bulbs which attract more attention when they are exhibited at shows and the group as a whole has acquired a certain aura about it. They are mainly Asiatic, from Turkey to Soviet Central Asia, but one species, *I. planifolia*, occurs in Mediterranean Europe.

The main characteristics of Juno Irises are in the bulb, which is covered with papery tunics and has thick fleshy roots from its base, in the flowers which have smaller standards than in most Irises, held out horizontally or reflexed rather than upright, and in the leaves which are channelled and produced in two ranks rather like those of a Leek. These features combine to form a group of some 55 species distinct from all other Iris groups. I discussed and described these species in some detail in *The Iris* (Batsford, 1981) and I cannot afford the space to repeat all the information here. Instead, I have included those most likely to be encountered in cultivation, with a brief mention of the more unusual ones under the nearest related or similar species.

It is wrong of me to give the impression that they are all difficult plants to cultivate for some of them are perfectly easy garden plants and require only sun and good drainage.

All species flower in spring, mostly mid to late spring, and unless mentioned otherwise it must be assumed that they prefer bulb frame or alpine house cultivation, with as much ventilation as possible given during their growing period; in summer they can be dried off, but not baked in the sun, and watering should start again in late autumn, keeping them cool and just damp until growth appears in spring. At repotting or replanting time, care must be taken not to break off the thick basal roots – or the bulb will be weakened.

Although some of the following exceed the height limits which I had intended for this book, this is such an interesting group of species that I feel that bulb enthusiasts will expect to find them here.

On the whole, the small reflexed standards have little diagnostic value and I have only mentioned them when there is a particular point of interest about them. The shape of the falls is however of great significance and I will mention in each case the shape of the lower portion (the haft) and mainly whether its margins are winged or not; in the latter case they are therefore more or less parallel. In some cases the edges are folded downwards.

I. aitchisonii   A slender species to 30cm, with narrow leaves well spaced out on the wiry stems. The flowers are yellow with a brown suffusion, or wholly purple, about 4–5cm diameter, with the haft of the falls winged and the blade rather pointed. It is one of the most eastern species from N. Pakistan on rocky hillsides. The yellow form is in cultivation but tests the skill of the best cultivators.

I. alata   See **I. planifolia**

I. albomarginata (I. caerulea)   An excellent plant for the bulb frame which might well succeed in the open, although I have not yet tried it. The forms in cultivation are about 20–30cm in height, with many fairly wide leaves up the stem and bright blue flowers about 4–5cm in diameter. The haft of the falls has unwinged, almost parallel margins and the blade has a white ridge with a yellowish surround in the centre. A central Asiatic species from the Tien Shan and Ferghana mountains.

I. aucheri (I. fumosa, I. sindjarensis)   A robust species 15–40cm tall with broad leaves densely packed on the short stem at flowering time. There are up to six flowers in the upper leaf axils, each about 6cm in diameter, pale bluish-lilac to nearly white with a yellow ridge on the falls, which have a broadly winged haft. The commercially available form is a particularly good colour, in a strong blue, and it is a vigorous plant suitable for outdoor cultivation in a well drained sunny site. It is a native of S.E. Turkey, W. Iran, N. Iraq and Syria, south to Jordan in rock crevices and flat open areas.

I. nusairiensis from Syria is very similar and undoubtedly closely related. The large flowers are pale blue with a pale yellow ridge on the falls, and the margins of the falls are somewhat undulate giving the flowers a 'frilly' appearance. It seems to be particularly easy to grow, for a Juno, and is becoming quite well known in specialist circles.

I. 'Sindpers' (*I. aucheri* × *I. persica*) is a very vigorous dwarf plant with broad leaves and lovely pale azure flowers.

I. baldschuanica   See under **I. nicolai**

I. bucharica   One of the most frequently cultivated Junos, easy in an open sunny border. It is a leafy plant with broad glossy green leaves, usually about 20–40cm in height at flowering time with several flowers in the upper axils. These are about 5–6cm in diameter, creamy white with a yellow blade to the falls, which have an unwinged haft. There is also a wholly deep yellow form which is in cultivation under the name of *I. orchioides* but the true species of this name is not the same.

I. bucharica is a native of Central Asia in Tadjikistan and N. Afghanistan.

I. caerulea   Syn. **I. albomarginata**

I. capnoides   A little known species from Soviet Central Asia, only 8–15cm in height with sheathing leaves on the stem and one to three smoky greyish-green flowers with a yellow crest on the falls; the haft is widely winged and the standards are said to be three-lobed and pale violet.

I. carterorum   An Afghan species, probably not in cultivation. It is only 7–10cm in height with narrow grey-green leaves and small yellow flowers spotted with black on the haft of the unwinged falls; the standards are reduced to bristles.

I. caucasica   One of the easiest of the smaller Junos to grow and will probably succeed in a raised sunny bed outdoors. The greyish-green leaves sheath the stem at flowering time and the plant is no more than 10–15cm tall but as the capsules are produced it elongates and the leaves become spaced out. The one to four flowers are a lovely shade of translucent greenish-yellow with a yellow ridge on the falls; the haft is only slightly winged.

I. caucasica subsp. *turcica*, which is widespread in E. Turkey, has glabrous-margined leaves whereas subsp. *caucasica* from N.E. Turkey and the Caucasus has ciliate leaves; they both inhabit mountain slopes.

I. schischkinii is probably a synonym of *I. caucasica*.

I. atropatana from Transcaucasia is probably just a variant of *I. caucasica* in which there is a narrowed portion between the haft and the blade of the falls; in *I. caucasica* the transition is gradual, so that the blade and haft merge imperceptibly.

I. pseudocaucasica differs in having a very wide wing to the falls and is in general a shorter plant, not elongating much in the fruiting stage. It can be yellowish-green or pale blue in colour; the area of distribution is in S.E. Turkey, N. Iraq, W. Iran and S. Caucasus, on rocky mountain slopes.

I. cycloglossa   A completely distinct Juno which is easy to grow in the open border. It is a tall slender plant to 40 or 50cm in height with scattered long narrow leaves and one to three large clear bluish-violet flowers about 8–10cm across. In the centre of the falls is a yellow blotch and the haft is widely winged but the really unique feature is the upright position of the standards which are rather large and obovate, falling outwards as the flower matures. Another characteristic is a strong clove-like fragrance. It is a native of N.W. Afghanistan in wet places, unlike most other species which occur on rocky hillsides.

I. doabensis   A lovely species which I named in 1972, sadly now probably lost to cultivation. It is short and stocky, with broad leaves clasping and concealing the stem, only 10–15cm in height to the top of the flowers. These are long-tubed and wholly deep yellow, such a rich colour that Paul and Polly Furse, who first discovered it in the Doab area of the Hindu Kush Mountains of Afghanistan, called it 'Doab Gold'. The flowers have a fruity fragrance; the haft of the falls has down-turned margins indicating that it is a relative of *I. nicolai*.

I. drepanophylla   See under **I. kopetdagensis**

I. edomensis   This rare species is not at present in cultivation and will probably be very difficult to grow outside its semi-desert home. It is less than 10cm tall with very narrow wavy-margined leaves coiled on the ground and has one or two flowers about 4–5cm across. These are prominently blotched and streaked deep purple on a white ground with a yellow crest on the falls, the haft of which has a narrow wing. It is a native of Jordan in dry scrubland.

I. eleonorae   Syn. **I. galatica**. See under **I. persica**

I. fosteriana   This beautiful species can scarcely be confused with any other since its flowers have yellow falls and styles, contrasting sharply with the large and completely reflexed bright purple standards. It is a compact plant, 10–15cm in height when in flower, with several narrow leaves clustered basally. The haft of the falls is not widely winged. It is a native of the Kopet Dağ range in N.E. Iran and adjacent parts of USSR and Afghanistan.

   I. narbutii (*I. dengerensis*, *I. hissarica*), from Soviet Central Asia, is of similar habit, perhaps slightly smaller in all its parts, and also has large strongly deflexed purple standards. The falls and style branches are however differently coloured; the falls have a deep violet blade with a yellow patch in the centre and a creamy crest, while the style branches are pale yellow shading to greyish blue on the lower parts. It occurs wild in Central Asiatic USSR in the Pamir-Alai, and, thanks to the skills of Norman Stevens and Tony Hall, is now in cultivation.

I. graeberiana   A good 'garden' Juno for a sunny position with sharp drainage, where it will increase into clumps. It is one of the taller species, 15–35cm at flowering time, with the broad leaves clustered at first but later spaced out up the stem. There are up to six flowers in the upper axils, and these are about 6.0–7.5cm across, blue-lavender overall in colour but with a white, dark-veined area around the white crest on the falls; the haft is widely winged. It is from Soviet Central Asia, where most of the more easily cultivated Junos originate.

   I. hippolyti is a little known species which, from its description, sounds like a shorter version of this with some yellow colouring in the centre of the falls. It is also from Central Asia.

I. heldreichii   Syn. **I. stenophylla**. See under **I. persica**

I. hissarica   Syn. ***I. narbutii***. See under ***I. fosteriana***

I. inconspicua   Unfortunately this is, as yet, unknown in cultivation. It is a dwarf species with the leaves grouped together at the base of the stem and one to three pale lilac flowers with green spotting on the blade of the falls; the crest of the falls is white and the haft is not winged. It is from Central Asia, in the Tien Shan range.

  I. leptorhiza, from its original description, sounds rather similar, with dimensions very close to this. The flowers are said to be of a violet-green mixture. It is also Central Asiatic.

I. kopetdagensis   This is rare in cultivation at present, but is to be seen in a few specialist collections. It is a variable species 10–35cm in height, with rather narrow leaves closely arranged at first but spaced out as the plant matures. In the upper axils are up to nine green flowers each 4–5cm across with a yellow crest on the falls; the haft is narrow and unwinged while the standards are so reduced as to be bristle-like. It is a Central Asiatic species from N.E. Iran, adjacent USSR and N.W. Afghanistan.

  I. drepanophylla, with a similar distribution, is like this in overall appearance but the flowers are more of a yellowish-green and the haft of the falls has down-turned margins.

  I. drepanophylla subsp. *chlorotica* from N.E. Afghanistan differs in having silvery green flowers.

  I. xanthochlora is on the whole slightly smaller than *I. kopetdagensis* and differs mainly in the haft of the falls, being wedge-shaped, widening from base to apex; in the latter the haft has nearly parallel margins. It occurs in N.E. Afghanistan.

I. linifolia   This is probably not in cultivation and is little-known as a wild plant. It is a dwarf species 5–10cm in height but even so the few narrow leaves are spaced out on the stem. The small flowers are said to be pale yellow, darker yellow on the blade of the falls, with a white crest; the haft is not winged. It is yet another species from Soviet Central Asia.

I. magnifica   Suitably named, this is one of the showiest and easiest of species for growing in the open garden, suitable for a well drained sunny position. It is robust, 30–60cm, with wide shiny green leaves scattered up the stem and up to seven large flowers in pale lilac with a yellow area in the centre of the falls, which have a widely winged haft. There is also a white form 'Alba' which, however, retains the yellow patch on the falls. It is a native of the Pamir-Alai range in Central Asia where I have seen it looking spectacular in rock crevices.

  I. zenaidae is related but said to differ from *I. magnifica* in having darker violet-blue flowers, strongly spotted violet on the haft of the falls.

I. maracandica   A rare species in cultivation but now to be found in specialist collections. It is of stocky habit, 10–15cm with rather wide leaves packed near the base of the stem. The large flowers are completely yellow and have a wide wing on the haft of the falls. It grows wild in the Pamir-Alai Mountains of the USSR.

  I. svetlanae seems to me to be almost identical.

I. microglossa   One of Paul Furse's introductions of the 1960s, still around in cultivation but very uncommon. It is a slender plant, 10–40cm tall, with markedly grey-green leaves scattered on the stem and one to four flowers in pale lavender or silvery blue with a white or pale yellow crest; the haft of the falls is widely winged. It is known only from N.E. Afghanistan. Because of its locality and colour Paul and Polly Furse dubbed it 'Salang Blue'.

I. narbutii   See under **I. fosteriana**

I. narynensis   A poorly known species, said to have a stem only 5cm tall with sickle-shaped leaves and one or two pale violet flowers, darker on the blade of the falls and with a white ridge; the haft is not winged. One of the many species recorded in the Tien Shan range of Central Asia.

I. nicolai   A superb plant, not easy to keep for long but far from impossible in a bulb frame or alpine house; probably new bulbs should be raised from seed frequently in order to keep it going. It is certainly worth every effort. It is a short plant, only 10–15cm at flowering time, with the leaves only just visible but expanding afterwards and becoming very broad. The flowers have a very long tube (8–11cm) and are strikingly marked; the ground colour is whitish or pale lilac but the falls have a deep violet blade and a bright orange crest. The margins of the haft are folded downwards, a characteristic of this and several related species mentioned below. It occurs wild in the Pamir-Alai range and adjacent parts of N.E. Afghanistan.

   I. rosenbachiana, also from the Pamir-Alai, is very similar in overall appearance and shape but the flowers are of a rich deep purple with a bright orange crest. The leaves are usually rather more developed at flowering time than they are in *I. nicolai*.

   I. popovii is unknown in cultivation and is, from its Russian description, very similar to *I. nicolai*.

   I. cabulica from Afghanistan is related to *I. nicolai* and its main features are similar, but it has arching, well-developed leaves at flowering time and the flowers are white to very pale lilac throughout, with a yellow ridge on the falls.

   I. baldschuanica also belongs to this group and structurally is like *I. nicolai*. The flowers may be yellowish with violet veining or, in the plants cultivated in Britain from a Paul Furse collection, creamy coloured with pinkish-brown staining. It grows in N. Afghanistan and adjacent Tadjik SSR.

   I. zaprjagajevii   Although clearly very closely allied to *I. nicolai*, this beautiful Juno has its flowers pure white throughout, except for a thin golden yellow ridge in the centre of the falls. Like *I. nicolai* it appears to be short lived and I have currently lost it unfortunately. It occurs in the Pamir Mountains of the USSR.

I. orchioides   I refer to the true species here, not the bright yellow *I. orchioides* of commerce which is a form of *I. bucharica*. True *I. orchioides* from the Tien Shan in Soviet Central Asia is 20–35cm in height, with the leaves packed together at first but soon becoming spaced out up the stem. There are three or four flowers in the upper axils, pale yellow or yellow-green, with a pale purple suffusion as they age. The crest is yellow and the haft of the falls is widely winged, thus differing from *I. bucharica* forms. I have seen this in the USSR growing in rather harsh rocky places, but it appears to take to cultivation in ordinary well-drained soil quite well.

I. parvula   This small Central Asiatic Juno is rather rare in cultivation at present. It is only about 10cm tall with the few narrow leaves widely spaced and distinctive in that they are abruptly narrowed at the apex (in most species they taper to a point). The small flowers are yellowish green with the standards reduced nearly to bristles; the haft of the falls is unwinged.

I. persica (I. bolleana, I. haussknechtii, I. issica)   One of the best known of the small Junos, although it is not particularly easy to grow and is best kept in a bulb frame or alpine house. It is only 10cm in height when in flower, with a few narrow sharply pointed leaves at ground level, never becoming very long. The flower has a long tube (6–8cm) and is about 5–6cm across. Although the colour varies considerably it is usually in pale shades of silvery-grey, or sandy-yellow with a darker purple or brown blade to the falls, which have a yellow crest and a widely winged haft. In spite of its name it is not from Iran, being mainly a plant of rather hot dryish places at lower altitudes in southern Turkey, northern Syria and northern Iraq.

I. hymenospatha is, however, from S. Iran and is closely related. It has nearly white flowers with a yellow crest surrounded by a purple patch. The main difference is in the two bracts which are like silvery-transparent tissue paper; in *I. persica* one of the bracts is stiffly erect and green. *I. hymenospatha* seems to be as near to impossible to grow as any bulb I know! Its subsp. *leptoneura* has wider leaves without the very prominent close veining which is characteristic of subsp. *hymenospatha*.

I. galatica (*I. purpurea*, *I. eleonorae*), from central and northern Turkey, is allied to *I. persica* and in some forms does approach it in colour. It is extremely variable and may be basically greenish-yellow or reddish-purple throughout, and sometimes a silvery-grey colour. The blade of the falls is normally darker, often deep purple and the crest is yellow. It is in the bracts that it differs from *I. persica*, having two green bracts sheathing the tube; in the latter they are unequal, one papery and the other erect and green, not sheathing the tube. *I. galatica* is from cooler higher altitudes and is much easier to cultivate than its southern relatives.

I. stenophylla (*I. heldreichii*, *I. tauri*) is another ally of *I. persica* and is similar in overall habit. The flowers are however violet-blue or lilac-blue with a much darker blade to the falls which spread out almost horizontally giving a wide flower. There is a yellow crest surrounded by a white, violet spotted zone. The two bracts of *I. stenophylla* are both green and sheath the tube like those of *I. galatica*, but this species never has flowers in the violet-blue colour range. *I. stenophylla* grows on rocky hillsides in southern Turkey in the Taurus mountains at fairly high altitudes and is not as difficult to cultivate as *I. persica*, although it still requires a bulb frame or alpine house. Its subsp. *allisonii*, which I named after a good friend, John Allison, has six to ten leaves per bulb (usually four or five in subsp. *stenophylla*) and pale blue flowers with very prominent dark spotting on the falls.

I. planifolia (I. alata, I. scorpioides) This has the distinction of being the only European species, distributed on rocky hillsides and banks in Portugal and S. Spain to Sardinia, Sicily, Crete and North Africa. It is a short, leafy plant, flowering very early, sometimes in winter, with many rather broad bright green leaves tapering gradually to a point. There are one to three large flowers 6–7cm across, normally bluish-violet with a yellow crest, but lovely white forms are known also. The perianth tube is long, 8–15cm, and there is a wide wing on the haft of the falls. It is not difficult to cultivate in a bulb frame or alpine house, but must have plenty of ventilation when it is in growth in the winter and early spring when humidity is high, for it is very susceptible to botrytis attack.

I. palaestina is very closely allied to this and is structurally almost identical; it, however, normally has green flowers and inhabits lowland areas of Israel and Lebanon.

I. porphyrochrysa A small Juno from central Afghanistan, probably now lost to cultivation. It is about 10cm in height at flowering time, with narrow grey-green leaves clustered at the base and concealing the stem. There are one to three bronze-coloured flowers with a deep yellow blade to the falls, which have a narrow unwinged haft and a conspicuous orange crest. The colour is distinctive and prompted Paul Furse to call it 'Shibar Bronze' when he collected it in the 1960s.

I. postii A desert Juno from Iraq, Syria and Jordan, apparently very difficult to cultivate, although there has been some success in well-ventilated alpine house conditions. It is 10–20cm in height with narrow, long-tapering leaves, very white-margined and clustered towards the base of the stem at first, though spaced out later. The flowers are heavily blotched dark violet on a pale lavender ground with a yellow crest; the haft of the falls is widely winged.

I. stocksii from hot dry regions of S. Afghanistan and W. Pakistan is similar in structure to this, but the flowers are lavender or bluish-violet without the very prominent dark blotching. Both have a bulb which is distinctive in being deep-seated in sandy soil, with a long neck of papery tunics reaching to the surface, probably an adaption to the semi-desert conditions.

I. odontostyla may also be included here since it has a similar bulb and similar flower structure. The colour is a greyish or silvery violet with an orange-yellow crest, and a distinctive feature is the conspicuous toothing on the style branches. It is a native of W. Afghanistan, another of the 1960s introductions of Paul Furse.

I. platyptera was called 'Old Smokey' by Paul and Polly Furse when they saw it in eastern Afghanistan, since its flowers are a somewhat smokey translucent purple or brownish-violet; the style branches are not markedly toothed.

I. regis-uzziae   One of the most southerly-occurring Junos, in S. Jordan and the Negev region of Israel. It is about 10cm tall when in flower with up to seven leaves packed together at the base of the stem. The flowers vary from pale blue to a translucent greenish-yellow with a yellow crest and there is a wide wing on the falls. It is very rare in cultivation and not too easy, being from such a hot dry habitat.

I. sindjarensis   See **I. aucheri**

I. subdecolorata   One of the poorly-known Central Asiatic species, possibly not in cultivation at present. It is a small plant only 5–10cm high with narrow arching leaves. The flowers are only 3.0–3.5cm across and are said to be translucent green, suffused violet with a whitish crest which is much-dissected, almost like a beard. The haft of the falls is not winged. It is a native of Uzbekistan.

I. tadschikorum   This is another of the little-known Central Asiatic species which I have not yet flowered from seed sent several years ago. It is short; the stem only 5cm at flowering time and concealed by the leaves which are packed at its base. There are up to four pale violet flowers with a dissected white crest on the falls which have an unwinged haft. It occurs in the Pamir-Alai Mountains.

I. tauri   See **I. stenophylla**, see under **I. persica**

I. tubergeniana   An attractive species which was in cultivation for at least 50 years but is probably now lost. It is a stocky leafy plant 10–15cm in height with broad glossy green leaves concealing the stem. The one or two large flowers are yellow with a beard-like crest on the falls, the haft of which has no wide wing. It is from the Syr Darya range in Soviet Central Asia.

I. vvedenskyi is also a short yellow-flowered species from the Pamir-Alai range. It is little known and not in cultivation. The crest of the falls is said to be toothed and the haft is narrow and unwinged. From the description it sounds as if the flowers are smaller than those of *I. tubergeniana* and the leaves are narrower.

I. vicaria   This was for many years confused with *I. magnifica*, but the true plant has now been introduced and they are certainly not similar. It is of medium to tall slender habit (20–50cm) with the leaves spaced out up the stem and several flowers in the upper axils. These are about 4–5cm across and pale bluish-violet, or nearly white, with a yellow blotch in the centre of the falls around the very prominent paler crest; the haft is unwinged, unlike that of *I. magnifica*, which is very widely winged. It seems to be fairly widespread in the mountains of Soviet Central Asia and has appeared several times in recent years in collections of seed and bulbs from the area. It appears to be fairly easy to cultivate and worth trying in the open garden in well drained sunny positions.

I. vvedenskyi   See under **I. tubergeniana**

I. warleyensis   A lovely species, which has been in cultivation since 1902 and which is relatively easy to please, probably in similar open sunny positions where *I. magnifica* and *I. bucharica* would grow, although I have not yet tried it outside; it certainly does very well in a bulb frame. It is 20–45cm in height with several leaves spaced out up the stem and up to five flowers in the upper axils. These are colourful, with a pale violet or lavender ground colour with a deep violet blotch on the blade of the falls, which have a bright yellow, very prominent, crest; the haft is not winged. It is Central Asiatic, from the Pamir-Alai range, where I have had the pleasure of seeing it in large numbers on rocky hillsides.
    I. 'Warlsind' is said to be a hybrid between this and *I. aucheri*; it is similar to *I. warleyensis* in appearance.

I. wendelboi   This is named after a great friend, Per Wendelbo, who studied the Afghan and Iranian floras and with whom I had the honour of collaborating on a study of Irises from the region. It is only 10cm in height, with three or four narrow grey-green leaves, curled on the ground or strongly arching. The flowers are deep clear violet with a golden yellow crest on the falls, which have an unwinged haft. It is a native of S.W. Afghanistan and was introduced from there by Chris (Kit) Grey-Wilson and Tom Hewer, but was always very rare in cultivation and may now have been lost.

I. willmottiana   A lovely species, in cultivation since the nineteenth century but very rare now. It is a short but robust plant, 15–25cm in height, with the broad glossy leaves tightly packed together at the base at flowering time. The four to six large flowers, 6–7cm across, are pale lavender-blue with a large white area on the falls around the creamy crest, which has dark violet lines and blotches alongside it; the haft is winged. It comes from the Pamir-Alai Mountains, like so many of the more impressive Junos. Although seldom seen, it does not seem to be difficult to grow and I suspect that it will flourish in an open sunny well-drained position. As yet I have not had enough to risk the experiment. There is a so-called 'white form' in cultivation, which I think may be a form of *I. bucharica*, but there is also a rare albino of the true species.
    I. kuschakewiczii from the Tien Shan Mountains looks almost identical, and the plants which have flowered in cultivation under this name appear to be just slightly smaller versions of *I. willmottiana*.

I. xanthochlora   See under **I. kopetdagensis**

I. zaprjagajewii   See under *I. nicolai*

I. zenaidae   See under *I. magnifica*

Ixiolirion

A small genus of Middle Eastern bulbs which have been pushed about from family to family until the only logical solution seems to be to recognize the Ixioliriaceae! There are between two and four species, but a lack of knowledge of two of these prevents any decisions being made at present about their authenticity. Only one is in general cultivation, *I. tataricum*, and this is most attractive in the wild, but seldom does well in cultivation. Its bulbs should be planted deeply in a position where they will be warm and dry in summer.

I. tataricum (I. pallasii, I. montanum)   The bulbs have brown tunics and give rise to linear basal leaves early in the year; the flower stems reach 20–40cm in height and carry more leaves and several flowers, normally in early summer. They are bluish-violet, funnel-shaped with a short tube and are about 3–5cm in length, several of them carried in an umbel, often also with a few others on branches below the umbel. It is widespread in Asia, from Turkey to the USSR, east of the Caspian and as far as Kashmir, growing in fields and rocky places.

   I. kolpakowskianum has shorter paler flowers with no tube; it occurs only in central Asiatic USSR.

Lapiedra

A monotypic genus in the Amaryllidaceae, of interest to bulb enthusiasts but of no great beauty and with short-lived flowers, so that it is unlikely to become widely known as a garden plant.

L. martinezii   The Daffodil-like bulbs produce strap-shaped dark green leaves through autumn, winter and spring, after the flowers. After summer dormancy the leafless inflorescence appears in early autumn, an umbel on stems to 15cm of small white flowers which open out flat, with six free segments; each one lasts only about a day, but they are produced in succession. It is a native of Spain and Morocco, in rocky places.

   Although it is apparently fairly hardy, its bulbs require a warm dormancy in summer to induce them to flower, so it is best to grow *L. martinezii* in a pot in the alpine house.

Leontice

Only one species of this unusual member of the Berberis family is cultivated, and this is very rarely seen, although common enough in the wild. It has a very large cork-like tuber deep in the soil, and this rests in a dormant state through the later summer months, producing leaves and flowers in spring and early summer. In cultivation it requires a warm sunny situation, planted at least 20cm deep. It flowers more reliably in a bulb

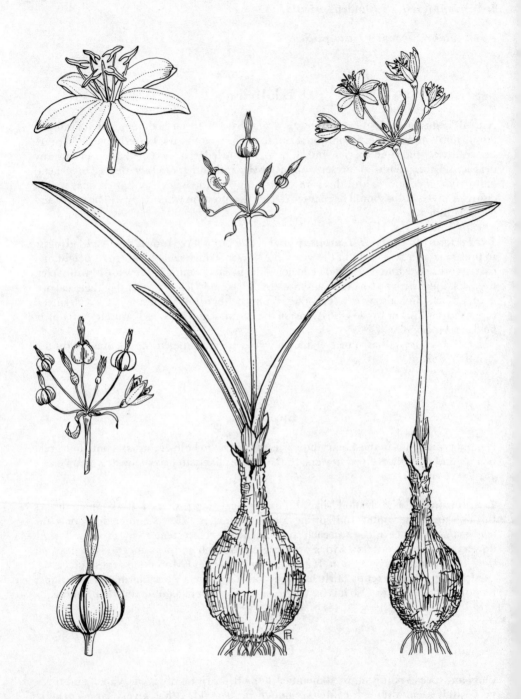

LAPIEDRA MARTINEZII

frame in areas which have cooler summers. Propagation is by seed, which takes several years to produce flowering-sized tubers.

L. leontopetalum   The tuber may be as much as 10cm in diameter, producing grey-green many-lobed leaves and a large branched inflorescence 20–80cm in height, which carries many small six-petalled yellow flowers followed by inflated capsules up to 3cm long. It occurs in the Balkans and N. Africa eastwards to Iran, often in open fields.

Subsp. *ewersmannii* is occasionally seen in cultivation and is very similar, but has narrower leaflets and smaller capsules. Soviet Central Asia, Iran, Afghanistan and Pakistan.

L. armenaica (*L. minor*) is a much more attractive plant which I saw in Iran many years ago but unfortunately no longer possess. It is a genuine dwarf, usually 10–20cm, with an unbranched flower stem and short-stemmed leaves carried near ground level. Iran, N. Iraq, S. Caucasus.

Leucojum

A small genus of beautiful Amaryllids, probably most closely related to the Snowdrops, but clearly differing in their six equal perianth segments – not three large outer and three small inner as in Galanthus. They are mostly white-flowered (but pink in *L. roseum*) and they are either autumn- or spring-flowering. The small species are on the whole best grown in an alpine house or bulb frame, but the robust *L. vernum* and *L. aestivum* are tough garden plants for damp soils.

Key to Leucojum species

A   Flowering in winter, spring or early summer .... B
    Flowering in autumn.. I
B   Flowers small, white or pink, less than 1cm diameter, stem solid . C
    Flowers large, white with green or yellow tips to segments, stem
      hollow... H
C   Outer three perianth segments with a sharp or thickened point at
      apex... D
    Outer three segments not furnished with a point.................. F
D   Leaves 6–8mm wide...................................... *L. fontianum*
    Leaves 2.5mm or less wide.. E
E   Pedicel up to 4cm long, flowers two to four .... *L. trichophyllum*
    Pedicel less than 2cm long, flower often single.......... *L. nicaeense*
F   Pedicel up to 4.4cm long, leaves usually shorter than scape ...... *L. tingitanum*
    Pedicel up to 2.5cm, leaves usually longer than scape .... *L. longifolium*
H   Flowering in winter to early spring; a short plant with one to two
      flowers per stem.. *L. vernum*
    Flowering in late spring or early summer, a tall plant with two to
      five flowers per stem .... *L. aestivum*
I   Flowers wholly pink.................................... *L. roseum*
    Flowers white, sometimes flushed pink at base .... J
J   Perianth segments furnished with sharp, thickened points at
      apex... *L. valentinum*
    Perianth segments with no such points at apex, usually blunt
      with 3 shallow notches .... *L. autumnale*

L. aestivum   Summer Snowflake, Loddon Lily. This blooms later than *L. vernum* but is
by no means a summer plant, usually flowering in April and May. It has a daffodil-like
bulb and long strap-shaped green leaves. The flower stems can reach 90cm in really
vigorous forms, bearing umbels of pendent bells, white with green tips to the segments;
each is about 3–4cm in diameter. It is a widespread species from Europe, including
S. Britain and Ireland east to the Caucasus, growing in moist meadows.

Var. *pulchellum* (*L. hernandezii*) from the Balearic Islands and Sardinia has smaller
flowers, a smaller capsule and is said to flower slightly earlier than var. *aestivum*.

The natural variation in *L. aestivum* means that some forms are better than others from
the garden point of view, and one of the best is 'Gravetye Giant' from the Sussex garden
of William Robinson.

L. aestivum is a fine plant for a damp position and does particularly well on clay soils,
increasing rapidly into clumps.

L. autumnale   A graceful little autumnal species with slender stems 10–15cm tall,
carrying one to four small white pendent bells in which the outer segments are toothed at
the apex; the leaves appear shortly after and are filiform. It differs from other species by
having only one spathe subtending the flowers – although a var. *diphyllum* with two
spathes has been described from the Atlas Mountains. It is a native of rocky places in
Portugal, Spain, Sardinia, Sicily and N. Africa. Flowering September–October.

Some forms produce seeds freely while others increase by bulb division rapidly and
produce seeds rarely. It grows best in light soils, in a sheltered position in full sun.

Var. *pulchellum* from N. Africa has three-toothed outer and acute inner perianth
segments, leaves present at flowering time and the pedicels arching over at the apex; var.
oporanthum from the Rif Mountains has both the outer and inner segments three-toothed,
leaves absent and the pedicels arching from the middle or base.

L. fontianum   This is a little-known species from North Africa, probably not in
cultivation. It is described as having four to five leaves produced with the flowers in April
and they are 6–8mm wide which makes them rather wider than most of the small-
flowered species. The 10–12cm stems carry two spathes and four white flowers
1.0–1.5cm long, which have a sharp point on the tips of the segments. In most respects it
seems to resemble *L. nicaeense* but F.C. Stern in 'Snowdrops and Snowflakes' considered
it to be a robust form of *L. tingitanum*.

L. hiemale   See **L. nicaeense**

L. longifolium   In overall appearance this resembles *L. autumnale* but is spring-
flowering. Its slender leaves overtop the small white flowers, which lack sharp tips to the
segments (unlike *L. nicaeense* and *L. trichophyllum*). It is a native of Corsica in rocky places
below 1000m and is not very hardy, requiring alpine house or bulb frame treatment in
cold districts.

L. nicaeense (L. hiemale)   The best of the small spring species, easy to grow and
hardier than most. The flower stems reach about 10cm in height and carry one or two
white flowers, which have sharp tips to the perianth segments. The leaves are present at
flowering time and are dark green with a greyish 'bloom'. It is a native of S. France and
Monaco on rocky hillsides and blooms in early spring. Although hardy in a sheltered
sunny position it is seen best in the alpine house or bulb frame on account of its size.

L. roseum   This is like a shorter version of *L. autumnale* but with lovely pale pink flowers subtended by two spathes; the slender greyish-green leaves appear just after flowering, which is in early autumn or even late summer. Seeds are produced freely. In frosty districts it is best grown in the shelter of an alpine house where its delicacy can be more closely appreciated. It grows wild in Corsica and Sardinia in dryish rocky or sandy places.

L. tingitanum   A spring-flowering species with four to five small white flowers on long nodding pedicels on a scape up to 45cm tall. It resembles *L. longifolium*, but the linear leaves are shorter than the flowering stem. It is a native of Morocco and Tangier below 1500m, so is not very hardy in cultivation and is also very rare.

L. trichophyllum   In general appearance this resembles *L. autumnale*, but has two spathes subtending the flowers. The filiform leaves are about equal to the scape, which is usually 10–25cm tall. There are two to four flowers and these may be white or pink; one form given to me by Paul Christian is a good pink; the perianth segments have sharp tips but are not toothed. It is wild in Spain, Portugal, Morocco and Tangier, in sandy places.

It flowers in winter or very early spring and is best grown in the alpine house and given a long warm dryish period during its summer dormancy. It tends to divide up into many non-flowering bulbs, but this can be discouraged by planting the bulbs deeply, near the bottom of 'long tom' pots, or at a depth of 15cm or so in a bulb frame.

There are several subspecies, varieties and forms noted by Maire in *Flore de L'Afrique du Nord*: forma *broteri*, white or pale pink flowers less than 2cm long; f. *purpurascens*, flowers pink, stained purple at the base, less than 2cm long; var. *grandiflorum*, flowers white, 2.0–2.5cm long; ssp. *micranthum* flowers white, only 7–12mm long.

L. valentinum   Another of the small white autumnal species which is superficially similar to *L. autumnale* but is in fact more closely related to the spring-flowering *L. nicaeense*. The perianth segments are 11–14mm long and are furnished with sharp points (at least the outer ones) and there are two spathes present. Like *L. nicaeense* there is a six-lobed disc situated at the base of the ovary, a feature which *L. autumnale* does not possess. It has a curious distribution in Spain near Valencia and in the Ionian islands of Levkas and Kefallinia, where it occurs in sunny rocky places. Plants from Kefallinia were known in the nineteenth century and provisionally named *Acis cephalonica* by J. Gay, but it has now been shown that they belong to the same species as those from Valencia.

A bulb given to me by Prof. J. Damboldt has flowered and increased well in the last few years and, although this species probably requires the protection of an alpine house it is a delightful and easily-cultivated autumn bulb.

L. vernum   Spring Snowflake. This is one of the best and most useful species, easy to grow in sun or semi-shade, especially in damp places and in grass. It flowers in winter or early spring, along with the Snowdrops, and has one or two large flowers per 10–20cm stem, accompanied by the glossy green strap-shaped leaves which elongate later. The pure white bell-like flowers are tipped green, or yellow in var. *carpathicum*. Var. *vagneri* is robust, with two flowers per stem. It is a native of south and east Europe, in dampish meadows or woods.

Lloydia

A fairly large genus in the Lily family but almost unknown (and not easy) in cultivation. All the species are natives to the northern hemisphere with one, *L. serotina*, very widespread, from the Arctic to the Alps. They are all tiny, slender plants with bell-shaped semi-pendent flowers. The best chance of success seems to be in a cool, gritty-peaty soil mixture with moisture available through the summer, since these are winter-dormant, summer-growing plants. The Mediterranean species *L. graeca* is now considered to be a *Gagea*.

L. flavonutans   This delightful little plant is just about in cultivation from material introduced by the Alpine Garden Society's expedition to Sikkim. It is less than 15cm in height with thread-like leaves and small deep yellow bells, almost like a little yellow Fritillary. It is a native of peaty turf in the eastern Himalaya, where it receives summer monsoon rainfall.

L. serotina   This has small elongated bulbs, producing two slender basal leaves and wiry 5–15cm stems carrying one, sometimes two widely bell-shaped white flowers about 1.0–1.5cm long, conspicuously purple-veined. Widespread in rock crevices in European mountains, and throughout the Arctic, and also a rare British native in N. Wales.

In addition to these there are several others, especially in the Himalaya and China, which are beautiful plants but not, unfortunately, in cultivation.

Merendera

This small genus will be found in most recent literature separated from *Colchicum*, although some botanists, for example Dr Karin Persson of Goteborg, regard the two as inseparable. The species are very Colchicum-like, but differ in that they have no proper tube to the flower – the six segments being separate from each other. They are on the whole not very showy and are best grown in a bulb frame or alpine house, where their smallish flowers are protected from the elements and can be seen at close range.

The bulbs are elongated with a 'toe' at the base, just like those of a *Colchicum*, and the leaves also are similar to the spring-flowering Colchicums; there are no autumnal Merenderas which produce leafless flowers followed by very large leaves, although this type of growth is quite common in Colchicum and gives us some of the best species for the garden. With some of the small spring-flowering species such as *M. trigyna* it is not easy to tell at a glance whether the plant is a Merendera or a Colchicum, so similar are they, but a check on whether there is a tube or not will clarify matters. *M. montana* (*M. bulbo-codium*) is the only species in general cultivation but there are several others of interest to the specialist. The Ethiopian species *M. longifolia* and *M. abyssinica* are, understandably, not hardy.

M. attica   A late autumn-flowering species with narrowly linear leaves, produced with the white or pale pink flowers which have very narrow perianth segments; these fall apart very easily in windy weather and in consequence it often looks a mess in the wild! The flowers rest on the ground and are about 3–4cm in diameter, several per corm, with blackish anthers. Greece and W. Turkey, in open stony areas.

M. androcymbioides from S.W. Spain is very similar but has yellow anthers.

M. filifolia   An attractive little species, but one which I do not find easy to cultivate. It has thread-like leaves, appearing after the flowers which come in early autumn. These are produced at ground level, about 4–5cm across and bright pinkish-purple. The corms require a good warm dry rest period in summer. Balearic Islands, N. Africa and S. France, in stony places at low altitudes.

M. kurdica The most showy species and very rare in cultivation. Thanks to Erich Pasche I have grown this handsome plant but find it surprisingly tender, even in a bulb frame. It has the broadest leaves of any species, up to 4cm wide at maturity, but fairly short at flowering time. The bright pink flowers, produced in spring, have wide segments, giving a substantial appearance and a diameter of about 4–6cm. It is a native of S.E. Turkey on mountain slopes.

M. montana (M. bulbocodium, M. pyrenaica) This is the best-known and most easily obtainable species, which is a pleasing little early-autumn flowering bulb for the alpine house or sunny rock garden. The large widely funnel-shaped flowers rest on the ground, about 4–6cm in diameter, in bright rosy-lilac with a white centre, followed shortly by the narrowly linear leaves in a rosette. It is a native of meadows and rocky slopes in the Pyrenees, Spain and Portugal.

M. robusta (M. aitchisonii, M. persica) A vigorous species, but not very attractive, having three to six erect linear leaves, together with untidy pink or white flowers which have very narrow segments, falling apart to spoil the 'wine glass' shape which is so characteristic of most Colchicums and their relatives. It is spring flowering and comes from N. Afghanistan and adjacent USSR and Iran.

M. hissarica from the same general area differs most obviously in having two leaves per corm.

M. sobolifera A rather insignificant dwarf species which spreads by means of horizontal stolon-like corms, very easy to cultivate in the alpine house or frame. It has linear leaves and small white flowers with narrow segments only 1.5cm or so long. It is widespread from S.E. Europe to Afghanistan in meadows.

M. trigyna (M. caucasica) One of the more attractive species, very widespread and variable and looking very like *Colchicum szovitsii* in the wild, but it has, of course, no perianth tube. Its funnel-shaped flowers appear in spring, together with the narrow leaves which are usually three per corm, and they are most frequently rosy-lilac with rather narrow segments, about 3–5cm in height. It occurs in Turkey, Iran and the Caucasus on hillsides and is best cultivated in the alpine house or frame, where its corms can be dried out in summer.

M. raddeana looks very similar to this but has two leaves per corm. E. Turkey.

Moraea

This large genus may be regarded as the African equivalent of Iris, for the flowers are very similar in structure, although on the whole are rather smaller. The underground part consists of a corm which is covered by fibrous coats, or tunics, whereas Irises have rhizomes or, in the case of some groups, bulbs. The species, which are about a hundred in number, may be conveniently divided into those which occur in the winter rainfall area of the S.W. Cape and those which occur in the summer rainfall Eastern Cape region, including Lesotho. The Tropical African species can be added to the latter, since in cultivation in cooler climates they tend to behave as summer growing plants, although in their native haunts they have wet or dry seasons rather than summer versus winter. Since this book is devoted to hardy bulbs for temperate climates, all the S.W. Cape species must be excluded. They are fascinating plants and many of them are beautiful, but they are not at all hardy and I grow them in a greenhouse kept at about 10°C (50°F). The Tropical African species are very poorly known in cultivation and are of course very tender, so these too can be discounted for the purposes of this book. It is therefore the E. Cape ones which offer us the best garden plants for temperate gardens, of which unfortunately only a few have been introduced, and these are mostly among the taller ones suitable for the summer border. The metre-high yellow *M. spathulata* (*M. spathacea*) is quite well known in cultivation, and the similarly easy *M. huttonii*, also yellow-flowered, is becoming more widespread since it produces such large quantities of seed.

Of the smaller species only one is known to any extent, *M. stricta*, and this is really only in the hands of a few specialists. Obviously this is a genus which would repay further investigation as a source of garden plants.

M. stricta (M. trita)   This dwarf species has been in cultivation a considerable time, possibly since the 1930s when Mrs Milford introduced some interesting plants from the Drakensberg Mountains, including *Rhodohypoxis*. *M. stricta* is a good alpine house plant, only 5–10cm in height with one rush-like basal leaf and a succession of small purple flowers which have a golden splash of colour in the centre of the three outer segments (called 'falls' in an *Iris*). They are flattish and about 3cm across, large for the size of the plant.

Muilla

In case anyone has not noticed, this is *Allium* spelled backwards! This is an indication of its allegiance to the *Brodiaea–Triteleia* group of genera, which in turn is related to the onions. *Muilla* is a small North American genus, interesting but not of great garden value and best grown in a bulb frame in order to ripen the bulbs in summer. The flowers, as is typical of the group, are carried in umbels in spring or early summer.

M. maritima   This is the most likely one to be encountered. It is 10–15cm in height when in flower, with a tuft of very narrowly linear basal leaves and several flower stems per bulb. These carry small hemispherical umbels, rather loose with 5–35 flowers each about 1cm across, greenish-white with blue or green anthers; the filaments are thread-like, and not fused together at the base. California, especially coastal regions, south to northern Baja California.

M. coronata from the Mojave Desert, California has the filaments wide and flattened giving a corona-like appearance in the centre of the flower.

M. transmontana has white flowers with the filaments wider than in *M. maritima* and they are united at the base. E. California, W. Nevada.

Muscari

The Grape Hyacinths are a comparatively large group of species, rather difficult to distinguish in many cases until the salient features are pointed out. They have true bulbs, giving rise to one to several basal leaves which in general are fairly narrow and linear,

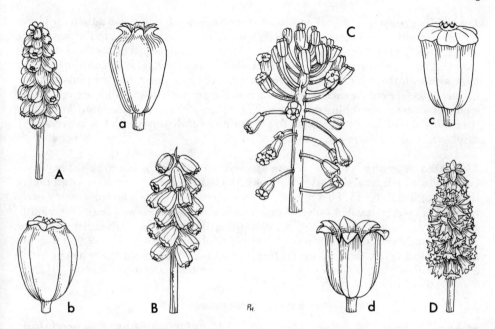

MUSCARI

Various types of Muscari *:* (A) *Typical* Muscari *with inflated flowers constricted at the mouth, the Grape Hyacinth* (B) M. macrocarpum *of the Muscarimia group with a corona surrounding the minute 'teeth' of the perianth segments* (C) *A Leopoldia type of Muscari,* M. comosum, *showing the tuft of up-turned sterile flowers at the apex* (D) M. azureum, *representing the Pseudomuscari group with bell-like flowers not constricted at the mouth*

although there are exceptions. The flowers are carried in dense to loose racemes. The species can be divided into fairly distinct groups which have been distinguished as separate genera by some authorities, or as subgenera or sections by others. Hence names such as *Muscarimia, Botryanthus, Leopoldia* and *Pseudomuscari* will be found in literature. Here I have kept these together under *Muscari* but have grouped them, with an explanation of the salient features of each group, and with notes about cultivation since the various groups do not need exactly the same treatment.

The four groups are as follows:

Botryanthus group (p. 126) (the true Grape Hyacinths)   These all have pale blue to blackish-blue flowers (apart from the occasional albinos), usually globose to obovoid in shape, with a very constricted mouth; they are carried in racemes which are compact and dense with the flowers almost touching, although they may become spaced out later on. The colour of the perianth lobes ('teeth') should be noted. These are mostly easy to cultivate and include some of the best-known species such as *M. armeniacum* and *M. neglectum*. They flower in early spring.

Pseudomuscari group (p. 127)   These have, like the above, flowers in shades of blue, often pale or rather bright blue, and are mostly smallish plants with fairly densely flowered racemes. The characteristic feature is that the bell-shaped perianth is not constricted at the mouth. They are also early spring-flowering and easily cultivated.

Leopoldia group (p. 128)   These are on the whole much taller plants than the above two groups, with the flowers more widely spaced on the raceme. The fertile flowers are longer, usually urn-shaped or tubular with angular 'shoulders' just below the constricted mouth. The colour is usually some shade of whitish, yellowish, greenish or brown, never blue, although there is often a conspicuous tuft of bright violet, blue or pinkish sterile flowers at the apex of the raceme. The colour of the perianth lobes, which are very small, is important in distinguishing the species. The species of the Leopoldia group flower later than those of the above two groups, in late spring or early summer. They are relatively easy to cultivate in warm sunny situations.

Muscarimia group (p. 130)   There are only two species in this group. They have large bulbs with thick fleshy perennial roots which delve down into the rocky ground of their natural habitat in Turkey and the east Aegean region. The stout stems carry racemes of large elongated flowers, which have six projections just below the mouth, giving a corona-like effect. They have a strong fragrance and are either yellow or whitish, faintly tinged green or blue, with brown lobes which are so small that they are more like small teeth. Since they come from hot sunbaked hillsides they are best grown in a bulb frame or alpine house in a deep pot to accommodate the strong roots.

Botryanthus group

M. armeniacum (M. cyaneo-violaceum, ?M. dolychanthum, ?M. pendulum, M. polyanthum, M. sosnovskyi, M. steupii, M. szovitsianum, M. woronowii)
One of the most commonly cultivated species, of robust habit and increasing well. It is about 10–30cm in height with several long narrow channelled linear leaves, often grey-green above, and long densely flowered racemes of bright blue flowers which have whitish lobes. It is widespread in woods and meadows from Greece and Yugoslavia, east through Turkey to the Caucasus. Some selections have been named including 'Blue Spike', a double-flowered form making a very solid massive blue inflorescence, and a paler blue form called 'Cantab'. I have collected a white form in Turkey which is also quite attractive.

M. aucheri (M. lingulatum, M. sintenisii)   A charming species, easy to grow but not increasing very rapidly. It is usually not more than 10 cm but taller forms do exist and the plant grown as *M. lingulatum* is one such vigorous variant; *M. tubergianum* is also very similar and is either a very robust form or perhaps a hybrid of it with *M. armeniacum*. *M. aucheri* usually has only two or three rather wide leaves, grey-green on the upper surface with a hooded apex. The dense raceme has almost spherical or obovoid flowers in very bright blue with whitish lobes and is topped by a cluster of small paler ones, sometimes almost white, giving an attractive bicoloured effect to the raceme. It is a native of Turkey in alpine turf.

M. botryoides (M. heldreichii)   This is much less invasive than the common *M. neglectum* (below) and is rather more attractive. It has only two to three leaves per bulb, usually greyish-green and narrowly oblanceolate with a hooded apex. The 5–15cm stems carry dense racemes (elongating with age) of bright blue flowers which are almost spherical with white recurving lobes. C. and S.E. Europe, especially in the Balkans, growing in light woods and mountain meadows. I also have an attractive white form of this.
   M. longifolium and *M. kerneri* are narrow-leaved forms from Italy.
   M. lelievrii from C. France has a raceme which stays compact.

M. bourgaei   A distinctive little species with several very narrow leaves with a white stripe along the centre. The flower stem reaches only 5–10cm with short (2–3cm long) racemes of deep blue or violet blue obovoid flowers which have whitish lobes and a very constricted mouth. It is not difficult to grow but increases only very slowly. W. Turkey in alpine meadows.

M. *microstomum* from C. Turkey also has a white line on its narrow leaves. It is a taller plant, up to 20cm, and the flowers are a deep china blue, carried in dense racemes up to 8cm long.

M. commutatum   A distinctive species, because the flowers are blackish-violet with the lobes the same colour as the rest of the flower. It is 5–15cm in height with several narrowly linear basal leaves. The flowers are carried in dense racemes and are elongated, obovoid in shape with squarish 'shoulders' and a very constricted mouth. E. Mediterranean, especially S. and W. Turkey and the Balkans in rocky places.

M. latifolium   This is unusual in having usually one, rarely two, wide leaves (1–3cm) per bulb. The flower stems are rather tall, 15–30cm, and have long dense racemes of oblong blackish-violet flowers with a strongly constricted mouth and paler lilac lobes; the upper sterile flowers are much paler. W. and S. Turkey on slopes and in light woods.

M. neglectum (M. atlanticum, M. bucharicum, M. elwesii, M. leucostomum, M. racemosum)   The common Grape Hyacinth, which is sometimes too invasive in small gardens because of the many offsets which the bulbs produce. It has several very narrowly linear leaves, which have the margins rolled inwards, and 5–20cm tall stems – bearing dense racemes of very dark blue to blackish-blue ovoid-oblong flowers which, have white lobes. There is often a conspicuous cluster of paler sterile flowers at the apex. It is an extremely widespread species in a variety of habitats throughout Europe and eastwards through western Asia to the USSR.

M. *pulchellum* is the name given to very dwarf deep blue-flowered forms from Crete and possibly also other parts of Greece and S. Turkey. With me, these do not increase invasively by offsets.

M. *grandifolium* is probably related to M. *neglectum* – with its blackish-violet flowers with whitish teeth – but they are large, 6–8mm in length, and the greyish leaves are much wider, 0.5–1.5cm wide. N. Africa, in the Atlas and Rif Mountains.

M. *stenanthum* is a very rare species from Libya which has deep blue flowers and is clearly allied to M. *neglectum* – but the flowers are said to be almost cylindrical, not ellipsoid or ovoid like most species of this group.

Pseudomuscari group

M. azureum (Pseudomuscari azureum)   One of the most popular little Muscari species, often called *Hyacinthus azureus* in catalogues. It is only 4–15cm in height with two or three greyish oblanceolate leaves and dense racemes of up to 60 small (4–5mm long) bell-shaped flowers in bright sky blue, with a darker stripe along each lobe. Like all members of this group they are not constricted at the mouth like most Grape Hyacinths. There is also a white form, 'Album' in cultivation. This is a delightful plant for the rock garden or for planting between shrubs at the front of a border. N. and E. Turkey in alpine meadows.

M. *pseudomuscari* (M. *chalusicum*) is very similar but has longer leaves, often coiling on the ground, and dense racemes of larger flowers in a bright mid-blue. It is one of the best plants introduced by the Bowles Scholarship Expedition to Iran in 1963, of which I was a member, and is still thriving in my collection in an open sunny situation. N. Iran in rock crevices and light woodland.

M. coeleste is difficult to distinguish from *M. azureum*. It has a somewhat looser raceme of not more than 25 flowers which are suberect. N.E. Turkey.

M. pallens is a small alpine plant of the Caucasus similar to *M. azureum* but with very pale blue to almost white flowers with a slight constriction at the throat. I have received several colour forms collected in the Caucasus by Janis Ruksans, but some of these are very robust and darker-flowered and I suspect they may be hybrids with *M. armeniacum*.

M. caeruleum from the Caucasus is one I have not seen; it is described as having only a few blue 5mm long flowers with white lobes. *M. azureum* has lobes the same colour as the rest of the flower, but the two species must otherwise be very similar.

M. apertum is also one I have not seen but from its description it is obviously related to *M. azureum*. It has small pale blue flowers only 4mm long. Caucasus.

M. turkewiczii, described from N.E. Turkey, is said to have violet flowers 7mm long but otherwise seems to be very similar to *M. azureum*.

M. discolor   This is little-known in cultivation. It is only about 5–10 cm in height with narrow linear basal leaves and short dense racemes of blackish-blue bell-shaped flowers which have a distinct white rim at the apex, as well as the white lobes; they are only very slightly constricted at the mouth, or not at all. A most attractive species. E. Turkey.

M. inconstrictum   An easily recognized species since it has very dark violet-blue flowers, often appearing blackish-blue, with the lobes the same colour, not whitish as in other species. It is about 10–15cm in height with very narrowly linear leaves. Cyprus and S. Turkey east to Iran in rocky places.

M. parviflorum (M. autumnale)   This is the only autumn-flowering Muscari but is unfortunately not very striking and is really only of interest as an alpine-house or bulb-frame plant. It reaches 10–20cm in height with almost thread-like leaves produced at flowering time and a small loose raceme of five to twelve flowers only 2–3mm long. They are almost bell shaped, very slightly constricted, and are pale to sky blue with paler or whitish lobes. It is widespread in the Mediterranean region but not easy to find, being small and autumn-flowering and growing amongst scrub.

Leopoldia group

M. comosum (Leopoldia comosa, L. charrelii, L. cousturieri, L. curtum, L. holzmannii, L. trojana, Muscari pharmacusanum)   The Tassle Hyacinth – so called because of the tassle of long-stalked sterile flowers at the apex of the inflorescence. It is a tallish species, 20–60cm, with several long-tapering basal leaves and long loose racemes of urn-shaped flowers 5–10mm long. The colour of the fertile flowers when mature is pale brown with cream or beige lobes; the upper smaller sterile flowers are bright violet, on long violet stalks up to 3cm long. I also have a white form which has a tuft of brownish sterile flowers, not an attractive plant! *M. comosum* is a widespread and common species in southern Europe, eastwards to Turkey and Iran, often in fields.

There is a cultivated form known as 'Monstrosum' or 'Plumosum', in which the flowers have all become sterile and transformed in branching purple threads, so that the whole inflorescence forms a feathery purple mass.

M. caucasicum (Leopoldia caucasua) is very similar in appearance and flower colour but the sterile flowers are as long as the fertile ones, and are longer than the shortish pedicels which carry them. The leaves are abruptly narrowed at the tip. It has a more eastern distribution in E. Turkey, the Caucasus and N.W. Iran.

M. cycladicum (Leopoldia cycladica)   This is one of a group of species which are similar to *M. comosum* but have brownish or greenish flowers with bright yellow perianth lobes or 'teeth'. They are mostly smaller more slender plants than *M. comosum* and are little-known in cultivation, at most in the hands of a few enthusiasts. In *M. cycladicum* the fertile flowers are carried directly on the main stem, without pedicels. Cyclades in rocky places.

The following also have yellow lobes to the flowers.

M. gussonei (*Leopoldia gussonei*), from S. Italy and Sicily, has the fertile flowers on very short pedicels, less than 1.5mm long.

M. weissii (*M. theraeum, Leopoldia theraea, L. weissii*) has pedicels up to 1cm long and always more than 2mm. S.E. Greece, Crete, S.W. Turkey.

M. dionysicum (*Leopoldia dionysica*) occurs only on certain very small islands in the Aegean Sea; it is like *M. weissii* but has even longer pedicels to the fertile flowers, 1.0–2.5cm long.

M. spreitzenhoferi (*M. amoenocomum, M. creticum, Leopoldia spreitzenhoferi*) has, like *M. weissii*, longer pedicels but may be distinguished from the latter by having few sterile flowers, or none at all (many in *M. weissii*). Crete and Algeria.

M. maritimum (*Leopoldia maritima*) also has flowers with bright yellow perianth lobes but the rest of the flower is yellowish as well, whereas in the above species they are greenish or brownish at maturity. The pedicels are about 5–7mm long, the leaves narrow (5mm or less) and the sterile flowers are on very short pedicels. Unlike other 'Leopoldias' the anthers are held just within the mouth of the flower near the lobes, not down inside the tube. It comes from Tunisia, Algeria and Morocco in rocky places.

M. longipes (Leopoldia longipes)   A robust species with several long linear grey-green basal leaves, which are often twisted, and flower stems 20–60cm in height with up to 200 flowers in a loose raceme; these are oblong, about 7–12mm long and carried on pedicels which are 2cm or more in length, elongating rapidly after the flowers are fertilized to 4–9cm; the fruiting head can thus be 8–18cm in diameter. The colour of the lower fertile flowers is mauve or pale brown with blackish perianth lobes, while the upper sterile ones are violet. It is widespread in the Middle East in S.E. Turkey, Syria, Iraq and Iran on open hillsides.

In the bud stage the inflorescence is dense and a bright blue-violet; this prompted Paul and Polly Furse to christen it the 'Blue Hot Poker' when they saw it in Iran. It needs hot sunny conditions to do well in cultivation.

Subsp. *negevensis* from S. Israel has leaves 2–4cm wide (up to 2cm in subsp. *longipes*).

M. deserticolum (*Leopoldia deserticola*) is related and has similar flower colours, but the pedicels are shorter, elongating to at most 2cm in fruit. Israel, Jordan, Syria.

M. bicolor is also allied to *M. longipes* and has yellowish flowers with blackish lobes but has shorter pedicels, up to 1cm long in the flowering stage. The sterile flowers are rather inflated and in this way it differs from *M. deserticola* which has narrow tubular ones. N. Egypt, Israel, S. Lebanon.

M. eburnea is a curious species with only one leaf per bulb. The flowers, like the above three species, have blackish or dark purple lobes, but the tube is ivory coloured and they are carried on short pedicels only 1–3mm long. S. Israel, Egypt in dry open areas.

M. massayanum   I have a particular affection for this species, since it was one of the plants found on the Mathew-Tomlinson expedition to Turkey in 1965 and this helped to solve the long-standing question of what *M. massayanum* was and where it came from. It has two to four thick-channelled grey-green leaves, often arched or coiled on the ground, and stout stems about 15–20cm tall, carrying a dense raceme of cylindrical flowers on short pedicels 5mm or less long. The colour is pink or purple in the bud stage, changing to greenish-yellow with blackish-brown lobes as they reach their peak. The cluster of sterile flowers at the apex is pink or bright purple-pink. It is a native of S. Turkey in rocky places. I find that its bulbs require a hot summer dormant period to induce them to flower; it is a handsome species for the bulb frame.

M. tenuiflorum (M. alpinum, Leopoldia tenuiflora)   This is the most common of those species which have brown or blackish perianth lobes (as opposed to yellow ones). It has several long narrow basal leaves and 20–60cm stems, bearing long loose racemes of narrowly oblong flowers which are carried on pedicels about 1.0–1.5cm long (rarely a little more); these do not elongate in fruit. The colour of the fertile flowers is violet in bud, changing to ivory or pale brown at the peak of condition, with dark brown or blackish lobes. The upper sterile flowers are bright violet and very conspicuous. A very widespread species in E. and C. Europe, to the Caucasus, Turkey and Iran, often in fields.

Muscarimia group

M. macrocarpum (Muscarimia macrocarpa, M. moschatum var. flavum)   A lovely species, requiring a hot dryish summer if it is to flower well. The large bulbs have thick fleshy roots. It is a stout plant with several channelled grey-green leaves and 10–15cm stems bearing fairly dense racemes of long tubular flowers 1cm or more long which are a dull violet in bud, but yellow when fully open, with brownish lobes. A bonus is the very strong fragrance, a little like bananas. It is a restricted plant in the wild, in E. Crete, the Islands of Amorgos and S.W. Turkey, growing in dry rocky places.

M. muscarimi (M. moschatum, Muscarimia moschata)   This is similar in overall appearance to *M. macrocarpum* but has shorter flowers (7–9mm long) greyish white when fully open, sometimes with a bluish tinge. The scent is like musk. S.W. Turkey in rocky places.

   M. ambrosiacum is sometimes offered in nursery catalogues. This is probably a selected form of *M. muscarimi* with very pale pearly blue flowers.

Narcissus

There is no need to describe the general characteristics of this popular and delightful genus for the various species and their hybrids are known to all who love plants. There are not a great many wild species but most of them hybridize freely so that there is an enormous number of cultivars – thousands in fact have been raised in the past, although at any one time only a proportion of these are to be found in catalogues, and new ones are being raised all the time. A classification of the garden varieties has been made depending upon the shape and size of the corona (cup or trumpet), whether the flower is bicoloured, whether single or double and how many flowers per stem. Some groups refer back to the wild species which played a part in their make-up, for example the Cyclamineus hybrids, based on *N. cyclamineus*. However, here I am concerned with the true wild species and I have included nearly all of them, since there are not too many and

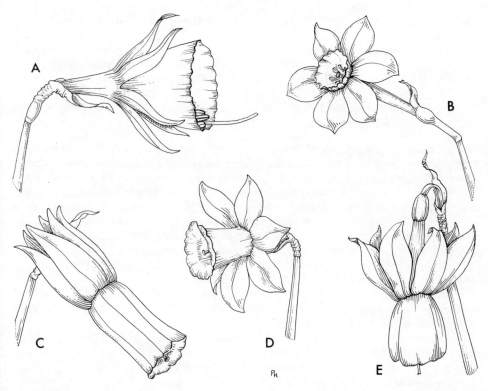

NARCISSUS

Flowers of various Narcissus *to show the wide differences in structure:* (A) N. bulbocodium *group* (B) N. jonquilla *group with a long tube a small cup* (C) N. cyclamineus *with its long trumpet and reflexed segments* (D) *Typical trumpet Daffodil,* N. pseudonarcissus (E) *Pendent flowers with reflexed segments, a characteristic of* N. triandrus

it is difficult to draw the line between short and tall – for there are dwarf variants of the normally larger species such as *N. pseudonarcissus* and *N. tazetta*.

The taxonomy of Narcissus is, to say the least, chaotic, and few genera have been subjected to such varied treatments by botanists from the very 'splitty' to the very 'lumpy', so there is a very variable number of species depending upon which authority one follows. I prefer the type of approach taken in *Flora Europaea* vol. 5, where D. A. Webb took a conservative view and 'lumped' considerably, and I suspect that this is a fairly true state of affairs; that there are rather few species but they are each extremely variable. This ability to vary is the very reason that there are countless garden selections and hybrids today. If one takes a very 'splitty' view of the genus and accepts a large number of species there are almost insurmountable problems in defining them and it seems that however narrow the concept of a species it still overlaps in its characters with the most closely related ones. I well remember Frank Waley, a great Narcissus enthusiast, telling me that standing in an alpine meadow on one occasion in Spain he was either surrounded by *N. bulbocodium* or, if he followed another classification, several related species all mixed up together, such was the extreme variation.

The main area of distribution of Narcissus is in W. Europe and North Africa, especially Spain, Portugal and the Atlas Mountains. A few species occur eastwards as far as Turkey but beyond that there are introduced ones only which have become naturalized.

For further reading there are several accounts, such as *Flora Europaea* 5: (19); F. G. Meyer, 'Narcissus species and wild hybrids' in *American Horticultural Magazine* 45:47–76 (1966): A. Fernandes, 'Key to the identification of native and naturalized taxa of the genus Narcissus L.' in *Daffodil and Tulip Yearbook* 1968, 33: 37–66 (1967), and for a classic, E. A. Bowles, *A Handbook of Narcissus* (1934). The recent *European garden Flora* 1: 301–309 (1986) is also very useful.

N. assoanus (N. requienii, 'N. juncifolius')   A small Jonquil type up to 25cm in height with narrow (1–2mm wide) semi-cylindrical green leaves and one or two fragrant flowers per stem; these are usually deep yellow, 1.4–2.5cm in diameter with a corona (cup) about 1.0–1.5cm in diameter and about 5mm deep. The perianth tube is straight and about 1.5–2cm long. Paler yellow forms have been called *N. pallens*. It is a native of south and east Spain and south-west France. March–April. Although hardy enough, this seems to thrive best as an alpine-house or bulb-frame plant, although it can be grown in a sunny part of the rock garden; it flowers in mid spring.

This has been subjected to a nomenclatural merry-go-round, and is still most likely to be found in catalogues and other literature as '*N. juncifolius*'.

N. gaditanus (*N. minutiflorus*) is related to *N. assoanus* but has thread-like leaves and smaller flowers, with a corona only 4–8mm wide, and a curved perianth tube. Early spring. S. Portugal and S. Spain.

N. fernandesii from S. Portugal is very similar to *N. assoanus*. It differs in having a spathe which is shorter than the pedicel of the flower (if more than one flower, take the longest pedicel). In *N. assoanus* the spathe is longer than the pedicels.

N. cordubensis is a recently described species, said to be more robust than *N. fernandesii*, up to 28cm in height but with prostrate leaves 3–6mm wide. The tube is 21–23cm long and the corona 6mm deep. Cordoba province of Spain.

N. willkommii from S. Spain and S. Portugal; like *N. fernandesii* this has the spathe shorter than the longest pedicel. It has two or three flowers per stem, slightly wider leaves (2–3mm) than in *N. assoanus* and a shorter tube (1.0–1.5cm) than in *N. fernandesii* (1.5–2.3cm).

N. marianicus from Toledo, Spain is very similar to *N. fernandesii* and, since I have not seen it, I feel unable to comment.

N. asturiensis ('N. minimus')   The smallest of the trumpet daffodils and a delightful, very popular, easily cultivated little plant for the rock garden. It is under 10cm in height with two or three narrow grey, strap-shaped leaves and solitary flowers which are deep yellow throughout; the trumpet-shaped corona is about 1.0–1.5cm long, flared out at the mouth and undulate or lobed. It is a native of mountain meadows in Spain and N. Portugal and flowers in early to mid spring.

N. lagoi from N.W. Spain is apparently a very small-flowered variant with taller stems and larger leaves.

N. broussonetii   A seldom-cultivated tallish species, rather tender. It has broad grey-green leaves and up to 12 flattish pure white flowers in an umbel; these are 2–3cm in diameter with a long tube, about 2–3cm long, and appear to be almost without a corona it is so small. It is a native of Morocco and flowers in autumn to winter.

N. bulbocodium   The Hoop Petticoat Daffodil, so called because of the broad funnel-shaped corona with a frilled edge; the six perianth segments are narrow so that it is this wide corona which forms the conspicuous part of the flower. It is distinct from most other

Narcissus species, except for a few closely related ones which have sometimes been treated as variants of it, such as the white *N. cantabricus*.

It is an extremely variable species 5–15cm in height with several narrow dark green leaves, sometimes almost thread-like. The solitary flowers are usually held more or less horizontally and have a corona up to 2.5cm long and a tube up to 2.5cm, so that the largest forms can have flowers 5cm in length. The perianth lobes are usually linear and smaller than the corona and are held out obliquely, usually not spreading widely. The whole group, including this and related species, is distinct in having stamens which curve down towards the lower side of the corona and then turn upwards at the tips. The anthers do not usually project beyond the corona. There is a lot of variation in size and shape of the corona and in the colour, which is in varying shades of yellow from pale sulphur to deep butter-yellow. Various varieties and subspecies have been named and a complex hierarchy exists, which is not entirely convincing!

N. bulbocodium and its variants are superb early-spring flowering bulbs for the alpine house or bulb frame. They can also be grown on the rock garden and some vigorous forms will take to the humus-rich conditions of a peat garden. In the wild, it often grows in mountain turf and it is sometimes successful in gardens growing in grass; the ideal site seems to be a grassy bank where there is plenty of water available in the spring months. The whole group is native to mountain meadows in W. France, Spain, Portugal and North Africa.

Subsp. *bulbocodium* var. *bulbocodium* has deep yellow flowers up to 3.5cm long, carried on a pedicel up to 2cm long. The leaves are very narrow, not more than 1.5mm wide. Widespread.

Subsp. *bulbocodium* var. *conspicuus* is also deep yellow but the flowers are large, more than 3.5cm long with a corona 2cm wide; the pedicels are more than 2cm long and the leaves are up to 2.5mm wide. W. France and Spain.

Subsp. *bulbocodium* var. *serotinus* is even larger than the above with flowers 3.5–5.0cm long and a corona about 3cm wide. The pedicel is more than 2cm long. It has wider leaves up to 4mm and they are usually recurved. W. Portugal. I have not seen this in cultivation.

Subsp. *bulbocodium* var. *nivalis* is usually a much smaller plant only 5–8cm in height with a rather narrow corona. It has the leaves and the scape longitudinally ridged which var. *bulbocodium* has not. The pedicel is less than 2cm long and the flowers less than 3.5cm long. Spain and Morocco.

Subsp. *bulbocodium* var. *citrinus* has large pale yellow flowers in spring, 3.5–5.0 cm long. Spain.

Subsp. *bulbocodium* var. *graellsii* also has pale yellow flowers but they are less than 3.5cm long and the stamens in this case usually protrude beyond the corona. It is a dwarf plant. Spain.

Subsp. *praecox* var. *praecox*, as its name says, is early-flowering, in winter. It is rather robust with pale yellow flowers, the stamens not exserted from the corona. Morocco.

Subsp. *praecox* var. *paucinervis* is like var. *praecox* but the perianth segments have only three nerves, whereas in the latter there are six in each segment. This variant is unknown to me.

Subsp. *obesus* (*N. obesus*) has very narrow (1mm) prostrate leaves often coiling on the ground. The deep yellow flowers have a large corona up to 3.5cm in diameter at the mouth and it is often somewhat constricted at the throat where the segments are attached. Portugal and Morocco. An unpleasant name, but a good vigorous plant!

N. romieuxii is very similar to some forms of *N. bulbocodium* but is distinguished by having a very short pedicel 5mm or less long and stamens normally protruding from the corona. The flowers are pale yellow, rather sulphur coloured in the form most frequently

frequently cultivated but it is variable in the wild. It is very early flowering, often in winter, and is an excellent subject for the alpine house. It is a native of Morocco.

Several variants of this have been given names:

Subsp. *romieuxii* var. *romieuxii* has pale yellow flowers with a spathe like white tissue paper; the pedicel is usually 2–3mm long and the perianth segments are about as long as the corona, or slightly shorter. Var. *mesatlanticus* looks very similar and is probably synonymous. A plant given to me under this name by Mr H. Esslemont has proved to be one of the most vigorous members of this group which I grow, increasing well.

Subsp. *romieuxii* var. *rifanus* is similar but has a brownish violet spathe and the perianth segments are longer than the corona.

Subsp. *albidus* var. *albidus* has very pale yellowish-white flowers with the perianth segments longer than the corona. A collection of this made by Jim Archibald many years ago does very well with me.

Subsp. *albidus* var. *zaianicus* is like this but the pale flowers are tinged greenish and the perianth segments are equal to or shorter than the corona. I have not seen this variant.

N. hedraeanthus is a very small member of this group, often only 5cm in height, with thread-like leaves only 1mm wide. The pale yellow flowers have no pedicel and are usually held slightly above the horizontal or even obliquely upwards and the stamens protrude a long way beyond the corona. The flower is quite small, usually 2.0–2.5cm long, smaller than the majority of *N. bulbocodium* or *N. romieuxii* variants. It grows wild in Spain in Cazorla, flowering in early spring and is a pleasing little plant for the alpine house.

N. cantabricus (N. clusii)   It is fortunate that this follows *N. bulbocodium* alphabetically, since it is very closely related! The flowers are very similar in overall appearance but are white with a corona which has a pleasing frilly margin and in some variants is very widely flared at the mouth; the pedicel is 3–9mm long and the stamens are always shorter than and held within the corona. It is very early flowering, usually in late winter and in its various forms is a superb plant for the alpine house. Like *N. bulbocodium* and *N. romieuxii* it is variable and several subspecies and varieties have been recognized:

Subsp. *cantabricus* var. *cantabricus* has more than one leaf per bulb, these more or less prostrate on the ground and 1.5mm or less wide. Spain.

Subsp. *cantabricus* var. *foliosus* has three to eight, more or less erect, narrow leaves and the flowers are large, 3.5–6.0 cm long. Morocco.

Subsp. *cantabricus* var. *kesticus* has normally two suberect leaves per bulb and the white flowers are tinged with green and less than 3.5cm long. I have not seen this variant. Morocco.

Subsp. *cantabricus* var. *petunioides* is a lovely plant with a large very widely flared corona. It is much sought-after by bulb enthusiasts. North Africa.

Subsp. *tananicus* differs from the above varieties in having wider stiff leaves, 1.0–2.5mm wide, three to five per bulb. The six stamens are very unequal, whereas in other variants they are more or less equal. Morocco. In cultivation this seems to be a very vigorous plant, increasing well.

Subsp. *monophyllus* has, as its name says, only one leaf per bulb, rarely two, and very narrow, 1mm or less wide. S. Spain and North Africa.

N. cyclamineus   So called because the perianth segments reflex sharply leaving the trumpet protruding. The leaves are bright green, narrowly linear. There is only one pendent flower on a stem, 15–30 cm tall, deep yellow with a trumpet 1.5–2.0 cm long, with a slightly expanded ragged margin, and the reflexed segments are also about 1.5–2.0cm long. Moist alpine meadows in Portugal and Spain. This delightful plant has unfortunately become rather scarce in cultivation recently and it is not very readily obtainable. It seems to do best in rather moist conditions, in a peat garden or damp grass.

N. cyclamineus has imparted its attractive characteristics to a range of 'Cyclamineus hybrids' which are very popular. Cultivars include the well known 'February Gold', 'Little Witch', 'Tête-a-Tête', 'March Sunshine' and 'Peeping Tom'. Like the species itself, these are early-flowering in spring before the main flush of daffodils.

N. jonquilla   The much-loved Jonquil is known mainly as a winter cut flower with its strong fragrance. It is 15–30cm in height with dark green, almost cylindrical rush-like leaves and umbels of two to five yellow flowers. These have a long slender tube, 2–3cm long and are flattish, about 2.0–3.5cm in diameter with a small shallow cup about 1.0–1.5cm across and only 2–4mm deep. It occurs in Spain and Portugal in damp grassy places but in cooler countries like Britain does not thrive unless given a sheltered sunny spot. Var. *henriquesii* is an attractive smallish version, only 10–15cm in height as grown by me.

N. baeticus from Cordoba province in Spain is a recently described species I have not seen. It is said to be smaller than *N. jonquilla*.

N. minor (N. pumilus, N. nanus)   This is a dwarf trumpet daffodil similar to but larger in all its parts than *N. asturiensis* (described above). It has grey-green leaves and stems 15–25cm tall, bearing solitary horizontal or semi-pendent flowers about 2.5–4.0 cm long and 3.5–5.0 cm across, deep yellow throughout. It occurs in France and N. Spain and its fairly variable in size. There is an excellent early-flowering form in cultivation as 'Cedric Morris' which produces its flowers in mid winter. *N. nanus* is probably just one of the forms of *N. minor*. All the variants are excellent little plants for the rock garden.

N. eugeniae, a recently described species from Zaragoza province in Spain, seems to be related. It is 15–20 cm in height with flowers 3.5–4.0 cm long, concolorous or the segments slightly paler. Even more recently it has been proposed as a subspecies of *N. pseudonarcissus*.

N. papyraceus   The Paper-White Narcissus, well known as a winter cut flower. I shall not dwell on this and its relations since they are tender plants not on the whole suitable for cultivation in the cooler countries, and in any case rather tall. *N. papyraceus* is very variable, 15–45cm in height, with greyish strap-shaped leaves and up to 20 fragrant white flowers in an umbel. They are 2.5–4.0 cm in diameter with a small cup and usually appear in winter or early spring. It is a native of the western Mediterranean region at low altitudes in stony places.

Subsp. *polyanthus* from S. France has green, not glaucous leaves.

Subsp. *panizzianus* is smaller-flowered than subsp. *papyraceus*, usually about 2.0–2.5cm across, W. Mediterranean.

N. pachybolbus has even smaller flowers, about 1–2cm across with blunt perianth segments. N. Africa.

N. canariensis from the Canary Islands is like *N. pachybolbus* in size, but the perianth segments are acute.

N. dubius is rather different from all the above in its flower proportions and general size. It grows to 20 cm in height with narrower grey leaves and has no more than six flowers; the cup is about half the length of the segments, whereas in all the above species it is less than a third as long. The flowers are small, about 1.0–1.5cm in diameter.

N. poeticus   The Poets' Narcissus, the latest of all species to flower and well known in its old garden form, the Pheasant's Eye. It is a tallish species, 20–50cm, with grey strap-shaped leaves. The solitary, very fragrant flower is flattish, about 4–5 cm in diameter with white or creamy perianth segments and a very shallow cup which is yellow or greenish, usually with an orange or red frilled margin. It is a widespread plant in southern Europe, often in very damp mountain meadows. An unforgettable sight for me was a water meadow in Yugoslavia filled with *N. poeticus* in flower and this form (subsp. *radiiflorus*) seems to grow best in cultivation if given a wettish position.

It is a very variable plant and many of the variants have been named. One of the most convincing of these is subsp. *radiiflorus* (subsp. *angustifolius*). This has the perianth segments narrowed at the base into a claw so that they are scarcely overlapping, whereas in subsp. *poeticus* they are broad and overlapping – giving a more substantial flower. It occurs in Switzerland, Austria and Yugoslavia.

N. verbanensis was a name given to variants from the Switzerland-Italy borders, which are intermediate between the two subspecies.

N. hellenicus from N. Greece is another variant with small flowers with a corona 2mm deep.

N. pseudonarcissus   This is the wild species from which many of the large trumpet daffodil cultivars have been raised by selection and hybridization. It is extremely variable from dwarf plants of 15cm to robust giants of 90cm, and the colour may be anything from wholly white to wholly yellow or bicoloured. Such a complex group is fairly difficult to classify and the treatments range from 'sinking' most variants together to 'splitting' them into 20 different species. I think the approach of Webb and Chater in Flora Europaea was a fairly realistic one, in having one species with several subspecies, and I am largely following this system. They are inhabitants of mountain meadows and sometimes light woodland.

All the variants are easily cultivated in the open garden.

Subsp. *pseudonarcissus* has strap-like, usually grey-green leaves, and solitary flowers which are held horizontally or drooping, bicoloured with the perianth segments pale to mid yellow and the trumpet deeper yellow, 2.0–3.5cm long; it is a little flared and frilled at the mouth. The perianth tube is 1.5–2.5cm long and the pedicel 3–12mm long. It is widespread in Western Europe.

Subsp. *pallidiflorus* (*N. pallidiflorus, N. macrolobus*) is similar but has paler yellow flowers, although still bicoloured; the trumpet is 3–4cm long, distinctly flared and lobed at the mouth. Pyrenees and N. Spain.

Subsp. *nobilis* (*N. leonensis, N. gayi*) is often a fairly dwarf plant with large bicoloured flowers which are horizontal or even held facing upwards. The segments are pale yellow, the trumpet very deep golden yellow, 3–4cm long and flared and lobed at the mouth, the pedicel is 8–15mm long. N. Portugal and N. Spain. Dick Brummitt and Arthur Chater collected a few bulbs of this and it is one of the more distinct forms I have, with its very strikingly bicoloured flowers.

Subsp. *major* (*N. hispanicus*) has flowers which are deep golden yellow throughout, carried on a pedicel 8–30mm long: S. France, Spain and Portugal. In its largest forms this is one of the tallest of all the various *N. pseudonarcissus* forms.

Subsp. *portensis* also has the flowers the same deep yellow throughout, but the trumpet is not flared out at the mouth. It has short rather narrow leaves, 7mm or less wide. N. and C. Spain, N. Portugal. This is a pleasing smallish variant worth growing at the front of a border or rock garden. I have Mr Sipkes of Holland to thank for some bulbs.

Subsp. *obvallaris* is uniformly deep yellow and is close to subsp. *major* but tends to be slightly smaller in leaf and flower, although there is an overlap in all measurements. It is of unknown origin but is naturalized in South Wales as the Tenby Daffodil.

Subsp. *nevadensis* is a smallish-flowered variant, often with two to four flowers per stem. They are bicoloured, with pale yellow segments less than 2cm long, and a deeper yellow trumpet 1.5–2.5cm long, which is not noticeably flared at the mouth. The leaves are usually green rather than grey. S. Spain, in the Sierra Nevada. I have not grown this interesting plant.

Subsp. *moschatus* (*N. alpestris*) has uniformly coloured flowers in white or pale cream held in a pendent position; the segments often lie alongside the trumpet giving a rather droopy appearance to the whole flower. Pyrenees and N. Spain. I think that this is my personal favourite in the whole group, perhaps not quite so vigorous a garden plant and fairly short, so ideal for the rock garden.

In the last few years several other subspecies have been described but in the absence of specimens I have been unable to assess them.

N. radinganorum has been recently described from Valencia Province in Spain. It is 25–40cm tall and has a corona 19mm long, so is apprently rather small-flowered. I have not seen it, so cannot comment on its relationships.

N. bicolor (*N. abscissus*) should perhaps also be treated as a subspecies of *N. pseudonarcissus* although, as I grow it, it is very distinct and causes no confusion. It is a stocky plant, not more than 40cm (but usually much less), with leaves which, in the form I have which was collected by Kit Grey-Wilson, are very rounded at the apex. The bicoloured flowers (rarely wholly yellow) have cream or pale yellow segments and a deep yellow trumpet, 3.5–4.0 cm long, which is more or less straight-sided, not flared out at the apex and hardly lobed or frilled so that it appears to have been trimmed straight across the mouth. In my garden it flowers much later than all the *N. pseudonarcissus* variants, not starting to push through the ground until they have almost finished flowering.

N. longispathus is another trumpet Daffodil, but distinctive in having a long green spathe, 6–10cm in length (in *N. psuedonarcissus* the spathe is smaller, papery and semi-transparent). It is a tall plant, up to a metre or more, with one or rarely two upward-facing flowers which have yellow perianth segments and a deeper yellow trumpet 2.5–3.0cm long with a flared mouth. It is a native of wet stream-sides in the Sierra de Cazorla mountains of S. Spain.

N. lobularis is the name given to a short stocky garden form of *N. pseudonarcissus* with rather broad leaves and bicoloured flowers in two shades of yellow.

N. rupicola   A delightful little species like a dwarf Jonquil. It is about 10–15cm in height with erect or almost prostrate grey-green leaves which have two keels on the back, making them squarish in cross-section. The fragrant flowers are usually solitary, deep, yellow, 1.5–3.0cm in diameter with a small cup only 2–4mm deep with six shallow lobes at its mouth; the perianth tube is 1.8–2.5cm long and is straight. It occurs in rocky places in Spain and Portugal and is an excellent alpine-house or rock-garden plant for a sunny, well-drained position.

Subsp. *pedunculatus* differs mainly in having the flower on a pedicel 3–12mm long (usually less than 3mm in subsp. *rupicola*). C. Spain.

Subsp. *marvieri* from Morocco has green leaves, not greyish, and the perianth tube is 2.3–2.7cm long.

N. cuatrecasasii probably belongs here with *N. rupicola*. It usually has solitary flowers 2.2–3.0cm in diameter with a cup which is about twice as wide as deep. C. and S. Spain.

N. calcicola is similar but has usually two to five flowers in an umbel and these are often smaller, 1.5–2.5cm in diameter, deep yellow with a scarcely lobed cup 5–8mm deep; the perianth tube is 1.3–1.8cm long. It occurs in rock crevices in Portugal and is a lovely alpine-house plant.

N. scaberulus is like *N. rupicola* but the leaves are usually prostrate or coiled and have rough teeth on the angles (smooth in *N. rupicola* and *N. calcicola*). The one to three small flowers have pedicels 8–15mm long, are 1.2–1.7cm in diameter and have a perianth tube 1.2–1.7cm long. The cup is 2–5mm deep; in this it differs from the deeper-cupped *N. calcicola*. It occurs in Portugal.

N. serotinus An autumn-flowering species about 10–15cm in height with slender (1mm wide) rush-like leaves which are not present at flowering time. There are one to three scented flowers per stem, flattish and about 2–3cm in diameter, white with a very small yellow-orange cup which is six-lobed and only 1–2mm deep and 3–4mm across. It is widespread in the Mediterranean region, flowering in autumn at low altitudes in rocky places or in scrub. The best way to grow it is in an alpine house where the pots can be almost dried off and the bulbs given a good baking in summer. Herbert and Molly Crook have acquired the technique and flower it much better than I can.

N. elegans is also autumn-flowering but is a larger plant, to 35cm with wider (2.5cm) grey, channelled leaves which are contemporary with the flowers. There are two to ten scented flowers about 2–3cm in diameter and these have somewhat recurved, usually narrow and pointed, white or cream perianth segments and a small yellowish-green cup. It occurs in the western Mediterranean region.

Several variants have been given names, including var. *intermedius* from Morocco and Algeria which has wider, blunt, segments; var. *flavescens* with cream segments (Algeria); var. *fallax* from Morocco and Algeria with greenish-white segments and forma *aurantiicoronatus* which has an orange cup (Libya).

I have not had the opportunity to try to grow *N. elegans* but imagine it to be similar to *N. serotinus* in its requirements.

N. tazetta A very widespread and popular species for many centuries and cultivated as far afield as Europe and China since very early times. It is a cluster-headed type of variable height from only 10–15cm up to about 50cm. The leaves are strap-like, often greyish and there are up to 20 very sweetly scented smallish flowers in an umbel. These usually vary from about 2.5–4.0cm in diameter and are bicoloured with white perianth segments and a yellow cup 3–6mm deep and 6–11mm across. Although it is essentially a spring-flowering species I have seen it in bloom in November in the Peloponnese and it can be found at almost any time through the winter. In cultivation in cooler climates these early forms revert to spring-flowering although the species does, of course, force very readily for a display indoors. It is probably a native of rocky places in the central and western Mediterranean, but is widely naturalized eastwards in several places as far east as China and Japan. In cooler countries away from its Mediterranean home it is not free flowering, unless it can be given a hot sunny sheltered spot.

Subsp. *italicus* has large (4–5cm diameter) flowers with cream or yellow coloured segments and a bright orange-yellow cup. Italy, Greece and Yugoslavia. The frequently-cultivated plant sold as *N. canaliculatus* is probably a small form of this. Subsp. *lacticolor* is probably a variant of subsp. *italicus*.

Subsp. *aureus* has bright yellow segments and a deeper yellow or orange cup. S. France, N.W. Italy.

Subsp. *patulus* is a dwarf version with prostrate leaves; the white and yellow bicoloured flowers are 1.8–2.4cm in diameter. Widespread.

Subsp. *corcyrensis* usually has solitary or at most 3 flowers with narrow white perianth segments and a deeply lobed yellow or orange cup. It was described from Corfu.

Other species which have been described but which are probably best treated as slight variants of *N. tazetta* include:

N. cypri: a vigorous plant which has large flowers 4–5cm in diameter, white with a yellow cup which is rather expanded at the mouth. Cyprus.

N. ochroleucus has flowers 2.5–3.0cm in diameter, white with a pale lemon yellow corona about 4mm deep. S. France.

N. bertolonii is probably a form of subsp. *italicus* with yellow segments and a yellow cup, but is smaller, the flowers about 3.5cm across. Italy. Varieties of this have been described in North Africa, with flowers in varying shades of yellow and orange bicolor (var. *algericus*, var. *primulinus*, var *discolor*).

N. cupularis is very much the same as subsp. *aureus*, but is said to have grey-green leaves whereas those of subsp. *aureus* are green. S. France, Italy, Sardinia.

N. triandrus   The Angel's Tears Narcissus is a delightful small species for early spring, excellent for growing in grass – or on the rock garden or peat garden. It is 10–25cm in height, with narrow dark-green, semi-cylindrical leaves and one to six pendent white flowers with strongly reflexed perianth segments; the corona is cup shaped, about 1.0–1.5cm deep in subsp. *triandrus*, and the same wide. It is a native of Spain and N. Portugal in mountain areas, moist in spring but dry later on.

Subsp. *capax* (*N. capax*) was maintained by Flora Europaea for variants which have a longer corona, 1.5–2.5cm deep. N.W. France.

Subsp. *pallidulus* (*N. concolor*) has solitary (rarely to three) bright yellow flowers, smaller with a cup only 5–10mm deep. Widespread in Spain and in central Portugal. The plant cultivated as var. *aurantiacus* is presumably a form of this.

Var. *cernuus* is a name given to pale yellow or creamy forms with two or three flowers per stem.

Slightly bicoloured forms sometimes occur with the corona paler yellow than the perianth segments and these have been called *N. pulchellus*.

In addition to these wild forms there is a race of charming white-flowered hybrids in cultivation which have several flowers per stem. Cultivars include *N.* 'Thalia', 'Liberty Bells', 'April Tears', 'Silver Chimes' and 'Tresamble'.

N. viridiflorus   A curious autumn-flowering species with green flowers, difficult to grow in cool districts for its bulbs need a good warm rest period if they are to flower. In such cases a deep pot in the alpine house offers the best chance of success, or a bulb frame. The dark green cylindrical leaves appear after the flowers are finished; these are carried in umbels of two to five on stems up to 25cm in height and are scented, about 2–3cm in diameter, with rather narrow pointed perianth segments which are often slightly reflexed. The cup is very shallow, only 1mm in height, and is six-lobed. It is a native of S. Spain, Gibraltar and Morocco in rocky places.

N. viridiflorus occasionally hybridizes with *N. elegans*.

N. watieri   One of the most delightful of the dwarf Narcissi and excellent in the alpine house or bulb frame, but usually not flowering freely in the open, unless the summers are dry and warm, for the bulbs must be ripened well in summer. It is about 10cm in height with grey, narrowly linear leaves and solitary flattish pure white flowers about 2.0–2.5cm in diameter with a shallow saucer-shaped corona. N. Africa, in the Atlas Mountains in rocky places and scrubland.

N. atlanticus has larger creamy-white fragrant flowers. Morocco.

Hybrids   In addition to the wild species of Narcissus there are countless hybrids and selections, far too numerous to list. Most species, if not all, will hybridize; even *N. bulbocodium*, which is one of the most distinct, will cross occasionally with

N. pseudonarcissus (*N.* × *bakeri*) and *N. jonquilla* (*N.* × *abilioi*) and I have seen hybrids between it and *N. triandrus* in gardens where they grow together.

Some of the more well-known hybrids which have been given names are:

N. × *incomparabilis* – *N. poeticus* × *N. pseudonarcissus*
N. × *intermedius* – *N. tazetta* × *N. jonquilla*
N. × *medioluteus* – *N. poeticus* × *N. tazetta*
N. × *odorus* – *N. jonquilla* × *N. pseudonarcissus*
N. × *rogendorfii* – *N. elegans* × *N. tazetta*
N. × *tenuior* – *N. jonquilla* × *N. poeticus*

Nothoscordum

I mention this Allium-like plant from South America mainly as a warning, for at least one of the species, *N. gracile* (*N. fragrans*, *N. inodorum*), is an awful weed to be avoided at all costs. They are tallish plants, mostly 25–70cm, with linear basal leaves and scapes bearing umbels of small whitish flowers, yellow in some species, which are very like some Alliums. The bulbs often produce many small offsets which crumble away from the parent at a touch, hence the weedy nature of *N. gracile*. The following one I have grown and this appears to be non-invasive, and for the enthusiast has some value – but the rest look rather uninteresting from the garden point of view.

N. andicolum   Usually about 10–15cm in height, with a tuft of grey-green linear leaves 2–3mm wide and an umbel of up to ten flowers which are white, striped purplish on each segment, about 1.0–1.5cm long, not opening out flat but remaining rather funnel shaped. It is a native of Peru, Bolivia and Argentina and seem to be a winter-growing, summer dormant plant whereas *N. gracile* is the reverse. It is thus best treated as an alpine house plant.

Odontostomum

An American genus containing only one species which is suitable for bulb frame cultivation, or for deep pots in the alpine house. In mild areas with warm dry summers it could be tried outside in a well-drained situation. It is interesting rather than showy.

O. hartwegii   This grows to 15–35cm tall with a few long erect linear basal leaves and a branched many-flowered inflorescence. The flowers are white and small, only 5–7mm in diameter, with the segments sharply reflexed above the 6mm long tube. It is a native of California, at low altitudes of not more than 500m in rocky places, and it flowers in spring or early summer.

Ornithogalum

A very large and confusing genus which is still in need of a great deal of study before the classification is understood. There are many in Europe and West Asia and in South

Africa, with rather fewer in the connecting link through Tropical Africa. Needless to say, most of the African species are very tender and hardly any of them are cultivated in temperate climates except for the Chincherinchee, *O. thyrsoides*, which is treated in the same way as *Gladiolus* and planted out for the summer months only. The northern hemisphere species are very uniform in their overall appearance, with starry white flowers, which are usually green on the outside, giving rise to the common name Star of Bethlehem. Some of them are excellent garden plants and I propose to describe a few of the best of the smaller species. This is certainly not the place to go into the involved points of distinction between the species, for the observation of some of the features involves slicing up the bulb itself! Other important characters are the cross-sectional shape of the ovary and the behaviour of the pedicels (flower stalks) in the fruiting stage. Clearly, a book intended primarily for keen gardeners is not the place to go into such dull topics and I will pass lightly, and thankfully, over these erudite matters and talk about aesthetic value.

Of the taller species, *O. arabicum* is well worth growing in a hot sunny place; it has flat-topped racemes of large creamy-white flowers with a blackish ovary giving a dark eye to the flower. *O. narbonense* is a common Mediterranean species which just qualifies as being worthwhile on account of its long slender racemes of small starry flowers. *O. pyrenaicum*, the Bath Asparagus, is rather dull, with long dense racemes of greenish flowers, but is of interest since its young inflorescences are said to be edible, and they certainly look like Asparagus! *O. reverchonii* is an unusual species from Spain, which can be a metre in height with long racemes of large, widely bell-shaped flowers which are wholly white, not striped with green. *O. arcuatum* is worth searching for; it has long racemes of upward-facing flowers each carried on a long pedicel which arches gracefully upwards in the fruiting stage.

The smaller species are mostly easy to grow and nearly all spring flowering, some lasting to early summer. The rock garden is an ideal spot, or the front of a border, but very vigorous ones such as *O. umbellatum* are best kept for naturalizing under shrubs or in grass, since they may increase invasively in a rock garden.

O. balansae A well-known and excellent dwarf early spring species. It has only two or three rather wide leaves in bright green and few-flowered racemes to 10cm at most. The flowers are large, up to 2.5cm across, pure white with the outside almost wholly bright green. N. and E. Turkey and Caucasus in alpine meadows.

O. brevipedicellatum is similar, often a little taller, and has several upward-facing flowers on short pedicels, giving a dense but short raceme. S. Turkey and possibly Iran.

O. fimbriatum An attractive dwarf species with very narrow grey-green leaves covered with short backward-pointing hairs. The raceme is wide and rather flat-topped, only 5–15cm tall, and carries flowers about 1.5cm in diameter. S.E. Europe, Turkey in stony places.

O. lanceolatum One of the most attractive of the dwarf species, with flattish rosettes of broad shiny green leaves (2cm or more wide) which taper gradually to the tip. The raceme is very compact and near stemless, so the large flowers, which are up to 2cm diameter, rest in the centre of the rosette. It is a native of S. Turkey, Syria and Lebanon in damp mountain meadows and rocky places.

O. montanum is similar but taller, with racemes 10–25cm in height, with a rosette of rather narrower leaves 1–2cm wide at their base. S. Europe and Turkey.

O. platyphyllum is much the same but the leaves are more erect. Turkey, east to Iran and USSR.

O. nutans   A 15–25cm tall Star of Bethlehem, which is very distinct in having a spike of short-pedicelled, slightly pendulous silvery-white flowers about 2.0–2.5cm long, with the pointed segments curved outwards at the tips and greyish-green on the outside. The leaves are long and linear, dying away at flowering time. It is an attractive species, useful for naturalizing under shrubs or in grass. Widespread in Europe, mainly in woods.

O. oligophyllum   A small, slender species with two erect grey-green oblanceolate leaves and a 7–15cm tall stem with a short raceme of two to seven flowers which are the usual white with a green stripe on each segment. Greece and W. Turkey in mountain woods and meadows.

O. orthophyllum (O. kochii, 'O. tenuifolium')   A very variable species ranging from dwarfs of only 5cm up to a vigorous 30cm. The leaves are narrowly linear, with a white line along the middle of the upper surface, and the raceme of white flowers is wide and rather flat-topped. Unlike the next species, *O. sibthorpii* and its relatives, the pedicels do not bend downwards in the fruiting stage. It is very widespread in grassy places from S. Europe east to Iran and the Caucasus.

O. umbellatum, the common Star of Bethlehem, is a coarse version with the flowers on very long pedicels, 5–9cm in length. The bulbs produce many small offsets which *O. orthophyllum* does not have.

O. sibthorpii (O. nanum)   An attractive very dwarf species, only 5–10cm in height when in flower, with the very narrow grey-green leaves having a white stripe on the upper surface. The flowers are carried in a flat-topped raceme which rests almost stemless in the rosette of leaves. After flowering the pedicels bend downwards and press the developing capsules on to the soil surface. S.E. Europe and Turkey in grassy places.

O. sigmoideum from N. Turkey is very similar and regarded by some authorities as a synonym.

O. exscapum from Mediterranean Europe is closely related to *O. sibthorpii* and differs in details of the shape and size of the ovary, and it generally has smaller flowers.

O. sintenisii is also similar, a most attractive compact plant from the mountains of Iran.

O. refractum is slightly larger and differs in having many bulblets around the parent bulb. Europe.

O. unifolium   This is unusual in having only one linear leaf per bulb. It is a small species only 5–10cm in height with a few flowers on short pedicels in a tight spike; they are about 1.5cm in diameter and almost wholly white without a green stripe on the outside. It is a native of Spain and Portugal.

O. concinnum is a larger version with more flowers on the spike and two or three leaves per bulb. Portugal.

Oxalis

This very large genus of around 800 species, which contains annuals, fibrous-rooted and tuberous-rooted perennials, and even has some shrub-like members, is one which charms and infuriates. Some species are among the world's worst weeds while others are beautiful and rare, requiring the care and attention of an alpine enthusiast to maintain them in cultivation. In my present garden I spend such a considerable portion of my gardening life digging up clusters of tiny bulblets which, if left, blanket out all other low-growing plants with their foliage. I have been almost at the point of banning all Oxalis! However, there are a few tuberous ones which are so attractive and well behaved that my fury is somewhat tempered. There are many species unknown in gardens, especially from temperate South America, which I have seen as herbarium specimens only, and it is clear that some of these would be worth introducing. Certain others are much safer left as herbarium specimens!

Oxalis are distinctive in their clover-like leaves, although sometimes these are divided into more leaflets than three, and widely funnel-shaped flowers which open out flat in the sunshine and have the petals twisted around each other, umbrella-like, in bud.

O. adenophylla   This has a large rootstock, consisting of small tubers covered by a mass of fibrous leaf bases, making a soft felt-like ball around them. The whole plant is usually less than 5cm, with greyish leaves up to 2cm in diameter with many narrowly obovate leaflets. There are many flowers per 'bulb' just overtopping the leaves in early summer, about 3–4cm in diameter and varying from near-white to a light magenta, although only a pale pinkish lilac form is in general cultivation; this has a large purple eye in the centre. It is a native of S. Chile and Argentina and is very hardy but requires full exposure and excellent drainage.

O. depressa (O. inops)   This has small tubers with shell-like tunics. It is usually about 5cm in height, with grey-green three-lobed leaves which are bilobed or notched at the apex. In early summer these are overtopped by 2cm diameter bright rosy pink flowers and it is very free-flowering, so can be very showy. It is from South Africa and is not entirely hardy, but is a delightful plant for the alpine house.

O. enneaphylla   This is closely related to *O. adenophylla* but has a more elongated rhizome-like rootstock. It can be up to 10cm in height but the form generally seen in cultivation is very dwarf. The leaves are up to 2.5cm in diameter, grey-green with narrow obovate leaflets and flowers up to 4.5cm in diameter; the forms in cultivation are mostly in shades of lilac-pink but there is also a white, 'Alba'. S. Chile and the Falkland Islands. Like *O. adenophylla* it does well in full sun in a gritty soil.

O. laciniata   I think this is my particular favourite in the genus, at least of those I have grown to date. Its rootstock consists of strange elongated scaly rhizomes looking like pinkish-white maggots; these give rise in spring and summer to small blue-grey leaves with many narrowly linear leaflets which are usually undulate-edged. The early summer flowers are 3.5–4.0cm across and a dark steely purple-blue in the form generally grown but, again, it is very variable in the wild and other forms could well be introduced varying from pink to maroon. It is wild in Patagonia and is thus very hardy. I have grown it successfully in a peat garden while others find it a good alpine house plant or for growing in sink gardens. *O.* 'Ione Hecker' is a beautiful hybrid between *O. laciniata* and *O. enneaphylla*, intermediate in character.

O. lobata   This has small woolly-coated tubers producing green leaves up to 1cm across, with a few obovate leaflets. It is only 4–6cm in height with bright yellow flowers 1.5–2.0cm in diameter produced in early autumn. It is a most attractive plant but I find it not fully hardy and it needs the protection of a frame or alpine house. Temperate South America.

O. obtusa   This has small tubers, pointed at both ends and covered with a shell-like coat. The neat grey-green leaves have three leaflets, each notched at the apex, and these are overtopped in mid summer to autumn by large flowers on 4–6cm stems. They are bright pink with reddish veining and a yellow centre, to about 3cm in diameter. It is from South Africa and is a fine plant for the alpine house, but not hardy in cold districts.

O. purpurea (O. speciosa)   A most attractive and variable species from South Africa, not hardy enough for the open garden in cold-winter countries but a lovely alpine-house plant. It makes densely leafy rosettes of three-lobed grey green leaves overtopped in spring or summer by large rounded flowers 3–5cm across. The lovely yellow-flowered form has been named 'Ken Aslet', after the well-known and knowledge-able superintendant of the rock garden at Wisley in the 1960s. In the wild there are also purple and white forms which would also be well worth growing.

O. tetraphylla (O. deppei)   A larger plant than most of those described, usually about 10cm with tufts of green leaves with four leaflets, each of which has a reddish zone near the base. The flowers are carried in small umbels in summer, a lovely shade of light carmine-red. A form of this with very conspicuous leaf markings is called 'Iron Cross'. The species is a native of Mexico.

Pinellia

An interesting little group of hardy 'Arums', of which I have grown three and find to be very tolerant little plants, worth having on the peat garden or semi-shaded border for their green spathes in summer. They have tuberous roots and are dormant in winter.

P. cordata   This is a delightful little plant sent to me many years ago by Don Elick in Japan. It is very low-growing, the leaves held just above the ground on short purplish petioles; it is a pleasing foliage plant, for the leaves are beautifully cream-veined, lanceolate with a cordate base and about 3–5cm long. In summer these are overtopped by tiny green, purple-veined spathes, no more than 3cm long, which have the apex hooded over at right angles to the tube; the spadix, which does an S-shaped bend to clear the mouth of the spathe, has a long, slender, vertically-erect tip standing up to 7cm above the spathe. A bonus is a pleasant fruity fragrance, although you need to be an athlete to get down low enough to detect it! It is a native of China. Apart from increasing by tuber division, a small 'bulbil' is produced on the leaf base where the veins meet.

P. ternata (P. tuberifera)   Probably the most widely cultivated species, this is 10–20cm in height, with tri-lobed leaves and green or purplish spathes, narrowly cylindrical with a slightly hooded apex. The long slender spadix is exserted from the spathe by at least 2cm, and often much more. Extra tiny tubers are produced on the stem near ground level. China and Japan.

P. tripartita is more robust than *P. ternata*, to about 25cm, also with three-lobed leaves; but the leaflets are much broader with conspicuously undulate, almost crisped, margins. The pale green spathes are carried amid the foliage, and are long-tubular, up to 10cm long with a hooded apex and are thick, almost wax-like in texture. A prominent feature is the extremely long spadix standing vertically for up to 20cm above the top of the spathe. It is a Japanese native.

Puschkinia

A small genus, closely related to *Scilla* and *Chionodoxa*, but distinct in having a small cup or corona surrounding the style and stamens; the six segments are joined into a short tube as in *Chionodoxa*, not free as in *Scilla*. Only one species is grown to any extent and this may in fact be the only one, although several names exist.

P. scilloides (P. libanotica)   Grows to about 10–15cm in height with two linear oblanceolate basal leaves overtopped by a dense raceme of up to 20 flowers. These are bright but pale blue, with a darker blue line along the centre of each perianth segment; albino forms occur sporadically among the blue in the wild. It is a native of alpine meadows in E. Turkey, the Caucasus and N. Iran south to Lebanon, growing near the snowline. It is an attractive early spring flowering small bulb for the rock garden, doing best in a cool position, but well drained.

In E. Turkey and the Elburz mountains in Iran there is a greenish-flowered Puschkinia which may possibly be an undescribed species; it is, however, less attractive as a garden plant.

Rhodohypoxis

This is an exciting little genus from the eastern (summer rainfall) region of Southern Africa, mainly in the Natal and Lesotho Drakensberg, where they grow in damp grassy or rocky places at altitudes up to 3250m. They are dormant in winter, resting as small tubers in a relatively dry condition, since in their natural habitat there is little winter rainfall. In cultivation they are fairly frost hardy, especially *R. milloides*, which has not been killed in the 10 years out in my own garden; the temperatures have been as low as −17°C and the tubers are regularly frozen solid in the surface layers of the soil. *R. baurii*, the commonest and the most showy species, is less hardy than this and except in mild districts it is best regarded as an alpine-house plant. Rhodohypoxis can also be grown very satisfactorily in beds of a peat and sand mixture which are left open to receive rain from April through to autumn, then covered by frame lights for the winter and left to dry off. If grown in pots they should be repotted annually.

The most noteworthy feature in the appearance of Rhodohypoxis is the 'closed eye' effect, caused by the perianth segments bending inwards, so that no stamens are visible; this lack of a centre is criticized by some people as being unattractive, but any slight detraction from their beauty such as this is more than compensated for by their bright flowers borne over a very long period from about May to August.

Much of the work in selecting the colourful varieties of *R. baurii* was done by Mrs Susan Garnett-Botfield in the 1920s and later by her daughter Mrs Ruth McConnel, who introduced them to the public via her nursery at Knockdolian in Ayrshire. These range in colour from the pure white of 'Ruth' through various shades of pink ('Appleblossom', 'Maragaret Rose', 'Albrighton'), to deep reds such as 'Douglas' and 'Great Scott'.

Thanks to the field studies of Mr B. L. Burtt and Dr O. M. Hilliard much more is now known about *Rhodohypoxis* in the wild; they have discovered several new species and forms, and hybrids between the species and between *Rhodohypoxis* and *Hypoxis parvula*, a related plant which is somewhat similar but has an open centre to the flowers, thus showing off the yellow stamens. I am growing two of the bigeneric hybrids, a white and a pink, and these too have their stamens visible as an eye in the centre and show promise as attractive rock plants.

Propagation is by seed or by division of the tubers, whilst dormant in winter or in midsummer after the main flush of flowers is over.

R. baurii The most widely grown, in a range of colours. It grows 5–10cm in height with hairy greyish narrowly lanceolate leaves up to 1cm wide. Var. *baurii* has pink or red flowers 1.5–2.0cm in diameter. Var. *platypetala* is usually more robust and has flowers 2.0–2.5cm in diameter in white or pale pink. Var. *confecta* has white, pink or red flowers and differs mainly from the other two in having green, not greyish, leaves. The flower segments in *R. baurii* are joined into a very short tube, only 2mm long.

It is a native of Natal, E. Cape, Transkei, Orange Free State, Swaziland and Lesotho in grassy or rocky places up to 2900m.

R. deflexa This tiny species is barely known in cultivation but is less attractive than *R. baurii*, with very short-tubed flowers only 1cm or less in diameter in white, pink or red; the leaves are hairy or hairless and only 5mm wide. It occurs wild in Lesotho and the E. Cape in wet turf at up to 3230m.

R. incompta A dwarf species less than 5cm high, clearly worth growing but probably not yet in cultivation. It has white or pink flowers about 2.0–2.5cm diameter with a long tube (up to 3cm); the bright green hairless (or nearly so) leaves are very short at flowering time. Lesotho and Natal in wet places up to 2900m.

R. milloides A vigorous, stoloniferous, patch-forming species which has proved to be the hardiest in cultivation so far. It grows to 10–15cm in height, with narrow erect bright green hairless leaves and 2.0–3.5cm diameter flowers in bright magenta-red; pink and white forms are recorded in the wild. The flowers have a very short tube (2mm). It grows wild in Natal, Lesotho, Orange Free State, E. Cape and Transvaal up to 2440m in marshy places.

Although very easy to grow in a peat garden or humus-rich area of the rock garden it is less free-flowering than *R. baurii*.

R. rubella A tiny species, only 3cm tall and suitable only as an alpine-house plant, where it can be viewed at close range. The pink (rarely white) flowers are less than 1cm in diameter, accompanied by thread-like green hairless leaves; the flowers have a longish tube (1–2cm). Natal, Lesotho, E. Cape, in moist gravelly or silty places up to 3230m.

R. thodiana This was cultivated by Mrs Garnett-Botfield and Sir Frederick Stern incorrectly as *R. milloides*, but is now very rare in gardens. It is, however, less attractive than the similar *R. baurii* and is not a great loss! It is dwarf, only 3cm at flowering time and has spreading greyish-green hairy leaves; the pink flowers are 2.0–2.5cm across and have a longish tube, about 1cm long. It is rather shy of flowering in cultivation. In the wild it occurs in a small area of the Drakensberg in Lesotho and Natal in humus-rich damp soil at up to 3050m.

Romulea

A large but little-cultivated genus with two main centres of distribution, the Mediterranean region and South Africa, with a few connecting localities in the mountains of Tropical Africa. The southern hemisphere species are beautiful but nearly all far too tender to be grown outside, even in fairly mild countries such as Britain. The northern hemisphere species are much hardier but many are rather unexciting, so the choice becomes fairly limited. They require well drained situations in as much sun as possible, since the flowers require a lot of light and warmth to induce them to open out properly. They make good alpine house or bulb frame plants but in the latter some of them can become pests if the seeds are not gathered before they fall naturally.

Romuleas have funnel-shaped flowers rather like *Crocus* but with only very short perianth tubes, so they are instantly separable on this feature. The leaves are always very narrow and wiry and lack the white stripe on the upper surface which is so characteristic of *Crocus*. They are all very short plants with the flowers at ground level or on wiry stems at most about 10–15cm in height; each flower is subtended by two bracts, the appearance of which is important in distinguishing between the species.

R. bulbocodium (R. grandiflora) This is probably the best of the northern hemisphere species for garden value. The flowers are 2.0–3.5cm long and open out to 3cm or more across, usually bluish-lilac with a yellow throat and shaded on the outside green or purplish. There are also white forms with a yellow centre. The characteristic features are that the stigma overtops the stamens considerably and that the inner of the two bracts is a papery brown, not green. It is widespread around the Mediterranean in rocky or sandy places.

Var. *clusiana* (*R. clusiana*) has large flowers, lilac with a deep yellow centre. Spain, Portugal.

Var. *leichtliniana* is white-flowered with a yellow throat. Greece, Crete.

Var. *subpalustris* has lilac flowers with no yellow in the throat. Cyclades.

R. crocea, sometimes called *R. bulbocodium* var. *crocea*, has all the same structural features as the above but has yellow flowers. I have not found it easy to cultivate. S. Turkey, Syria in sandy soils.

R. tempskyana is also large-flowered with a membranous inner bract. The flowers are, however, deep purple with a purple, not yellow, throat and it differs as well from *R. bulbocodium* in having a longer tube over 8mm long (up to 8mm in *R. bulbocodium*). Turkey, Cyprus, Israel.

R. nivalis from mountains in Lebanon is rather similar to *R. bulbocodium* in being large flowered, lilac to violet with a yellow throat, but the inner bract is mainly green with only membranous margins. The leaves are often rather short at flowering time, and stiffly erect. There are good colour forms of this species which is among the best of all hardy Romuleas.

R. columnae A small-flowered species, scarcely worthy of cultivation. The flowers are white or very pale lilac, 1.0–1.5cm long with pointed perianth segments. The inner bract is membranous, spotted brown, and the style is overtopped by the stamens. W. Europe, in sandy and rocky places, and a rare native of S. Britain.

R. rollii is very similar and differs mainly in having very long thread-like leaves up to 30cm long. Central Mediterranean region.

R. ligustica A seldom-cultivated species with 2.0–3.5cm long lilac or violet flowers. The main characteristic is that the anthers which overtop the style are held well down inside the flower, less than half as long as the segments. The inner bract is papery, speckled reddish-brown. Corsica, Sardinia, N.W. Italy.

R. linaresii A rather richly-coloured little species with the flowers deep violet throughout with no yellow or paler zone in the throat, about 2.0–2.5cm long with rounded segments. The inner bract is papery, red-spotted, usually with a green median line; the stamens overtop the style. It is confined to Sicily.

Subsp. *graeca* has smaller flowers less than 2cm long with acute segments. Crete, Greece and W. Turkey. Stony situations at low altitudes.

R. melitensis is similar to *R. linaresii* but does have a yellow zone in the throat. Malta and Gozo Is.

R. revelieri is a relative of *R. linaresii* and has similar characteristics, but the flowers have a paler zone in the throat, but not yellow, and they are smaller, about 1.0–1.5cm long. Corsica, Italy, Capri.

R. macowanii (R. longituba)   This is sometimes cultivated under the erroneous name of *Syringodea luteo-nigra*. It is an attractive species producing a long tube to the flower like a *Crocus*. The colour is bright yellow, sometimes with creamy tips to the segments and sometimes shaded brown or purplish on the outside. It is a native of E. South Africa and Lesotho, in the Drakensberg mountains, and is hardier than the many winter-growing species of the South-West Cape region. It is a fine plant for the alpine house.

Var. *alticola*, which has a perianth tube 3.5–6.5cm long, is the variant usually found in cultivation, but there are other varieties differing in size of flower and length of tube.

R. ramiflora   A rather unattractive tall species, 10–15cm at flowering time and sometimes reaching 30cm by the time it is in fruit, with long narrow leaves. The flowers are pale to deep lilac with or without yellow in the throat, about 1–2cm long, and they differ from the other pale small-flowered species *R. columnae* by having a wholly green inner bract (sometimes a narrow brown margin). The style is overtopped by the stamens or they are about equal in length. It is widespread in the Mediterranean region. Although not showy I have found that this does well in a rough grassy patch and its starry lilac flowers in the turf are very welcome on sunny days in spring.

Subsp. *gaditana* from Spain and Portugal is like this but has larger flowers 2–3cm long, lilac or pinkish, and the style slightly overtops the stamens.

R. requienii   One of the most attractive of the European species, with the flowers wholly dark violet with no paler or yellow zone in the throat, about 2.0–2.5cm long with rounded segments; the inner bract is membranous with only a green line along its centre. The flower colour, and the fact that the style overtops the stamens considerably, makes this a distinct species. Corsica, Sardinia, S. Italy in stony places.

R. rosea   This is a tallish (up to 20cm) South African species which has become weedy in some parts of the world. It has long leaves reaching up to 30cm. The flowers are very variable, 1.5–4.5cm long and may be white, pink or cerise, usually with a central yellow zone. The corms can be distinguished from those of the northern-hemisphere species because they have tunics which split at the base into conspicuously bent teeth. It flowers in spring or early summer and is suitable for the alpine house or bulb frame – although in mild areas it may seed about far too freely.

R. thodei   The plant in cultivation under this name has deep violet flowers on stems up to 15cm in height. It is from E. Southern Africa, in the Drakensberg mountains, and is hardy enough to be grown in the alpine house.

In addition to these mentioned above there are many beautiful species in South Africa, some of which have proved to be hardy in an alpine house, during mild winters at least. However, the corms will not withstand being frozen and it is best if they are planted into beds rather than grown in pots. As examples, I have succeeded with the following lovely species for a time:

R. atrandra This has huge flowers 3–4cm in diameter, pinkish-magenta with a yellow throat, which sometimes has a very dark purple zone around it.

R. aurea A yellow-flowered species, dwarf with wavy thread-like leaves and large flowers up to 4cm across.

R. hirta This has long erect rather wide four-angled leaves and large yellow flowers with brownish markings forming a band-like zone around the centre.

R. sabulosa Very spectacular with enormous flowers varying from 4–10cm in diameter, bright red with black and yellow zones in the centre.

R. saldanhensis Has yellow flowers about 3cm across which have a shiny surface to the segments, like those of *Crocus korolkowii*. It is one of the easiest of the South African species to cultivate.

Roscoea

A fascinating group of tuberous-rooted hardy plants belonging to the Ginger family, Zingiberaceae. They are mainly Himalayan and Chinese and therefore occur in summer rainfall regions, spending the winter in cold dry conditions often under snow. They are on the whole easily cultivated in cool positions such as a peat garden provides, and flower in mid to late summer. There are, as recognized by Jill Cowley in Kew Bulletin vol. 36 no. 4 (1982), 17 species, but unfortunately some of these are not at all well known in cultivation and some have not yet been introduced.

Roscoeas are mostly fairly low growing, 10–25cm being the most frequent range of height when in flower, and they have distichous leaves (i.e. in one plane) which are tubular and sheathing at the base. The long-tubed flowers are produced in succession from the centre of the leaf cluster and are subtended by bracts, the characters of which are important to observe. In the Gingers as a whole the flowers are somewhat complex and this is not the place to go into great detail, but the main features of the *Roscoea* flower should be noted for interest's sake. Each flower has a tubular membranous calyx, a long perianth tube and an upper, usually hooded 'petal', two narrower lateral petals and a large lower lip which often bends downwards and may be bilobed at the apex. Near the base of the lip are attached two small petal-like staminodes (sterile stamens) and there is one fertile stamen which is furnished with two appendages on the filament. It sounds more complex than it is and it is well worth pulling a flower to pieces to identify the various parts.

All this aside, Roscoeas are excellent garden plants, easily increased by division or by seed, which may take a little finding, for it is often carried down in the tube formed by the leaves.

Some of the better known species are:

R. alpina A smallish species, usually 10–20cm, with one or two poorly-developed leaves at flowering time. The long-tubed flowers have an almost circular upper petal and an obovate bilobed lip about 1.5–2.0cm long; the colour is very variable from deep purple through lilac to pink or white. It is a rare species in cultivation and appears not to be very easy, especially in drier climates. Kashmir, Nepal, Sikkim and Bhutan in mountain pastures.

The easily grown *R. scillifolia* is often erroneously called *R. alpina* in gardens.

R. auriculata   The name is taken from the leaf bases which are auriculate ('eared') at the base of the blade where it begins to sheath the stem. It is a robust leafy species usually 25–40cm in height, with five to ten well-developed leaves at flowering time. The large flowers have a lip about 3.5–5.0cm long and are often a rich purple, although white or bicoloured forms occur in the wild. In gardens it is fairly late flowering, often into the autumn. Sikkim, Nepal and Tibet in lightly wooded places or open meadows.

R. capitata   An easily recognized species since it produces a head of flowers on a stalk which is raised above the leaves–giving a total height of about 15–30 cm. There are four to six linear leaves, fairly narrow and pointed. Like most species the flower colour is quite variable in the purple, magenta, bluish or pink shades and albinos are recorded. It is an easy species to cultivate, not large-flowered but quite showy, with several flowers open at a time. Nepal.

R. cautleoides (R. chamaeleon, R. sinopurpurea)   This is one of the best-known species in gardens and one of the earliest to flower, in early to mid summer, while the leaves are still poorly-developed, so that it makes quite a show. The fairly large flowers have a lip 2.5–4.0cm long and are yellow in the form most often seen in cultivation, but may be purple or white in the wild. It is a native of W. China, in Yunnan and Sichuan.

'Grandiflora' is a vigorous form with larger leaves, possibly a hybrid.

'*R. beesiana*' is also yellow flowered with an unattractive suffusion of purple; it is possibly a hybrid with *R. auriculata*.

R. humeana   A robust but stocky large-flowered species, flowering early, as the leaves are only just beginning to develop, usually about 10–25cm tall with purple or lilac flowers in the cultivated forms, but yellow or white are recorded in the wild. The lip is about 2.5–4.5cm in length, divided into two for more than half its length, and the upper petal is about the same length, giving a very substantial flower. Sichuan and Yunnan Provinces of China. A most attractive species, with several of the large flowers open at a time when there is little leaf development.

R. purpurea (R. procera)   An excellent strong growing species, 25–40cm in height when in flower, with four to eight well developed leaves and large flowers in shades of purple, lilac or bicoloured white and purple. There is usually only one flower open at a time on each shoot, but there is a long succession in mid to late summer. The lip is about 4.5–6.5cm long and this makes it one of the largest-flowered species, together with the similar *R. auriculata*. The main difference lies in the fact that the leaves of *R. purpurea* are not conspicuously auriculate (eared) at the point where the blade joins the stem, and the lip of the flower in *R. purpurea* is not as sharply deflexed as in *R. auriculata*.

R. purpurea is a native of Nepal and Bhutan and adjacent parts of N. India. The bicoloured forms are particularly attractive and one, which I formerly cultivated as '*R. procera*' is perhaps the finest Roscoea I have seen. It had white flowers with a large purple blotch in the centre of the lip.

R. scillifolia   A very easily grown species which can seed around a little too well and has become almost a weed in my peat bed. It is a smallish slender plant 10–25cm in height with the fairly narrow linear or lanceolate leaves quite well developed, and small flowers which may be a deep blackish-purple, pink or white, but I have not yet seen an albino form in cultivation; the lip is about 1.5–2.0cm in length. It is frequently seen as *R. alpina*, a much more uncommon species in cultivation which has little leaf development at flowering time, and a circular upper petal (elliptic in *R. scillifolia*), apart from several other differences. *R. scillifolia* is from China in Yunnan Province.

Apart from these, which may be found without difficulty in cultivation, it would be exciting to obtain the recently described *R. nepalensis* from Nepal, which has large white flowers, or the early-flowering *R. praecox* from China, which produces its large purple or white flowers before any leaves appear.

Scilla

The Squills and Bluebells belong to a quite large genus distributed through Europe and Asia and also in Africa and South Africa, although many of the African species have been transferred to the genus *Ledebouria*. These are all tender plants and I have not dealt with them in this book. Most of the hardy species are well worth growing, especially those like *S. siberica* and *S. mischtschenkoana*, which flower in the very early spring. They are nearly all fairly easy to cultivate and do not require hot dry positions, so are suitable for rock gardens and in some cases for planting beneath shrubs.

The botanical characteristics of Scilla are mainly in the flowers, the chief features being that the six perianth segments are free from each other, and the stamens have thread-like filaments, not widely expanded. In the related genera *Puschkinia* and *Chionodoxa* the segments are joined into a tube, and the filaments are expanded. The overall features of Scillas are the narrow leaves, all basal, and the leafless stems bearing racemes of flowers, usually blue, which can be bell-shaped to flat and starry. A few species have only one or two flowers per stem but in others there are many. The position of the Bluebells has caused considerable divergence of opinion, and here I have retained them in Scilla. The two main differences are (1) that each flower is subtended by one bract in the true Scillas and by two in the Bluebells, and (2) the fact that the bulbs have a different structure, more or less solid in the Bluebells and scaly in the Squills. The bulbs of the former are replaced each year by new ones, whereas those of the 'ordinary' Scillas go on year after year without change, other than to add new scales as they grow. Bluebells have been known as *Hyacinthoides* and *Endymion* as well as *Scilla* and may be found under these various names in literature. Some of the Mediterranean species which, because of the two bracts and bulb structure, should be associated with the Bluebell, *S. non-scripta*, do, however, look far more like the other Scillas with many small starry flowers. It probably makes more sense to regard them all as belonging to the genus Scilla.

The hardy northern-hemisphere Scillas are nearly all early to late spring-flowering, but there are a few autumnal ones as well, *S. autumnalis*, *S. obtusifolia* and *S. scilloides*. The few North African species which I have tried, such as *S. latifolia* and *S. villosa*, have proved to be very tender even in my southern English garden and only survived in a heated glasshouse; I have omitted these for both this reason and the fact that they are barely, if at all, in cultivation.

S. amoena A good garden plant of unknown origin. It produces several long linear leaves in spring – and shortly, after one to several 15–20cm flower stems per bulb, carrying loose racemes of three to six mid-blue flowers, which have a darker blue stripe along the centre of each segment. They are held almost erect and are about 1.5–2.0cm in diameter.

S. atropatana   From S. Caucasia, this has now been shown to be a *Hyacinthella*.

S. autumnalis   Although useful in that it is autumn flowering, this little plant is not showy enough to have any great appeal. The flowers are produced before the very narrow leaves appear and are carried in fairly dense racemes 5–15cm in height; each is only about 5mm in diameter and flattish when fully open. There is a wide range of colour variation from pale lilac to deep purple or violet, and albinos occur as well. It is very widespread at low altitudes in western and southern Europe east to Turkey, and is also an uncommon British native.

S. *obtusifolia* from N. Africa and S. *intermedia* from Corsica, Sardinia and Sicily are almost identical to S. *autumnalis* in flower, but the leaves are much broader, to 2.5cm wide with a ciliate margin. The two are probably indistinguishable from each other.

S. bifolia   One of the most frequently cultivated species, and indispensable as an early spring bulb for naturalizing in semi-shade or for the rock garden. It is a dwarf plant, only 5–10cm (rarely to 15cm) in height, with normally two oblanceolate or linear leaves and loose one-sided racemes of small (1.0–1.5cm diameter) starry flowers, each on a slender pedicel 1–3cm long. The colour is usually deep mauve-blue but very variable. It is very widely distributed in the mountains of Europe and Asia Minor and many local forms have been given names, sometimes as separate species. Some of the more distinct and valuable variants from a horticultural viewpoint are: 'Rosea', pink, 'Alba' white and 'Praecox', a very robust large-flowered purple-blue.

Var. *polyphylla* (*S. longistylosa*) from S.W. Turkey produces up to five narrow leaves per bulb.

S. *nivalis* should probably be regarded as another variant of S. *bifolia*; it is very similar and represents the small end of the range of variation.

S. *decidua*, S. *montenegrina* and S. *resselii* are so similar to S. *bifolia* that I can find nothing to say!

S. *khorassanica* from Iran is probably not in cultivation. It has been compared with S. *bifolia*, but has three leaves per bulb and larger flowers, 1.5–2.0cm in diameter.

S. bithynica   A good plant for naturalizing in sun or semi-shade. It is up to 15cm in height, with three to five linear leaves up to 1cm wide produced in spring, accompanied by fairly dense racemes, of starry horizontal to upright mid blue flowers about 1cm in diameter, on pedicels 5–10mm long. It grows wild in Bulgaria and N.W. Turkey in light woodland.

S. *messenaica* from S. Greece, in the Peloponnese, is very similar but has up to seven often slightly wider leaves and looser racemes. S. *albanica* from Albania is probably the same as S. *messenaica*.

S. furseorum   This was named after Paul and Polly Furse, who introduced so many interesting bulbous plants from Asia in the 1960s. It is a small plant, only about 10cm when in flower, and has distinctive very narrow leaves with a whitish stripe along the centre, several to each bulb. The short dense racemes bear deep bluish-mauve flowers which have a green stripe on each segment. It is a native of rocky slopes in Afghanistan and is perfectly hardy, but the bulbs seem to need a dry summer if they are to thrive, hence bulb-frame or alpine-house treatment is necessary.

S. *raewskiana* from Soviet Central Asia is obviously related to this; it has very few, only one to three larger deep violet flowers on each stem and these are carried on long pedicels. It does not appear to be very easy to cultivate.

S. parvanica is rather like *S. raewskiana* in having few dark violet-blue flowers, but they are close together on very short pedicels giving a tight raceme. Afghanistan.

S. bisotunensis (described from W. Iran) I have not seen; it is described as having a white stripe on the leaves and two to six violet flowers 1.0–1.5cm long.

S. hohenackeri   There is some confusion over this name and I can only repeat what seems to be the currently accepted position. *S. hohenackeri* is a charming smallish species about 10cm in height with narrow linear basal leaves, which are produced in spring just before the flowers. These are carried in a loose raceme, each in a pendent position but with the perianth segements reflexed in cyclamen fashion with the stamens protruding; the colour is a mid lilac-blue. This is the plant which my colleagues and I collected on the Bowles Expedition to Iran in 1963. It does very well in the peat garden and other cool positions. N.W. Iran and adjacent USSR, in the Talysh mountains in woods and shady rock crevices.

S. greilhuberi (which often goes under the name *S. hohenackeri*) is rather taller, with more flowers per stem. The main difference, however, lies in the longer leaves, which are produced in autumn and become rather untidy by flowering time. They are less than 1cm wide. N. Iran (Caspian region).

S. gorganica (*S. gorganensis*), from N.E. Iran, is similar in floral details and size to *S. greilhuberi*, but has broad shiny leaves up to 2cm wide with a hooded apex.

S. cilicica is very similar in overall appearance to *S. greilhuberi* and also produces its long linear leaves in the autumn. They are usually 1–2cm wide. The flowers are lilac-blue, with only slightly reflexed perianth segments. There are some small differences which indicate that they should be kept as distinct species, for example the fact that the bulb tunics in *S. cilicica* are dark violet while those of *S. greilhuberi* are brown. *S. cilicica* is a native of rocky places in Cyprus, S. Turkey, Syria, Lebanon and Israel. I find that it is not very hardy and much less vigorous than either *S. hohenackeri* or *S. greilhuberi*.

S. veneris described recently from Cyprus appears to be only a slight variant of *S. cilicica*.

S. griffithii   This is probably best compared with *S. hohenackeri* and its allies, since it too has loose racemes of mid bluish-lilac flowers with reflexed segments. The leaves are, however, distinct. They are produced in autumn, several per bulb, and they are very narrow with a pale stripe along the centre – a feature not shown by any of the above. It is from the mountains of Afghanistan and Pakistan and, although hardy, seems to do best in the protection of a frame or alpine house.

S. koelzii is probably not in cultivation. Desmond Meikle, in its original description, compared it with *S. griffithii* but gave as the differences the lower stature (5–11cm tall stems) and few flowers, usually only one or two per stem. S. Iran.

S. melaina, described from S. Turkey, is most nearly related to *S. cilicica* but is distinguished by its narrow leaves, usually less than 1cm wide, darker blue flowers and by the generally shorter bracts which are not furnished with a spur. It also has only two to four flowers per raceme. The bulbs have blackish-violet tunics.

S. mesopotamica also has bulbs with dark violet tunics like *S. cilicica*. It is distinguished from the latter by having leaves which are shorter than the flower stems (longer in *S. cilicica*) and is a very robust plant, sometimes reaching 35cm when in flower, but with few flowers, up to five in the raceme. It is a little known species from S. Turkey.

S. hyacinthoides   Although this is far too large to be included in a book on the smaller bulbs, I have mentioned it in passing for the sake of completeness, since nearly all the rest of the hardy Scillas are dealt with. It has enormous bulbs up to 8cm in diameter and when in flower in late spring reaches to nearly a metre in height with a long raceme of many blue starry flowers about 1cm across, carried on slender blue pedicels. The broad leaves are produced in erect tufts. It is a plant of rocky places in the Mediterranean region and, although hardy and forming large clumps, I find that it needs a hot sunny position if it is to flower well.

S. italica (Hyacinthoides italica) An easily cultivated hardy species for a sunny position. there are several linear leaves per bulb and 15–20cm dense conical or flat-topped racemes of small pale to deep blue flattish starry flowers about 1cm in diameter. Each pedicel has two bracts at its base, whereas all the other similar ones such as *S. verna* and *S. ramburei* have one. Italy, France, Spain and Portugal in stony and grassy places.

S. vicentina from S. Portugal (Cape St Vincent) is very similar but has yellow pollen (blue in *S. italica*).

S. reverchonii from Jaen Province of S. Spain has longer loose racemes of flowers which are more cup-shaped.

S. lilio-hyacinthus A squill which is recognizable from its bulb alone since it consists of loose yellowish scales more like that of a Lily. It has up to ten wide shiny green leaves up to 3cm broad, and 10–15cm stems with loose racemes of blue starry flowers 1.0–1.5cm in diameter. There is also a white form which is to my mind slightly more attractive. Spain, France in shady places. This is easy to grow in semi-shaded conditions but is not very showy, being rather leafy with small flowers.

S. litardierei (S. pratensis, S. amethystina) A most attractive species, later flowering than most, in early summer. It has several dark green narrowly linear leaves and dense racemes, usually 10–20cm tall, carrying up to 30 small (5–7mm diameter) starry blue flowers on pedicels 1.0–1.5cm long. It is a native of W. Yugoslavia in rocky places and in cultivation does best in full sun. The smaller flowers on longer pedicels distinguish it from *S. bithynica* and its kin.

In the Dalmatian coastal mountains of Yugoslavia I and Chris Grey-Wilson once saw a bright purple form of this – but unfortunately it was growing in a quite inaccessible position on a cliff so we could not introduce it to cultivation.

S. mischtschenkoana (S. tubergeniana, S. diziensis) This difficult name, for Western gardeners at least, is apparently the correct name for a much-loved early spring Squill, which will be found in most catalogues and literature as *S. tubergeniana*. It is a variable species and the more well-known name describes the largest-flowered form. It is a dwarf plant with up to six flowers, which are pale blue with a darker blue stripe on each perianth segment. They begin to open as they push through the ground and last until the racemes are 10–15cm in height, by which time the few glossy green oblanceolate leaves have developed. It is related to *S. siberica* but the paler blue flowers open out flatter to about 1.5cm in diameter. N. Iran and the Caucasus on stony hillsides. Some wild collected forms have much smaller paler flowers and are less attractive than the form sold as *S. tubergeniana*.

It is an excellent rock garden plant or for the front of a border and will do well in semi-shade.

S. monophyllos An unexciting species horticulturally, but interesting in that it has only one broad leaf per bulb, 1–3cm wide. The raceme is 5–15cm in height, with up to 15 blue flowers about 1cm in diameter, on long ascending pedicels 1.0–1.5cm long. S.W. Spain, Portugal and Morocco in stony places. It does best in a frame or alpine house.

S. morrisii   This is a fairly recently described species named by Desmond Meikle in 1975. It is most closely related to *S. cilicica* but is very distinct in having only one to three pale pinkish-lilac flowers which are bell-shaped. It has blackish-violet bulb tunics like *S. cilicica*. The height is usually about 15–20cm, sometimes more, with the long leaves well developed before flowering time. It is endemic to Cyprus in mountain scrub.

S. non-scripta (S. nutans. Hyacinthoides non-scriptas, Endymion non-scriptus)   The English Bluebell. Perhaps not to be recommended as plant for the small garden, for it can become a pest, but in countries where it is not native it can be difficult to grow: such are the vagaries of plants! It is of course a lovely bulb for naturalizing beneath shrubs and in grass. It grows about 20–50cm in height with narrowly basal leaves, not more tha 1.5cm wide. The fragrant flowers are deep violet blue, or less frequently pink or white, tubular (although the segments are not actually joined) with reflexed tips to the segments, about 1.5–2.0cm long and much less wide. The raceme has a characteristic shape, with the flowers borne all on one side and the apex drooping, points of distinction between this and *S. hispanica*. It has cream or yellowish stamens, another diagnostic feature. *S. non-scripta* occurs only in western Europe, including Britain, where it is a notable feature of spring woodlands.

   S. hispanica (*S. campanulata, Hyacinthoides hispanica, Endymion hispanica*)   This is the Spanish Bluebell, which is larger in all its parts than *S. non-scripta*. The leaves are broader, up to 2.5cm wide, the flowers unscented and broadly bell-shaped, 1–2cm long and as much wide, and they are carried in a loose raceme which does not nod at the apex and has the flowers borne all round the axis, not just on one side. It is a superb garden plant, forming showy clumps, and there are now selections with flowers in various shades of blue, pink or white. It is a native of Spain and Portugal.

   In gardens the distinguishing features between the two may not always be obvious due to the fact that they hybridize, resulting in intermediates.

S. odorata   A rare species in the wild and in cultivation. It is 5–15cm in height, with a few linear leaves and a loose raceme of deep blue fragrant flowers, which are cup-shaped or bell-shaped and about 1.5cm in diameter. This is an attractive plant but I have not found it easy to keep. S. Portugal.

S. persica   This species brings back pleasant and amusing memories from the Bowles Scholarship Expedition to Iran in 1963. We camped on a meadow which was a sheet of blue *S. persica*, but overnight storms turned it into a clay bog into which the Land Rover sank; this species requires a moist soil during its growing season! It is a tallish plant, up to 30cm, with five to seven erect bright green leaves 1.0–1.5cm wide. There are many flattish starry flowers in long loose racemes, carried on horizontal pedicels 2–4cm long. The colour is mid blue and they are about 1cm in diameter. S.W. Turkey, W. Iran, N. Iraq.

S. peruviana   A robust Squill, producing rosettes of many tapering lanceolate leaves well before the flowers, often in autumn, and they may look rather untidy by flowering time in early summer. The large, many-flowered racemes are on 5–25cm stems and are broadly conical, the 50 to one hundred flowers carried on long horizontal pedicels 3–5cm long. Each flower is about 1.5–2.5cm in diameter, flattish and normally deep violet-blue, although there are many variants; there is also an albino form, 'Alba'. It is a native of Spain, Portugal, Italy and N. Africa in rocky places at low altitudes, so in cultivation requires a hot sunny place if it is to do well. The bulbs should be planted near the surface.

It is a very variable species, differing in its leaf width and flower colour; the bracts may be hairy or not and the stems and leaf bases may be purple-spotted. To enumerate all those 20-odd slight variants which have been named, notably North African in origin, would serve no useful purpose, but a few of the more extreme might be noted:

Var. *killianii* has ciliate bracts and blue flowers.
Var. *flaveola* has yellowish-white flowers.
Var. *subalbida* has whitish flowers.
Var. *hipponensis* has pinkish flowers.
Var. *gattefossei* is a dwarf variant, less than 10cm in height.

Also probably best treated as varieties are;

S. elongata, which is like *S. peruviana* but with hairy leaves and bracts.
S. cupanii, a miniature variant with leaves 1.5cm or less wide and only five to 15 flowers on short stems.
S. sicula has long bracts, equalling the 4–6cm long pedicels.
S. hughii is a very robust plant with broad leaves, 4–6cm wide.

S. puschkinioides   An easy to grow hardy species, but not very showy. It is about 10cm tall, with narrowly linear leaves and a raceme of whitish or pale blue 1cm wide starry flowers with a darker stripe along the centre of each segment. It is a relative of *S. furseorum* and shares the feature of a white stripe along the centre of the leaves. It is a native of Soviet Central Asia on mountain slopes.

S. scilloides (S. chinensis, S. japonica)   An unusual species in that it is autumn-flowering and the flowers are pink. It is dormant for the summer, then produces linear leaves, which are followed shortly after by 15–20cm dense racemes of small starry flowers about 5mm in diameter. There is a little variation and the current form I have, which was given to me by the Royal Botanic Gardens, Edinburgh, is a really deep pink. It is a native of China and Japan and is a good garden plant for a sunny situation, or for the alpine house. Forma *albida* is a white-flowered form from Korea which I have not grown.

S. siberica (S. cernua)   A well-known species for its intense deep blue flowers in the early spring, suitable for the rock garden or for naturalizing in semi-shade. It is a dwarf species with two to four linear or oblanceolate leaves, which are overtopped by the flowers but elongate later. The stems are only 5–10cm, elongating during flowering to 10–15cm and carrying up to five pendent rather bell-shaped flowers about 1.0–1.5cm long. 'Spring Beauty' ('Atrocaerulea') is the deepest blue form, which can be found in the wild as well as in catalogues, but there are paler blues as well and a white form, 'Alba'. It is a native of the Crimea and Caucasus and N. Iran in woods and mountain meadows.

Subsp. *armena* from N.E. Turkey and the Caucasus is an attractive variant which has only one or two flowers, pale blue with a darker blue stripe along the centre of each segment; they are usually not as bell-shaped as in subsp. *siberica*.

S. monanthos from the same region is almost identical to subsp. *armena*, and *S. kurdistanica* from N. Iraq also looks pretty much the same.

Subsp. *caucasica* has three to five larger flowers per raceme. Caucasus.

Subsp. *otschiauriae*, also Caucasian, usually has only one large flower.

S. ingridae from S. Turkey is very similar to *S. siberica*. It has one to three pale blue flowers and is said to differ in its seeds, which are not furnished with a fleshy appendage as in *S. siberica*.

S. leepii from E. Turkey is like *S. siberica* subsp. *armena*, and from its description appears to differ mainly in having a longer style.

S. libanotica from Lebanon is like *S. siberica* but has up to eight flowers in a loose raceme.

S. mordakiae is one I have not seen, said to originate from Georgia, USSR. From a photograph it looks very similar to *S. siberica* subsp. *armena*, with only one or two flowers per stem.

S. winogradowii (*S. lazica*) is like a vigorous *S. siberica*, with leaves 1.0–2.2cm wide and 10–30cm stems, carrying up to five blue flowers 1.2–2.0cm long. N.E. Turkey. It is an easy and striking garden plant.

S. rosenii is a delightful plant but not easy to grow. It had one or two very large flowers with reflexed perianth segments up to 3cm long; they are blue with a white centre. Caucasus, N.E. Turkey in mountain woods and meadows. The secret of getting this to flower properly is to grow it in a cool place where it will not be stimulated into early growth in spring; in sheltered spots the stems do not elongate so that the graceful nodding flowers with reflexed segments are ruined by the soil. N.E. Turkey, Caucasus.

S. vvedenskyi ('*S. bucharica*') from Soviet Central Asia is probably also related to *S. siberica*. It is a vigorous plant with wide oblanceolate leaves and 15–20cm stems carrying a loose raceme of up to eight mid blue flowers.

S. verna   This dwarf species is not very showy and is surpassed by similar-looking species such as *S. italica*. There are several narrowly linear leaves per bulb. The flower stems are 5–20cm in height and carry up to 12 lilac blue to violet flowers in flat-topped racemes; they are small and starry, 5–10mm in diameter. It is widespread in W. Europe (including Britain) in stony and grassy places and the Spanish forms tend to be the best from a garden viewpoint, representing the upper range of measurements given, taller with larger flowers than the British form which is the smallest. There is only one bract per pedicel which distinguishes it from *S. italica* and its allies.

S. ramburei is like a very vigorous *S. verna*, and much more showy with up to 30 flattish flowers about 1cm across, in lilac blue. S. Spain and Portugal.

Sternbergia

Although having Crocus-shaped (i.e. like a wine glass) flowers, these lovely bulbs are actually more closely related botanically to the Daffodil. They are mostly yellow and autumnal but there are two spring ones, one of them a rarity with waxy white blooms. The Daffodil-like bulbs produce narrow, parallel-sided leaves which are greyish or deep green, either flat or slightly channelled, and these are either produced before the flowers or together with them or, in the case of some species, long after the flowers have finished. All species have six yellow stamens.

Sternbergias require sunny, well-drained situations where the bulbs will receive a warm dry period in summer whilst dormant; they are good on alkaline soils. The bulbs are usually planted in late summer or early autumn, but *S. lutea* and *S. sicula* can be satisfactorily lifted and divided while still in leaf in late spring, like Snowdrops. Propagation is normally by division of clumps or by cutting up the bulbs, providing each portion has a piece of basal plate attached; seed may be the only method in those species which do not increase vegetatively very readily. Only *S. lutea* and *S. sicula* are really satisfactory outside without protection, and they are best if given the shelter of a wall or fence which is facing the sun. The other species are best grown in a bulb frame or in deep pots in a cold glasshouse or frame.

S. lutea is sometimes offered in garden centres as the Autumn Daffodil, and is also known as Lily of the Field, although it is not at all certain that this represents the biblical plant of that name!

Key to Sternbergia species

A   Flowers white, produced in early spring with the leaves .... *S. candida*
    Flowers yellow in autumn or spring .... B
B   Flowers produced in early spring .... *S. fischeriana*
    Flowers produced in autumn C
C   Leaves absent at flowering and not appearing for a long time after ... D
    Leaves appearing before or with the flowers, or sometimes
      developing immediately after .... E
D   Flowers very small, less than 3cm (rarely 4–5cm) long with   *S. colchiciflora*
    narrow segments not overlapping; leaves only 1–4mm   and *S. alexandrae*
    (rarely 8mm) wide ....
    Flowers large with segments up to 7cm long; leaves 8–16 mm
    wide .... *S. clusiana*
E   Leaves 7–12mm wide, bright shiny green; perianth segments
    3.0–5.5cm long, 1–2cm wide .... *S. lutea*
    Leaves up to 5mm wide, dark green with a grey central stripe;   *S. sicula* (incl.
    perianth segments 2–4cm long, 3–12mm wide ....   *S. pulchella* and
                                                         S. schubertii)

S. alexandrae   See **S. colchiciflora**

S. candida   A recently discovered species, introduced in 1976 and named in 1979. It is
a spring-flowering plant with long greyish-green leaves, appearing before the flowers
and about 1cm wide, usually erect and slightly twisted. The lovely white flowers are
widely funnel-shaped and sometimes sweetly scented, and are carried on stems up to
20cm long. It is a native of S.W. Turkey, growing very locally at the edge of cedar woods
at about 1100m. The flowering period is normally January to February.

S. clusiana (Syn. **S. grandiflora, S. latifolia. S. macrantha, S. spaffordiana,
S. stipitata**)   The largest-flowered species, producing upright waxy goblets of
greenish-yellow, with overlapping segments up to 7cm long and a stiff tube up to 6.5cm
long. The leaves appear later on in winter and spring and are grey-green and about
8–16mm wide. It grows wild on dry stony hills and in fields in Iran, Iraq, Israel, Jordan,
Lebanon, Syria and Turkey, where it flowers in October or November. Although known
in cultivation since the sixteenth century it is not a common plant in gardens and is only
suitable for very hot sunny conditions or a bulb frame.

S. colchiciflora (S. aetnensis, S. dalmatica)   Although small-flowered and not all
showy, this widespread little species has a certain appeal for the bulb enthusiast and is
very easy to grow in an alpine house or bulb frame. The yellow flowers are about 2–3cm
long and funnel-shaped, resting almost on the ground since the tube is mostly
subterranean. The narrow leaves, often twisted, are produced later and are at most 4mm
wide. It is a native of Mediterranean Europe eastwards to the Caucasus and Iran, and
occurs in open dry stony places, flowering between September and November.

    S. alexandrae, which was described in 1936 from Azerbaijan SSR, appears to be a large-
flowered variant of *S. colchiciflora* with perianth segments about 4–5cm long; it is not in
cultivation at present.

S. fischeriana   This yellow-flowered spring blooming species is not unlike *S. lutea* in
overall appearance, but has narrower perianth segments giving the flowers a starry

appearance when fully open. The leaves are also a little different, being flat, somewhat twisted lengthways, and usually glaucous green. It flowers in February or March and occurs in stony places in Turkey, Iran, Iraq and the USSR. The bulbs need planting deeply (at least 15cm) and must be given a warm dry summer rest to induce them to flower.

S. lutea   The most common autumn-flowering species, and probably the best from the garden point of view. Its glossy green-channelled leaves appear just before the large deep yellow goblets, which are 3.0–5.5cm long. The flowering time is between September and November, depending on the season and locality. Planted in a hot sunny situation it can be very free flowering and increases well by division, but the bulbs must have a sunbaking in summer. It occurs widely in the Mediterranean region, usually in or near cultivated land.

S. lutea var. angustifolia is a name given in gardens to a form with narrow dark-green leaves. It is possibly a very vigorous form of S. sicula or a hybrid between S. lutea and S. sicula.

S. pulchella   Until recently a little-known species. Peter Boyce has now found it again in Syria and given me a bulb. It is very like S. colchiciflora in its flowers but it has narrow leaves well developed at flowering time in autumn. Unlike this species, S. pulchella has its seed pods on long stalks above ground (sessile in S. colchiciflora).

S. sicula (S. lutea var. graeca)   This is like a small version of S. lutea, more compact in all ways and really a more attractive plant. The narrow, deep-green leaves are usually less than 4mm wide and the deep yellow flowers are short-stemmed, but normally overtop the leaves at flowering time. For the size of the plant as a whole the flowers, in the best forms, are large and showy with segments up to 3.5cm long. It grows wild on limestone hills in Mediterranean regions, flowering in October or November. Like S. lutea its bulbs require planting in a sun-drenched spot if it is to flower and increase well.

S. schubertii from W. Turkey is similar but has a much longer perianth tube; it has not been seen again since its description in 1840 and was possibly a variant of S. sicula, which has not persisted.

Strangweia

The only species, S. spicata from Greece, has been shown by Prof. Per Wendelbo and Dr Karin Persson to belong to the genus Bellevalia, where it will be found on p. 14.

Syringodea

These delightful little South African members of the Iridaceae are rather like miniature Crocus, although their corms are more like those of Romulea, with a projection at the base. They are very little cultivated and are unfortunately not hardy, requiring a frost-free glasshouse. The name S. luteo-nigra will be encountered in literature and the plant may be found in cultivation, but it is correctly Romulea longituba var. alticola. This is hardy enough to be grown in an alpine house and a description will be found in Romulea, on p. 148.

Tapeinanthus

The only species, *T. humilis* (*Braxireon humile*), is now regarded by some botanists as a *Narcissus*. It was distinguished from the latter by having no corona (cup), but there is evidence of a vestigial corona in the form of small scales at the base of the segments. It is easy to grow in an alpine house but to encourage it to flower requires a very warm dryish summer dormancy.

T. humilis   The small Narcissus-like bulbs produce slender stems up to 10cm tall with solitary, flattish, yellow, narrow-petalled flowers about 20cm in diameter in autumn, followed by thread-like leaves which remain green until the following summer. It is a native of stony places in S.W. Spain, Algeria and Morocco.

   T. humilis occasionally hybridizes in the wild with the white-flowered autumnal *Narcissus serotinus* to produce an intermediate which has been called '*Carregnoa dubia*', although its correct name, if regarded as a *Narcissus* hybrid, is *N. perezlarae*. Thanks to Mrs Joy Hulme I now have this interesting little hybrid, although neither it nor its two parents can be said to be of earth-shattering beauty!

Tecophilaea

The Chilean Blue Crocus, *T. cyanocrocus*, is now thought to be extinct in the wild, probably through a combination of overgrazing and overcollecting. It is, however, not rare in cultivation, although it is justifiably expensive to obtain. It is spring-flowering and dormant in summer and, although fairly hardy, does seem to thrive best in an alpine house or bulb frame; there is no need to sunbake the corms in summer, but water should be withheld from the time it has ripened its seeds until the autumn. Propagation is mainly by seed, although some offsets also occur. The only other species, *T. violiflora*, is very small flowered and tender, requiring a frost-free glasshouse.

   The unusual name commemorates Tecophila Billotti, an Italian botanical artist.

T. cyanocrocus   From a corm with a matted silky tunic arise narrow basal leaves and usually one stem up to 10cm high carrying a solitary funnel-shaped intense deep-blue flower, 3cm in diameter. It is perhaps one of the most spectacular dwarf bulbs of all.

   Var. *leichtlinii* has paler but clear blue flowers with a large white centre.

   Var. *violacea* has deep purplish flowers.

   The country of origin of *T. cyanocrocus* was Chile, in alpine meadows above Valparaiso.

T. violiflora   Also from Chile, this has several small white, lilac or purplish flowers only 1.0–1.5cm in diameter.

Trillium

The delightful Trilliums, natives of Eastern Asia and North America, are easily recognized by their bare stems, carrying at the apex three leaves in a whorl and a solitary flower which has three showy petals and three smaller green sepals. The rootstock consists of a rhizome which is capable of developing lateral buds, producing clumps which can then be divided. Trilliums like cool growing conditions in damp – but not waterlogged-soil which is rich in humus. They are thus very suitable for a peat garden or semi-woodland situation, where they will not receive too much hot sun. They flower in spring or early summer and are dormant in winter. There are probably about 30 species, but many of these are little-known in cultivation and are distinguished botanically by features which are of little concern to the average horticulturist. I have included only those which are most likely to be encountered in gardens.

The species of *Trillium* can be grouped according to whether the flowers are carried on a stalk, thus separated from the rosette of leaves, or whether they are born erect immediately on the leaves, when they are said to be sessile. It is also convenient to distinguish two groups within the stalked ones, those in which the flowers are held above the leaves and those where the stalk (pedicel) is deflexed, thus holding the flower below the leaves. I shall follow these three groupings starting with (A) the sessile ones, followed by (B), the stalked or pedicellate ones with the flowers above the leaves and finally (C), the species with nodding flowers.

A. Sessile Trilliums, with erect stemless flowers (subgenus Phyllantherum)

T. chloropetalum   A robust Trillium, easily cultivated, 25–50cm in height, with broadly ovate leaves, usually beautifully mottled, and stalkless. The flower is very variable in colour, greenish, yellowish or purple in var. *chloropetalum* or white to reddish purple in var. *giganteum*. The three sepals spread out widely rather than remaining erect and the erect oblanceolate petals are about 5–10cm long. The form usually seen in cultivation has white flowers which stand out superbly against the dark mottled leaves. It is a native of California in woods.

T. cuneatum   Many of the plants grown in gardens as *T. sessile*, at least in Britain, appear to be *T. cuneatum*. Certainly the plant I used to grow as 'T. sessile rubrum' seems to belong to this species. It is a larger plant than *T. sessile*, 30–60cm in height, with beautiful large ovate stalkless leaves mottled pale and dark green to varying degrees. The flowers are about 5–10cm long with maroon-purple wedge-shaped petals and smaller, slightly spreading, green, purple-flushed sepals. In the wild there are other colour forms with brownish, greenish or yellowish flowers. S.E. United States.

T. decumbens   A most extraordinary species, not unlike *T. cuneatum* but the rosette of leaves rests flat on the ground, some 20–25cm across, and they are attractively mottled so it is a good ground cover foliage plant – although not evergreen. The flowers have deep maroon erect petals, 8.5–10cm, long and much shorter greenish sepals. S.E. United States. Unfortunately it is very rare in cultivation at present.

T. luteum (T. sessile var. **luteum)**   This is 15–45cm in height with the stalkless mottled leaves narrowed abruptly to a point at the apex. It has soft yellow or greenish yellow flowers 3–9cm long, the sepals slightly shorter than the erect petals and spreading widely. It is a lovely garden plant, not at all difficult. S.E. United States.

T. recurvatum   One of the less attractive of the sessile Trilliums, but still worthy of cultivation. It is up to 45cm in height and distinctive in having each of the leaves narrowed to stalk. The name derives from the fact that the sepals are reflexed to the near vertical below the leaves, while the petals remain erect; they are 2–5cm long and normally deep purple or maroon, although greenish and yellow forms occur in the wild. Widespread in the E. United States.

T. sessile   In this group this is one of the best-known names, although the plants cultivated in Britain are often *T. cuneatum* (above). It is 10–25cm in height, a shorter plant than *T. cuneatum* with broad mottled stalkless leaves; the flowers are about 2.0–4.5cm long and variable in colour from dark maroon to greenish with widely spreading sepals. It is not as showy as *T. cuneatum* but nevertheless well worth growing. E. and N.E. United States in rich woodland.

B   The stalked or pedicellate Trilliums with flowers held above the leaves

T. erectum   One of the better-known species in gardens in a range of colour forms, easily grown and an excellent plant. It is very variable, usually 25–50cm in height, with broadly ovate unmottled stalkless leaves. The flower is carried on a stalk up to 10cm long and this may be upright or held at an oblique angle, so that the flower can be erect or facing outwards to some extent. The flower size is variable with petals 3–8cm long and the colour too has a wide range; typically it is deep maroon red but white forms occur which are in cultivation as var. *album* and yellowish ones as forma *luteum*. The flowers, which may be flattish or cupped, are said by my very knowledgeable friend Fred Case to smell of wet dog, but I must confess to not having tested the aroma yet! It is a widespread woodland plant in the E. United States.

T. flexipes (T. declinatum, T. gleasonii)   Some of the plants being sold under other names turn out to belong to this species. It is a fairly strong growing Trillium up to 40cm in height with stalkless unmottled leaves, pointed at the apex. The long-stalked fragrant flowers are erect or held at an angle and are normally white with spreading, 2–5cm long petals, giving a flattish flower – or the petals may even be rather reflexed at the tips. It occurs in the central and northern United States in woods.

T. govanianum   One of the small-flowered Himalayan species, mainly grown for interest's sake. It is 10–20cm in height with ovate unmottled pointed leaves shortly stalked, overtopped by the yellowish, greenish or purplish flowers which have narrow petals only 1.0–2.5cm long. Kashmir, Nepal, Sikkim and Bhutan.

T. grandiflorum   Perhaps the best of all Trilliums for garden use, a gorgeous plant in the dappled shade of a woodland setting, forming large free-flowering clumps when growing well. It is usually 20–45cm in height with sessile broadly ovate unmottled leaves. The flowers are carried on stalks up to 7cm long and are pure white at first, shading to pink with age, the broad petals 4–9cm long and often somewhat undulate at the margins; there are also forms which have pinkish flowers as they open, but these are very rare in cultivation. It is a widespread plant in woods and thickets in eastern North America, and is extremely hardy. Forma *flore pleno* is the name given to double-flowered variants, which are almost as lovely as the single forms, especially in the tightly double one most frequently seen in British gardens.

T. kamschaticum   One of the better (garden-wise) Asiatic species, 25–30cm in height, with sessile unmottled pointed leaves and erect stalked white flowers with petals 2.5–4.5cm long; obviously it does not compare favourably with the large white American species but is quite acceptable. Eastern Asia in mountain woods.

   T. tschonoskii is similar but shorter, not more than 20cm with smaller flowers 1.5–3.5cm long, held facing outwards, not erect. Eastern Asia.

T. nivale   A delightful early dwarf species which is a must for the rock garden or alpine house but not, I find, all that easy to grow. It is usually only 5cm or so in height, elongating as it matures to 10–15cm. The stalked unmottled leaves are ovate, 5.0–7.5cm long, and a dark slightly bluish-green, overtopped by snowy white flowers with petals 2.5–4.5cm long; the pedicel of the flower is erect at first but bends down in the fruiting stage. It is a native of the S.E. United States in rather open situations on limestone and it is probable that my lack of success was caused by treating it like other Trilliums, as a woodlander in acid soil.

T. ovatum This is the western American counterpart of *T. grandiflorum*, with lovely large clean white blooms usually slightly smaller than those of the latter, with petals 2.5–6.5cm long. The flowers also tend to open more widely with the petals spreading from the base; in *T. grandiflorum* they are erect at the base and bend outwards higher up. *T. ovatum* is a variable 10–15cm with broad unmottled leaves pointed at the apex and the flowers are carried upright or outward-facing on 2–8cm pedicels. In Oregon I have seen colonies in which white and deep purple forms are growing side by side, but this is mainly due to the age of the flower; some forms do, however, appear to start life with some pinkish-purple colouration. Widespread in western North America from Canada to California, growing in forest clearings. Double-flowered forms are known.

T. hibbersonii (*T. ovatum* forma *hibbersonii*) is a lovely plant, like a small version of *T. ovatum* with pink flowers. British Columbia. It is very rare in cultivation.

T. rivale This is to me one of the most attractive of the Trilliums, possibly the one I would choose if I could have no other. It is very easy to raise from seed and will flower fairly quickly if the seedlings are planted out into a humus-rich soil. The raised beds on my peat garden seem to suit it admirably and it is very hardy. The height is usually only 5cm or so, but it may reach more after flowering. It has stalked unmottled ovate leaves, pointed at the apex, overtopped by the smallish flower which has white or pale pink petals 2.0–2.5cm long, spotted with pink towards the base, sometimes so strongly as to form an eye in the centre; a form like this has been given the name 'Purple Heart'. Although not as showy as the larger-flowered species it is perfectly proportioned and a most attractive little species for the smaller garden. It is a native of Oregon and California, often in rocky places near streams.

T. smallii Although coincidental, this is aptly named for it is very small and rather insignificant as a garden plant! Nevertheless is has its followers and I must include it for the enthusiast. It varies in height, usually 15–25cm, with stalkless leaves acute at the apex and unmottled. The flowers have green sepals and dark purplish-brown petals 2cm long and are held at an angle, not strictly erect. Japan.

T. undulatum A lovely, graceful Trillium 10–30cm in height with unmottled stalked leaves which have a narrow-pointed apex. The upright flowers are not large, with undulate-edged petals 2–3cm long, but are attractively coloured; the ground colour is white or pinkish-white, each petal with a red basal stain which runs out along the veins towards the tips. E. United States in acid bogs and dampwoods.

C The stalked or pedicellate Trilliums with flowers nodding below the leaves

T. catesbaei (Possibly also equals *T. nervosum*, *T. stylosum*) 20–45cm in height with unmottled, stalked leaves. The pedicel is slightly deflexed from the horizontal so that the flower is nodding below the leaves; it has reflexed petals about 2.5–5.0cm long in various shades of pink and the ovary is green. S.E. United States.

T. cernum   One of the best known of the pendent-flowered Trilliums and a good garden plant, best planted on a raised bed in a peat garden where the flowers can be seen from a low angle. It is about 25–50cm in height with unmottled stalked leaves and smallish white or pinkish white pendent flowers with petals about 2cm long, made more colourful by the purple anthers and dark reddish-purple ovary. N.E. United States and E. Canada.

T. vaseyi   A beautiful species, although you have to hunt for the flowers under the broad leaves. It is robust, up to 60cm in height, with wide stalkless leaves and large nodding maroon flowers with broad petals about 4.5–5.5cm long, spreading to give a flower some 10cm in diameter, with the tips reflexing. It grows wild in the S.E. United States.

Triteleia

This North American genus is closely related to *Brodiaea* and a general discussion will be found under the latter genus about the main differences between these and others such as *Bloomeria* and *Dichelostemma*. Most of the Triteleias I have tried seem to be easy to grow in a sunny position, where they will dry out in late summer. They flower in late spring to mid summer.

To assist with identification I have grouped them into two, those with yellow flowers and those with blue to white flowers. They all have long linear basal leaves which tend to die away by flowering time.

A   Yellow-flowered Triteleias

T. crocea (syn. **Brodiaea crocea** but not **Bloomeria crocea**)   This grows up to 40cm in height with spherical umbels 5–7cm in diameter, rather dense because there are many flowers on pedicels only 2.0–3.5cm long. The flowers are 1.5–2.0cm long with a narrow funnel-shaped tube, yellow. The six stamens are carried inside the tube at different levels, in two rows of three. Oregon and California.

T. hendersonii   This is 12–35cm in height, with rather loose umbels, the pedicels 1.5–4.0cm long, carrying 2.0–2.3cm long yellow flowers, which have a conspicuous purplish vein on each perianth segment. The stamens are attached all at the same level in the narrowly funnel-shaped tube. S.W. Oregon.

T. montana (*Brodiaea gracilis*) is related and differs in not having a very conspicuous dark stripe on the perianth and in the ovary being carried on a shorter stalk (in *T. hendersonii* the ovary is carried on a stalk which is twice its own length). Sierra Nevada, California.

T. ixioides (Brodiaea lutea)   The most well-known of the yellow species and an attractive garden plant. It is extremely variable and can be as small as 5cm up to 60cm. It has spherical or hemispherical umbels up to 12cm in diameter, carrying yellow flowers 1.0–2.5cm long with a tube 3–10cm long, which is much shorter than the segments. There is a greenish or purplish stripe along each segment. The filaments of the stamens are forked with two horn-like appendages at the apex, a feature useful in distinguishing it from some of the other species. California, in sandy places in coniferous woods. There are several subspecies but these are only slight variants and are of equal garden value.

Subsp. *unifolia* has just one rather short linear-lanceolate leaf per bulb (all the other subspecies have one or two long linear leaves).

Subsp. *cookii* has white or cream flowers, purple outside (the rest have yellow flowers).

Subsp. *anilina* has short appendages to the filaments and blue or cream anthers.

Subsp. *scabra* has long appendages and a short perianth tube 3–7mm long.

Subsp. *ixioides* also has long appendages but a longer tube, 7–10mm long.

T. dudleyi is like *T. ixioides* but the flowers are large, with the 12mm long perianth tube about the same length as the segments. California, in Tulare country.

T. lugens is similar to *T. ixioides*, but the filaments have no horn-like projections. The form of this which I grow is short, only 15–20cm with a small umbel 4cm across, quite an attractive little plant. California.

T. guadalupensis is closely related to *T. lugens* and differs from *T. ixioides* in the same way. It is, however, a larger plant than *T. lugens* and the perianth tube is broadly funnel-shaped whereas in *T. lugens* it is more tubular. It is Mexican, occurring only on Guadalupe Island, and I have not seen this rare plant. The flowers are described by Lee Lenz as being golden yellow with dark mid-veins on the segments.

B   Blue or White-flowered Triteleias

T. grandiflora   As the name says, this is a large-flowered handsome species 30–50cm in height with a rather dense hemispherical umbel 5–8cm across, carrying 2–3cm long deep to pale blue or rarely white flowers, rather bell-shaped with the tube rounded at the base and about the same length as the segments. It is widespread in the W. United States, especially Washington, Oregon and British Columbia.

T. howellii is similar but the stamens have tapering filaments whereas in *T. grandiflora* they are linear. British Columbia south to California.

T. hyacinthina (Brodiaea lactea)   This is well worth growing and is rather distinctive. It is variable, 15–50cm in height, with compact many-flowered umbels up to 8cm across, carrying short-tubed wide open white or very pale blue flowers about 1cm in length and 1.5–2.5cm in diameter. It is widespread from British Columbia south to California on hillsides and meadows, sometimes in rather wet areas.

T. lilacina (*T. hyacinthina* var. *greenei*) is also a pale-flowered species whitish with a suggestion of blue, but it has fewer flowers giving the umbel a looser more open appearance. California.

T. laxa   Probably the best-known species, and a showy garden plant for a sunny border in summer. It is 10–50cm in height, with many flowered umbels up to 16cm across which appear loose because of the longish pedicels, up to 9cm although they may be much shorter. The flowers are funnel-shaped, a variable 2–5cm in length with a long tube tapered to the base, usually a rich blue but occasionally white. It is a native of California and Oregon.

T. modesta has shorter flowers, less than 1.8cm long, and the stamens have unequal filaments (in *T. laxa* they are equal). It is very similar structurally to the yellow-flowered *T. crocea*. California.

T. bridgesii looks rather similar to *T. laxa* and the main difference lies inside the tube, where the six stamens can be seen to be attached at all the same level in a whorl. In *T. laxa* they are attached at two levels in two whorls of three. Oregon, California.

T. × *tubergenii* is a hybrid between *T. laxa* and *T. peduncularis*, which is very like *T. laxa* and shows little influence of the latter. It is a good vigorous plant with rich blue-lilac flowers on long pedicels.

The plant sold as 'Queen Fabiola' is similar, but I know of no reference to its parentage.

T. peduncularis   Perhaps less attractive as a garden plant than some of the others because of its enormous diffuse umbels. It is 10–40cm in height with the white, faintly blue-flowered, funnel-shaped flowers 1.5–3.0cm long, carried on pedicels up to 18cm long, giving the umbels a diameter of anything up to about 35cm – although they may be much less in shorter-pedicelled forms. The flowers are funnel-shaped with a tube equal to or shorter than the lobes. It is Californian but I find it completely hardy, surviving all the severest winters we have had.

T. clementina should also be mentioned here since it also has long pedicels, up to five times as long as the flowers. The flowers are pale blue. It occurs only on San Clemente Island, off the Californian coast.

Tulipa

The lovely and popular tulips are a large group of about a hundred species mainly from western and central Asia, with a few European ones. They have been cultivated for over 400 years and consequently there are countless garden forms, some of which have become naturalized in certain places and have been given latin names as if they were species. In spite of several recent works on the genus it still remains a very complex business to distinguish between the species, since most of them are very variable in colour, size and stature, even within one population. Individual selected forms are sometimes introduced and propagated by nurserymen, giving a false impression of what the species is like as a whole. For example, *T. vvedenskyi* from Central Asia first came to my notice as a tall plant with bright red flowers the size of soup bowls, but now a dwarf form has been introduced which has much smaller flowers on short stems only just above ground level.

The bulbs are important in the classification of Tulips, a difficult feature to observe in the growing state; their tunics may be hairless or lined to varying degrees with short to long hairs, sometimes only at the base or apex of the bulb. The stamens may or may not have hairs at the base of the filaments and it is useful to note this, apart from the more obvious features such as flower colour, whether or not there is a dark blotch in its centre and the general shape of the flower. The colour, number and degree of hairiness of the leaves, although they are often glabrous, may also be helpful.

Cultivation of most species is not difficult, but they do best if given a warm dry rest period in summer. In climates where there is a guaranteed warm, dry summer they can be left in the ground, which should be a site in full sun with good drainage. In cooler countries, and I would include here much of Britain, northern Europe and the more northerly States of North America, it is best to lift the bulbs as soon as the leaves begin to turn yellow and store them in a warm dry place until autumn, when they can be replanted again. Left in the ground I find that all but a few tough species such as *T. sprengeri*, *T. greigii* and *T. kaufmanniana* just dwindle away in two or three years. For the smaller species bulb frame cultivation is ideal, and they also make attractive alpine house plants, but in the latter case it must be remembered that deep pots are necessary, with the bulbs planted in the lower half as deeply as possible since most wild tulips normally grow with their bulbs at a considerable depth in the soil and will not perform well if they are shallow.

It is difficult to know how to arrange the species in a satisfactory manner, but I think one must accept the standard treatment whereby they are split into two major groups, based on the flower shape and whether or not the stamens have hairy filaments. Those with hairs near the base of the filaments have slender funnel-shaped flowers tapering at the base to the point of attachment to the pedicel; those with glabrous filaments tend to have larger flowers with a bowl-shaped rounded base.

For those who wish to delve deeper into the complexities of *Tulipa* species I can recommend the following works. Firstly there is A. D. Hall's *The Genus Tulipa* (RHS 1940) which is standard reading. For the many species from the USSR there is *Tulips* by Z. P. Botschantzeva (Balkema 1982) and for the Turkish species the account by W. Marais in *Flora of Turkey*, vol. 8 (Edinburgh 1984). *Tulipes sauvages et cultivées* is an excellent work, full of fascinating information, by Adelaide L. Stork (Geneva 1984), and most recently there is a useful study by V. A. Matthews and C. Grey-Wilson in *The European Garden Flora* vol. 1 (Cambridge 1986).

To describe in detail all the species which have been named would fill a book in itself and I have therefore been somewhat selective and have often not attempted to pick out the distinguishing botanical features. It is hoped that enthusiasts who have come across a name, or been given some seeds or bulbs, can at least get some idea on the following pages of what the plant might look like.

A   Flowers tapered to the base; stamens with hairs at the base of the filaments.

(*T. sprengeri* is an exception having a tapered flower with glabrous filaments).

T. aucheriana   This excellent little plant should probably be regarded as another variant of *T. humilis* (below). It is usually less than 10m in height, with a rosette of narrow basal leaves. The lovely 6–7cm diameter flowers of clear pink have a yellow centre, and the filaments are yellow also. It has segments which are rather pointed, giving a starry flower when fully open. The bulb tunic is hairy at the base and the apex only. N. Iran, on rocky mountainsides.

T. biflora   This is a smallish species about 10cm in height. It has the bulb tunics densely lined with hairs inside. There are normally two grey-green leaves, margined reddish, and one to three starry flowers up to 3.5cm in diameter, white inside with a central yellow eye, tinged on the outside with a greenish or purplish suffusion. Very widespread in rocky places from south-east Europe eastwards through the Middle East to Iran and the USSR. In E. Turkey I have seen yellow forms mixed in with the white.

T. polychroma seems more or less identical and was a name used for slightly taller plants from Iran and Afghanistan.

T. talievii and *T. turcomanica* from Soviet Central Asia are very similar to *T. biflora*.

T. turkestanica has up to 12 flowers and is 10–30cm in height, but otherwise like *T. biflora* and in few-flowered the specimens in the wild looks just the same.

T. bifloriformis, also from Central Asia, is similar to *T. turkestanica* with up to 15 flowers per stem. Plants which I saw near Tashkent varied so much, especially in size and number of flowers, that I felt several of these species could be lumped together. The stamens are often dark violet but may be yellow as in *T. biflora*.

T. orthopoda I have not seen, but it sounds a worthwhile variant for garden purposes. It has two rather short, blunt blue-green leaves at ground level and one or two flowers on stems only 3–4cm tall; they are similar to those of *T. biflora*. C. Asia (Kazakh SSR).

T. binutans from Uzbekistan sounds from its description much the same as *T. biflora* but the bulb tunics are hairy only at the apex and base.

T. cretica   A small species, probably related to *T. humilis*. It has the bulb tunics furnished with hairs at the base and apex only. There are two or three dark green shiny leaves and 5–10cm stems carrying one to three starry flowers about 5–6cm in diameter, which are white tinged pale pink with a yellow blotch on the inside, suffused pinkish, purple and green on the outside. Crete.

T. humilis   One of the best of the dwarf species, a superb plant for the sunny rock garden, bulb frame or alpine house. The bulb has tunics, which have hairs at the base and apex only. It is usually only 5–15cm in height, with two to five narrow linear grey-green leaves clustered in a rosette at ground level and usually solitary (rarely two or three) flowers which are up to 7cm diameter when fully open flat. They are extremely variable in colour and different forms have been described as species, the names being maintained in horticulture for certain clones but, certainly in Iran, I have seen many of these colour forms all growing together. *T. humilis* in gardens is the name given to plants with pinkish-magenta flowers with a yellow centre, yellow filaments and brownish anthers. The whole complex is distributed in S. and E. Turkey, N. Iraq, N. and W. Iran and adjacent USSR, growing on mountain slopes often near the snowline.

T. violacea is used for forms with purple flowers with a yellow or blackish centre and purple filaments and anthers.

T. pulchella has light crimson or purple flowers with a deep blue eye in the centre, margined white; the filaments are bluish and the anthers purple.

T. violacea var. *pallida* (*T. pulchella* var. *pallida*, *T. pulchella* var. *coerulea-oculata*) is a lovely variant with white flowers having a small bluish-purple eye in the centre.

T. kurdica is an attractive variant, apparently very closely related to *T. humilis*; this has brick-red or orange-red flowers with a greenish-black blotch in the centre, not margined with white or yellow. N.E. Iraq.

T. lownei from Mount Hermon in Israel is a whitish form, suffused pale pink, with a yellow centre and stained green and red on the outside. A variant I have not unfortunately had the opportunity to grow.

T. neustruevae   A delightful little Tulip which I grew successfully for several years in a pot in a cold frame. Its bulbs have blackish papery tunics. The stems usually reach about 10–15cm in cultivation and carry only two bright green leaves just above ground level. The one to three starry flowers are about 3–5cm across, bright golden yellow with a green stripe outside along the midrib with some purplish staining as well. Soviet Central Asia.

T. dasystemon, also from Central Asia, seems to be fairly similar with small yellow flowers, and *T. dasystemonoides* as well; the latter is described as having almost no stem at flowering time which would make it an attractive plant for alpine gardeners.

T. heterophylla (*Eduardoregelia heterophylla*) looks rather similar with small yellow flowers stained bronze or green on the outside and about 3–5cm across. It is only 5–12cm in height and looks really exciting, but I have not had the opportunity to try to grow it. It differs from the true Tulips by having a definite style between the stigma and ovary (stigma sessile in most other species) so is probably not very closely related to the above species and may be nearer to *Amana edulis* (p. 5). Also, as far as I can ascertain, the filaments are glabrous. Soviet Central Asia.

T. hissarica seems to be rather like *T. heterophylla* and also has the stigma on a style. Soviet Central Asia.

T. orphanidea A medium-sized Tulip, attractive with its muted colours, usually 15–30cm in height with hairy or glabrous stems and two to seven narrow glabrous leaves clustered on the lower part of the stem. The one to three flowers are 3.5–5.5cm in diameter, dull red, orange-red or orange-yellow with a blackish or dark green blotch in the centre and suffused greenish or yellowish on the exterior of the outer segments, very occasionally yellow with a reddish tinge on the outside; the anthers are brown or dark green. There are rather few hairs at the base and apex on the inner side of the bulb tunics. W. Turkey, Greece, Bulgaria on hillsides and in fields.

The following names have been given to variants falling within the above broad description and these are regarded as separate species by some authorities, but as minor variants not worthy of recognition by others. Horticulturally speaking some of these are worth acknowledging in some way. They are easily cultivated and in a quiet way attractive garden plants.

T. orphanidea Glabrous stem and glabrous ovary; flowers orange-brown suffused greenish outside. 'Flava' has the flowers yellow flushed red.

T. hageri Glabrous stem and glabrous ovary; flowers dull red tinged green outside. 'Splendens' has the flowers flushed scarlet outside.

T. whittallii Glabrous stem and glabrous ovary; flowers bright orange-bronze. Usually more vigorous, 30–35cm in height.

T. hellespontica Hairy stem and hairy ovary; flowers reddish.

T. thracica Hairy stem, but only in the upper part, and hairy ovary, flowers orange-red.

T. hayatii Hairy stem, glabrous ovary: flowers scarlet.

T. goulimyi is probably related to *T. orphanidea*; it has orange flowers with a darker eye and differs mainly in having bulb tunics densely wooly inside. S. Greece.

T. saxatilis A lovely Tulip which needs a hot sunny place where it can spread undisturbed to form patches, for its bulbs are stoloniferous; they have hairs on the inside of the tunics at the apex only. The leaves are broad and shiny green, overtopped by 15–35cm stems carrying one to four 6–8cm diameter pink or lilac-pink flowers which have a yellow eye in the centre; the anthers are purple, brown or sometimes yellow. Crete, S.W. Turkey in rocky places.

T. bakeri is the name given to darker purplish-pink flowered plants.

T. sylvestris A very easy species to cultivate in sun or partial shade, but it is not very free-flowering. The bulb tunics are hairy at the base and apex inside. It grows about 10–40cm in height, with two to four narrow leaves and solitary (rarely two) fragrant yellow flowers about 6–8cm diameter when fully open; there is some green suffusion on the exterior and the anthers are yellow. The origin is unknown but it is naturalized in woods and meadows in several countries in Europe including Britain, eastwards to Iran where a form was collected and given the name of 'Tabriz', said to be freer-flowering.

T. australis (*T. sylvestris* ssp.*australis*) is like a small version of *T. sylvestris* with small flowers suffused red on the outside. It is found in rocky places in the central and western Mediterranean region.

T. celsiana is also smaller, not more than 15cm in height, with narrow leaves which are twisted and prostrate on the ground; the flower is similar to that of *T. australis* but opening about a fortnight later in mid to late spring. Mediterranean region.

T. tchitounyi was described from E. Turkey but seems to be the same as *T. sylvestris*.

T. primulina is probably related but has one or two creamy coloured flowers shading to darker yellow towards the centre and flushed on the outside with green and pinkish suffusion; the flowers are on long pedicels which normally droop over to some extent rather than being stiffly erect. Algeria.

T. tarda ('T. dasystemon' of gardens*)* One of the most popular of the very dwarf Tulips, and easy to obtain and cultivate in a sunny situation. It is only 1cm or so high, with a rosette of narrow green leaves amid which nestle up to five flowers on each stem, so close together as to appear in a bunch, opening out flat and starry to 5–6cm in diameter. They have a very large central yellow eye which reaches to half way or more up the segments, the tips of which are white. Externally there is a greenish suffusion. The anthers are yellow and the bulb tunics more or less hairless. It is a native of rocky places in Soviet Central Asia, in the Tien Shan range.

T. urumiensis Another very good dwarf species for the rock garden, only about 10–15cm in height with a rosette of narrow leaves and one or two wholly bright yellow flowers, 5–7cm in diameter, tinged with bronze on the outside and opening flat in the sun to reveal yellow stamens. The bulbs have tunics which are slightly hairy inside towards the base. It was originally found in N.W. Iran near Lake Rezaiyeh (formerly L. Urumia).

Some wholly yellow forms of *T. biflora* which I saw recently in E. Turkey among the normal white forms seem to bear a remarkably close resemblance to *T. urumiensis*.

B   Flowers bowl-shaped or cup-shaped with a rounded base (T. sprengeri is an exception); stamens with no hairs on the filaments.

In this group, which contains many species with medium to large red flowers with a blackish eye in the centre, it is important to know the degree of hairiness of the inside of the bulb tunics. I have therefore made a comment about this in each case at the beginning of each description. They are often very gaudy plants, a lot of them from Central Asia, and require a good warm summer rest period, so it is best in the cooler temperate climates to lift and dry the bulbs for summer months.

T. armena (T. willmottae, T. suaveolens and probably **T. schrenkii)** Bulb tunic, with a thin layer of long hairs inside. 10–25cm in height. It has medium sized (4.0–5.5cm diameter) bright red or crimson red flowers with a small blackish eye and yellow or blackish stamens; the leaves are grey-green, often wavy at the margins. Yellow-flowered forms occur in Turkey and these have been called *T. mucronata* and *T. galatica*, the latter differing in having no black eye; *T. lutea*, also from Turkey, was the name given to a yellow-flowered form with a bluish eye. Turkey, N.W. Iran and S. Caucasus growing on open mountain slopes.

Subsp. *lycica* (*T. ciliatula*, *T. concinna*, *T. foliosa*, *T. heterochroa*) from C. and S. Turkey has a slightly different bulb tunic with hairs at the base and apex only.

T. schrenkii is probably a synonym of *T. armena*. It is widespread in C. and W. USSR, and extremely variable in colour, not only red and yellow but also white and pink forms are known. There is sometimes available, from specialist nurseries, a form with red flowers edged yellow, a very striking plant.

T. julia is a related species from Turkey, N. Iran and Transcaucasia, of similar appearance to *T. armena* but has the bulb densely lined with hairs forming a thick felt. It also has red and yellow forms, and sometimes intermediate ones with striped flowers which have been called *T. kaghyzmanica*.

T. ulophylla from N. Iran seems to be very close to *T. armena*, with only slightly hairy bulb tunics. It has about six very undulate leaves per bulb, whereas *T. armena* usually has only three or four. The flowers are red with a blackish eye.

T. altaica is like *T. armena* but always yellow-flowered with no basal blotch. Siberia and Central Asia.

T. batalinii   Bulb tunic hairy towards the apex inside. A lovely and popular dwarf Tulip ideally suited to the rock garden. The narrow grey-green leaves are very undulate at the margins and often form a basal rosette. The wholly yellow flowers are about 5–7cm in diameter, with yellow anthers, and are carried on stems only 5–15cm in height. It is probably a form of the red *T. linifolia* (below) and hybrids have been produced between the two with bronze or apricot flowers, such as 'Apricot Jewel', 'Bronze Charm' and 'Bright Gem'. *T. batalinii* is a native of Soviet Central Asia on stony hillsides.

T. clusiana (T. aitchisonii)   The Lady Tulip. Bulb tunics with a dense tuft of hairs at the apex. One of the most graceful of the smaller species, up to 30cm, with slender grey-green leaves. The one or two flowers are up to 10cm in diameter when fully open but have narrow acute segments giving a starry shape, white stained crimson-pink on the outside and with a central eye of dark crimson inside; the anthers are dark purple. Iran east to W. Himalaya and naturalized in some Mediterranean countries.

Var. *stellata* (*T. stellata*) has similar white flowers but the eye and the stamens are yellow.

Var. *chrysantha* is like *T. clusiana* in its bulb and general appearance, but has yellow flowers stained red outside.

T. ferganica   Bulb tunic with hairs only at the base and apex inside. A delightful smallish Tulip in the wild, usually about 10–15cm in height but taller in cultivation. It has undulate-margined blue-grey leaves at ground level and one, sometimes two flowers in bright yellow suffused pinkish on the outside; anthers yellow. Soviet Central Asia on bare rocky hillsides.

T. fosteriana   One of the better known of a large group of robust Asiatic Tulips having bulb tunics which are densely lined with hairs, and large red flowers, mostly with a blackish eye in the centre. They are difficult to distinguish and indeed some of them are probably not distinct species but just slight variants. There has been no thorough recent botanical study of them and I have more or less accepted things as they are at present.

T. fosteriana, 20–45cm in height, with three to six grey-green leaves which are hairy on the margins and finely hairy all over the upper surface. The solitary flowers can be up to 20cm across when fully open but fortunately are often much less, brilliant scarlet-red with a purple-black eye in the centre, bordered with yellow; the outside often has a yellow-gold or orange overlay and the anthers are blackish. Soviet Central Asia on rocky scrub-covered hillsides. There are various named clones and hybrids of *T. fosteriana* in cultivation including a white, 'Purissima', and a brilliant red, 'Madame Lefeber'.

T. lanata is very similar but has undulate-edged leaves. Soviet Central Asia.

T. tubergeniana also differs from *T. fosteriana* in having undulate-edged leaves and is very close to *T. lanata*. The stamens have filaments which are wholly black (black with a white apex in *T. lanata*). Soviet Central Asia.

T. hoogiana   Although the leaves are hairy at the margins they are not covered with hairs on the upper surface, as in *T. fosteriana*. Soviet Central Asia.

T. kuschkensis is very similar to *T. hoogiana* but the outer segments of the flowers have their margins folded downwards. Soviet Central Asia.

T. carinata is very similar to *T. tubergeniana*, but the leaves are undulate only towards the tips; some forms have a yellow rather than blackish 'eye' in the centre. Soviet Central Asia.

T. albertii is a very variable plant also from Soviet Central Asia which may have orange-red, pinkish or yellow flowers; they have a blackish, yellow-margined blotch and in their redder forms may look a little like *T. fosteriana*, but only the upper part of the bulb tunic is densely lined with hairs, the rest rather sparsely so.

T. ingens differs from *T. fosteriana* and the others above in having the black blotch in the centre not margined yellow. Soviet Central Asia.

Another group of Tulips with large red flowers with a blackish eye is found farther to the west, and these species may be conveniently dealt with here as well. They also have densely hairy bulb tunics (except *T. undulatifolia*).

T. agenensis (*T. oculis-solis*)   This has green leaves, not or only slightly undulate and hairless except on the margins. The red flowers have rather long narrow segments more than three times as long as wide with a yellow-margined black blotch in the centre. W. and S.W. Turkey, Aegean Islands and naturalized in S. France.

Subsp. *boissieri* (*T. sharonensis*) from Israel is very similar but usually has slightly smaller flowers, which have a very large deep olive green blotch in the centre covering almost half the length of the perianth segments.

T. aleppensis is like *T. agenensis* but has grey-green leaves and has flowers with a rather small blackish eye in the centre, usually not margined yellow. S. Turkey and Syria.

T. systola from Iran has upright rather narrow leaves; the red flowers have a black blotch in the centre which is often not margined yellow.

T. praecox is very closely related and similar to *T. agenensis*, but the segments are only about twice as long as wide and have a fairly small black blotch in the centre (a rather long narrow blotch in *T. agenensis*). W. Turkey, naturalized in parts of S. Europe.

T. stapfi is a rather short Tulip of this group with broad grey-green leaves lying almost on the surface of the ground. It is a native of W. and N. Iran.

T. cypria seems to be just a variable red tulip from Cyprus, some forms of which are nearly identical to *T. agenensis*.

T. undulatifolia (*T. boeotica*, *T. eichleri*) differs from the above species in having bulb tunics which have only a few hairs on the inside; otherwise it is similar to *T. agenensis* but with very undulate leaves, the upper ones of which are finely hairy. W. Turkey, Greece, S. Caucasus.

T. gesneriana   This is the name given to a confusing complex of Tulips of unknown origin but which are probably, at least in part, old garden selections which have sometimes become naturalized and give the impression of being distinct species; thus they are sometimes referred to as a group called 'Neo-tulipae'. The features of the complex as a whole are: Bulb tunic glabrous or with hairs just near the apex; tallish plants 30–60cm in height; leaves glabrous on the surface, but hairy on the margins near the apex; one large flower per stem in a wide range of colours, sometimes striped, with or without a blackish eye in the centre; anthers yellow or purple.

Some of the names which may be found in literature and catalogues belonging to this group are:

T. acuminata   This has a fascinating and curious elongated flower with long narrow pointed segments in yellow or pale red suffused green; anthers brown.

T. didieri   Red with a blackish-purple eye; anthers usually blackish.

T. elegans   Red with a yellow eye; anthers purple.

T. fulgens   Red with a yellow eye; anthers yellow.

T. galatica of gardens (not *T. galatica* Freyn which is a form of *T. armena*). Yellow with a green eye and suffused green outside; anthers yellow.

T. grengiolensis   A bicoloured flower, yellow with red margins to the segments; anthers yellow.

T. hungarica   Yellow with a darker eye; anthers purple.

T. marjolettii   Cream-coloured, flushed purplish on the outside and pinkish on the edges; anthers yellow.

T. mauritiana   Bright scarlet red with a yellow eye; anthers purple.

T. platystigma   Pink flushed with orange at the edges and with a darker bluish eye; anthers violet.

T. retroflexa   Yellow with the long-pointed tips of the segments curving outwards. This is one of the parents of the lovely Lily Flowered Tulips.

T. urumoffii (*T. rhodopea*) probably also belongs in this group. Scarlet flowers with a dark blackish-green eye margined yellow; anthers blackish-green.

T. variopicta   Red, striped orange and purple with a greyish eye; anthers violet.

T. viridiflora   The segments have broad green bands on the outside almost covering the surface except for a narrow yellow margin. This has given its name to a whole group of garden Tulips which are similarly marked green on the exterior with background colours of red or yellow.

T. greigii   Bulb tunics, hairy inside at the apex. A very striking tulip, 20–45cm in height, with broad grey-green leaves which are striped and dotted with purplish or reddish-brown, so it is attractive in foliage. The solitary flowers are widely cup-shaped, up to 15cm across when fully open, variable but usually red or yellow with a blackish yellow-margined eye in the centre and blackish stamens. Soviet Central Asia on mountain slopes in heavy soil.

There are now quite a number of cultivars in various shades, and hybrids between *T. greigii* and *T. fosteriana*. Two good ones are 'Red Riding Hood' with brilliant red flowers, and 'Donnabella', a pale yellow with a blackish eye.

T. micheliana is like this in having purple-striped leaves but the red flowers have violet or yellow anthers, not blackish. The bulb is usually extended into a long neck at the apex. N.E. Iran and adjacent USSR, often in fields.

T. kaufmanniana   Bulb tunic thinly lined with hairs, denser at the top and bottom. This is the well-known Waterlily Tulip, a superb garden plant for the early spring in all its many colour forms. It is a stocky species 10–25cm in height with broad grey-green leaves only partly developed at flowering time, carried in a basal rosette. The flowers open wide in the sun to 6–15cm in diameter and are often cream or yellow flushed with red on the outside and a deep yellow eye in the centre, but there are also forms with deep yellow, orange or red flowers. The long anthers are yellow and they split open from the apex downwards, twisting as they go, and this is a notable feature of the species. Soviet Central Asia in rich clayey soil in the mountains. This lovely species has been hybridized with others, especially *T. greigii*, to produce a wide range of excellent dwarf cultivars suitable for the rock garden or border. For example, 'Hearts Delight', a pink variety, 'Concerto', white, 'Chopin', lemon yellow.

T. dubia is very like *T. kaufmanniana* but is often even more dwarf, at most 10cm when in flower, and has very blue-green undulate leaves. It flowers slightly later, in mid spring, and the flowers are rather smaller, yellow with a pink suffusion on the exterior. The anthers do not coil on splitting. Soviet Central Asia.

T. tschimganica is also closely related and similar to *T. kaufmanniana*, and has as wide a range of colour forms. The anthers do not coil spirally on dehiscence, and it differs also in having minutely hairy leaves. Like the Waterlily Tulip it may be up to 25cm in height, with more or less straight-edge leaves. Soviet Central Asia.

T. butkovii looks rather like one of the red forms of *T. kaufmanniana*. It has rich, brick red flowers, with no conspicuous eye in the centre or any other prominent markings. The somewhat undulate leaves are hairy and overtop the flower, which is on a stem not more than 15cm tall. Soviet Central Asia.

T. subpraestans, like *T. kaufmanniana*, has spirally-twisted anthers but it differs from this and the others above in having glabrous bulb tunics. The flowers are orange-red opening to a starry shape with a tiny yelow eye in the centre. Soviet Central Asia.

T. kolpakowskiana   Bulb tunics thinly lined with hairs all over. An attractive small slender species, usually about 10–20cm in height, with erect narrow grey undulate leaves and a medium sized rather pointed flower, yellow with pinkish or greenish suffusion on the outside, opening out to about 6–8cm in diameter; it is darker yellow in the centre, but not with an obvious eye, and the anthers are also yellow. Soviet Central Asia on mountain slopes.

T. ostrowskiana with red flowers with an olive-green eye is closely related to *T. kolpakowskiana*, and similar in its overall size and shape – but differs in the flower colour and in the leaves which are often spreading rather than erect. Soviet Central Asia.

T. iliensis and *T. tetraphylla*, both Central Asiatic, appear to be very like *T. kolpakowskiana*, but the flowers are slightly smaller.

T. lehmanniana   Bulb with tunics densely woolly inside and with a long neck reaching the soil surface. A semi-desert Tulip which is rare in cultivation and not easy to cultivate, needing hot dry conditions after flowering. It has stems to 25cm and glabrous, undulate grey-green leaves. The flowers may be red, yellow or orange in the wild, furnished with a blackish or brownish eye in the centre, and yellow anthers. It is a native of N.E. Iran, Afghanistan and Soviet Central Asia, in rather dry stony places.

T. borszczowii is another species from the Central Asiatic deserts which is very like *T. lehmanniana* but has black or violet anthers. It was introduced at one time by Paul Furse in the 1960s but I do not know of it at present in cultivation.

T. linifolia   Bulbs with the tunics hairy at the apex inside. A very satisfactory smallish tulip for a sunny position in the rock garden or border. It is 10–20cm in height with narrowly linear undulate-edged grey leaves and 6–8cm diameter flowers in brilliant scarlet with a small dark purple eye in the centre and blackish anthers, opening out flat in the sun. Soviet Central Asia in rocky places. *T. batalinii* mentioned above (p. 171) is probably a yellow form of this and there are intermediate hybrids between them, all good garden plants.

T. maximowiczii is similar in general appearance, but the dark eye in the centre is bordered white; other differences are so slight that it appears to be just a minor variant of *T. linifolia*.

T. montana (T. wilsoniana)   Bulb with a tuft of hairs protruding from the apex. A Tulip for which I have particular affection, having seen it in countless numbers in the mountains of Iran, but it is not one of the easiest to grow. It is slender, 15–25cm in height, with narrow greyish wavy leaves and flattish red flowers about 8cm in diameter without an eye or with only a very small dark greenish eye in the centre and with yellow anthers; in the wild yellow forms occur, and sometimes orange intermediates. N. Iran and adjacent Central Asiatic USSR on rocky mountain slopes. The yellow forms have been called var. *chrysantha*, not to be confused with *T. clusiana* var. *chrysantha*.

T. praestans   Bulb tunics with a few hairs inside near the apex. An excellent garden Tulip, increasing well and flowering freely. As Tulips go it is quite distinctive, with stems up to 30cm carrying rather broad almost erect grey-green leaves nearly all the way up to the flowers. There may be only one flower but usually more, up to five, and these are bright orange-red with no darker eye in the centre, about 10–12cm in diameter with yellow or purplish anthers. Mountain slopes in Soviet Central Asia. 'Fusilier' is a good variety producing several smallish flowers per stem, while 'Van Tubergen's Variety' is a vigorous selection with larger flowers.

T. sintenisii   Bulb tunics with hairs at the base and apex inside. This resembles the large-flowered red Tulips with a blackish eye but does not have the densely woolly bulb tunics and the flowers are generally smaller, only 5–6cm in diameter. The blackish blotch in the centre does not usually have a yellow margin. It occurs always in fields in C. and E. Turkey and may not be a native plant although, if this is so, its true origin is not known.

T. sprengeri   Bulb tunics glabrous or very slightly hairy. A very attractive and useful Tulip, flowering long after all other species have finished, usually not until early summer. It is very easy to grow in a variety of situations in the semi-shaded peat garden, full sun or in grass. It produces an abundance of seeds which produce flowering bulbs in only three or four years (up to seven in many species). It is a slender species 30–45cm in height with erect shiny green leaves and narrow bright scarlet flowers with a paler yellowish-gold exterior; there is no darker blotch in the centre and the anthers are yellow. It is native of N. Turkey, known from only one small area and has, as far as known, not been rediscovered there during this century.
   Although belonging to Group B, because of the glabrous filaments it has a narrow-based flower more like those of Group A.

T. vvedenskyi   Bulb tunics lined with rather few hairs. I must confess to being confused about this species which I first knew some 15 years ago as a tall plant with straight-edged leaves and flowers the size of soup bowls, but more recently I saw a form in Tashkent Botanic Garden which had prostrate wavy-edged leaves and short-stemmed, much smaller flowers, a really excellent little Tulip. Something they have in common is the lively orange-red colour without a dark eye but instead a small yellowish centre. The dwarf form has now been introduced into cultivation and is well worth searching for. Soviet Central Asia.

T. zenaidae   Bulb tunics densely lined with hairs inside near the apex. A smallish species, 10–15cm, with quite broad grey-green hairy-edged leaves which overtop the short-stemmed flower. The solitary flowers are about 8–9cm in diameter, yellow with a small black blotch in the centre, carmine with yellow margins on the outside and with yellow anthers; the blackish eye is sometimes lacking. Soviet Central Asia.

Zephyra

Z. elegans   The only species, which produces from a silky-tunicated corm branched stems 10–25cm high, carrying many flowers which are white inside and pale blue on the outside, about 2cm in diameter. The narrow leaves are carried on the lower part of the stem below the level of the inflorescence. It inhabits rocky situations in Chile near the coast, about 100m in altitude and flowering in October in the wild. It requires cool greenhouse treatment in cold districts, but is probably hardy in the warmer areas of North America, New Zealand and Australia.

Zephyranthes

A genus of lovely small Amaryllids, unfortunately mostly not at all hardy. They have solitary, regular, rather Crocus-like or funnel-shaped flowers held more or less upright and with six equal stamens. In the related *Habranthus* they are carried at two different levels in the flower and are somewhat deflexed to the lower side; the flower is also usually held at an oblique angle, not erect as in *Zephyranthes*. The best position for the hardier species is in a sunny border by a wall, fence or greenhouse where there is some protection from cold winds and frost; otherwise they are best grown in a cool but frost-free house in pots.

Z. atamasco   This is said to be hardy in milder districts but is not in Surrey. It has white flowers in spring, produced on 20–30cm stems, about 7–8cm long and broadly funnel-shaped to about 10cm in diameter at the mouth when fully open. The leaves are strap-like. It is a native of the S.E. United States.

Z. candida   Undoubtedly this is the hardiest one and is a first rate autumn-flowering bulb for planting in a sunny border, where it receives plenty of summer warmth. It grows to about 10–20cm when in flower, with narrowly linear shiny green leaves which are nearly always visible, not dying away; the flowers are Crocus-like, about 3.5cm long, white shading to green at the base. It is a native of Argentina and Uruguay.

When growing well the bulbs produce offsets, and soon form clumps which can be divided from time to time.

Z. × *ajax* is thought to be a hybrid of *Z. candida*, with the yellow *Z. citrina*; it is similar to the former but has creamy-yellow flowers. *Z. citrina* is a tender one of unknown origin, cultivated to some extent in the West Indies.

Z. flavissima   This came to me first as an unidentified species collected by Dr Ray Harley in Brazil and has since also arrived from Argentina. It has filiform green leaves, accompanied in late summer by small yellow flowers about 2–3cm long, Crocus-like but with a short tube. It has survived several winters outside in a sandy border, but does better in a pot in the frost-free greenhouse.

Z. grandiflora (Z. carinata)   Although one of the most beautiful in the genus, this is rather tender and best grown as a pot plant in a frost-free house. It has narrow shiny green leaves and erect, funnel-shaped 6–7cm long flowers in bright pink with contrasting rich yellow stamens, produced in summer. It is a native of Central America but is widely naturalized in warm countries through the world and I well remember seeing it, looking very much part of the native vegetation, on the lower slopes of the Himalaya in Sikkim.

Z. rosea   A lovely smallish autumn-flowering species with narrow linear leaves and pink flowers about 3cm long, funnel shaped with a short tube. It grows wild in Guatemala and the West Indies and is, as might be expected, rather tender but worth a try in a sheltered position in mild areas.

Z. tubispatha   This summer-flowering species from Central America has 4–5cm long white flowers on 10–15cm stems. It is not very hardy but the optimist in favoured districts might try it against a warm sunny wall.

Z. verecunda   A smallish charming species, hardier than most. The white flowers are backed pinkish and are nearly stemless, but have a tube 2–3cm long. They are 3–5cm long and open out almost flat to 3–4cm in diameter. It grows wild in N. Mexico at up to 3400m altitude in moist grassy places. It flowers in late spring or summer.

Glossary

Acid   Soil with a pH of less than 7, often peaty
Acuminate   Long-pointed apex
Acute   Pointed apex
Alkaline   Soil with a pH of more than 7, often on chalk or limestone
Anther   Male organ of flower, producing pollen
Appendage   An extra attachment to an organ such as a lobe or swelling
Axil   Junction between leaf and stem
Axillary   Growing from an axil

Basal   Often applied to leaves, arising from the base of the stem or directly from the bulb, at ground level
Beak   Often applied to a capsule which is extended at the apex into a point
Bifid   Divided into two
Bipinnate or 2-pinnate (see Pinnate)   A leaf in which each division (i.e. leaflet) of a pinnate leaf is again pinnately divided
Biternate or 2-ternate (see Ternate)   A leaf in which each of the three primary divisions is again divided into three
Blade   The flat expanded portion of a leaf, petal or perianth segment (also Lamina)
Bract   Modified leaf subtending the flower stalk, usually much smaller than leaves
Bulb   Underground storage organ consisting of concentric fleshy scales, like an Onion or Daffodil
Bulbil   Small vegetative 'offset' produced on stem or in the leaf axils or inflorescence
Bulblet   Small 'offset' bulb produced around the parent bulb

Calcareous   Growing on chalky or limestone soils
Campanulate   Bell-shaped
Capsule   A dry seed pod which usually (in 'bulbous' plants) splits lengthways to shed its seeds
Chequered   Regularly mottled as in many Fritillaries
Ciliate   Edged with hairs
Claw   Usually applied to the lower part of a petal or perianth segment (especially in *Iris*) which is a different shape from the blade.
Clone   A plant propagated vegetatively so that all individuals are identical
Colony   A group of individuals of one species
Concolorous   Of a uniform colour throughout
Conical   Cone-shaped
Cordata   Heart-shaped
Corm   Underground storage organ consisting of solid tissue, not scaly like a bulb
Corolla   Collective name for the whorl of petals or perianth segments of a flower; in Daffodils, the outer whorl

Corona   Usually applied to Daffodils and their relatives, referring to the cup or trumpet inside the corolla

Crest   In *Iris*, the ridge in the centre of the falls, usually yellow or orange

Cultivar   A variant of a species or hybrid which is considered to be horticulturally interesting and distinct; it is given a non-latinized name

Cylindric   Tube-like with a round cross-section

Dilated   Swollen or expanded

Distichous   Arranged in two rows like the leaves of bearded Iris

Endemic   Confined to a given area such as one country or a mountain

Entire   Undivided, without teeth or lobes, usually applied to leaves or perianth segments

Falcate   Curved, like a sickle

Fall   Applied to the outer three perianth segments of an *Iris* which are held outwards and 'fall' downwards at the apex

Filament   The stalk of a stamen

Filiform   Very slender, like a thread

Free   Not joined

Fruit   A mature seed-bearing organ whatever its type (capsule, berry etc.)

Genus   A group of plants having a set of important features in common, all given the same (generic) name, e.g. *Narcissus*, *Crocus* etc., and subdivided into species

Glabrous   Smooth, without any hairs

Gland   In 'bulbous' plants, such as *Calochortus*, this name is applied to an area near the base of the perianth segments which secretes a sticky substance

Glaucous   Covered with a waxy greyish coat

Habitat   The type of conditions in which a plant grows

Haft   In *Iris* flowers, the lower part of the falls or standards (also Claw)

Hastate   Spear-shaped, with two basal lobes

Herbarium   A collection of dried specimens

Hybrid   A cross between two different plants, usually belonging to different species

Inflorescence   The whole flowering part of a plant, including flower stem and flowers

Involucre   A whorl of bracts or leaves surrounding a flower, like a ruff, as in Winter Aconite

Lamina   The flat expanded portion of a leaf or perianth segment (also Blade)

Lanceolate   Tapering at both ends but broadest just below the middle

Lax   Loose, spaced out on a stem

Leaflet   One of the lobes of a compound leaf

Linear   Narrow, with the edges more or less parallel

Linear-lanceolate   Very narrowly lanceolate, bordering on parallel-sided (linear)

Local   Referring to distribution, a species which is not widespread

Locule   One of the chambers of a seed pod

Monograph   A written account of one particular group of plants

Mouth   Usually refers to the open end of a perianth tube

Naturalized   Of foreign origin but reproducing and establishing as if a native

Nectary   An organ in which nectar is produced, usually from a gland near the base of a petal

Oblanceolate   Tapered at both ends but broadest just above the middle

Oblong   Much longer than broad, with nearly parallel margins

Obovate   Reversed egg-shaped, broadest near the apex

Obtuse   Blunt at the apex

Offset   Small, vegetatively produced bulblet at the base of a parent bulb

Opposite   Usually referring to leaves, when two arise at the same level on the stem, one on each side

Orbicular   Having a circular outline

Ovary   The female part of the flower containing ovules, which after fertilization become the seeds

Ovate   Egg-shaped

Palmate   With several lobes, spreading like the fingers of a hand

Panicle   A much-branched inflorescence

Pedicel   The stalk of a single flower

Peduncle   The main stalk of the inflorescence, each flower then carried on a separate pedicel

Perianth   The outer, usually showy part of a flower, in monocotyledons normally consisting of six segments, often in two whorls

Perianth segment   Usually applied to monocotyledons, which have six of these making up the flower, not with separate sepals and petals like many dicotyledons

Perianth tube   The basal portion of the flower where the segments are joined together forming a tube or cup

Petiole   The stalk of a leaf

Pinnate   A compound leaf which has its leaflets arranged on either side of a common petiole

Plicate   Pleated, with lengthwise concertina-like folds, or folds along the margins as in some *Galanthus*

Pubescent   Hairy, the hairs rather short

Raceme   An elongated inflorescence of flowers with each flower carried singly on a pedicel, as in Bluebell

Rhizome   A 'rootstock' which is capable of producing both roots and shoots, with lateral buds sometimes developing; may be below ground or at ground level and usually creeps horizontally forming clumps or patches

Rosette   A cluster of leaves densely packed together, usually flat on the ground as in Dandelion

Sagittate   Arrow-shaped with the basal 'barbs' well-developed into long lobes

Scale   One of the fleshy 'leaves' of a bulb

Segment   See Perianth segment

Sepal   One of the segments or lobes which make up the calyx of a flower; not usually applied to monocotyledons but sometimes used for the outer three segments of *Calochortus* and *Trillium* flowers

Serrate   Having teeth on the margin

Sessile   With no stalk

Spadix   The thick pencil-like organ within the spathe or Arums which carries the flowers at its lower end and is elongated into an 'appendix' at the apex

Spathe   A modified leaf, often much-reduced and papery, enclosing the whole inflorescence in the bud stage; in Arums it is the expanded most prominent feature of the whole inflorescence, often cowl-like

Species   A natural grouping of plants contained within a genus (e.g. *Crocus*); each species is given a separate specific name (e.g. *C. vernus, C. malyi* etc.)

Spike   A raceme in which the individual flowers are attached directly to the main axis with no pedicel, as in some *Muscari*

Spur   A basal elongation of one or more of the petals of a flower, as in *Corydalis, Dicentra* and *Aquilegia*

Stamen   Male part of the flower consisting of anther and filament

Staminode   A sterile stamen, producing no pollen and often modified and enlarged

Standards   Popular term in *Iris* for the inner three perianth segments which 'stand up' as opposed to the falls which arch outwards and downwards

Sterile   A flower which is incapable of producing seeds; sometimes also applied to stamens

Stigma   The tip of the female part of the flower which receives the pollen

Stolon   An underground stem which may give rise to a new plant or bulb at its apex

Style   The 'stalk' separating the stigma from the ovary

Subspecies   A taxonomic group within a species not sufficiently different to be given a higher status

Synonyms   Another name for a species(etc.) which already had a valid name

Taxonomy   The classification of plants and other organisms

Tendril   An outgrowth or extension, usually of a leaf, which is capable of twining around objects for support

Ternate   In threes, usually applied to a leaf which is divided into three leaflets or lobes, as in clover

Tessellated   With a square, chequered, pattern as in flowers of some *Fritillaria* and *Colchicum* species

Throat   The interior upper part of a perianth tube

Trifid   Divided into three

Trifoliolate   With three leaflets

Tripinnate   Pinnately divided (see above) three times

Trumpet   In Narcissus species, often used to denote the corona when it is longer than cup-shaped

Truncate   An apex of leaf, petal etc. which ends abruptly and squarely, not rounded or obtuse etc.

Tube   see Perianth tube

Tuber   A swollen organ, often capable of producing shoots from dormant lateral buds

Tunic   The coat of a bulb, corm etc.

Umbel   An inflorescence in which all the flowers arise at the same point like the spokes of an umbrella, as in *Allium* species

Variety   A category of plants subordinate to species and subspecies

Whorl   Usually applied to leaves, more than two of which arise at the same level in a circle around a stem, as in Crown Imperial and some Lilies

Widespread   Distributed over a wide area but not necessarily common

Index